The New Industrial Economics

The New Industrial Economics

Recent Developments in
Industrial Organization,
Oligopoly and Game Theory

Edited by

George Norman

Tyler Professor of Economics
University of Leicester

and

Manfredi La Manna

Lecturer in Economics
University of Leicester

Edward Elgar

Published by
Edward Elgar Publishing Limited
Gower House
Croft Road
Aldershot
Hants GU11 3HR
England

Edward Elgar Publishing Limited
Distributed in the United States by
Ashgate Publishing Company
Old Post Road
Brookfield
Vermont 05036
USA

A CIP catalogue record for this book is available from the
British Library

Library of Congress Cataloging-in-Publication Data

The New industrial economics: recent developments in industrial
    organization, oligopoly, and game theory/edited by George Norman
    and Manfredi La Manna.
        p.   cm.
    Includes index.
    1. Industrial organization (Economic theory)   2. Oligopolies.
3. Game theory. I. Norman, George, 1946– . II. La Manna,
Manfredi.
HD2326.N42   1992
338.8–dc20   91–28153
                                                                CIP

ISBN 1 85278 139 4

Printed in Great Britain by
Billing and Sons Ltd, Worcester

Contents

Figures

Tables

Contributors

Mark Casson, Department of Economics, University of Reading, UK

Ian Domowitz, Department of Economics, Northwestern University, USA

Françoise Forges, CORE, Université Catholique de Louvain, Belgium and Fonds National de la Recherche Scientifique

Gérard Gaudet, Départment de sciences économiques, Université du Québec à Montréal, Canada

Norman J. Ireland, Department of Economics, University of Warwick, UK

Alexis Jacquemin, CRIDE, Université Catholique de Louvain, Belgium

Manfredi La Manna, Department of Economics, University of Leicester, UK

George Norman, Department of Economics, University of Leicester, UK

Stephen W. Salant, Department of Economics, University of Michigan, USA

Margaret E. Slade, Department of Economics, University of British Columbia, Canada

Jacques-François Thisse, CORE, Université Catholique de Louvain, Belgium

Roger Ware, Department of Economics, Queen's University, Kingston, Ontario, Canada

Acknowledgements

All chapters in this volume have been especially commissioned to bring 'frontier' research in industrial economics, usually confined to specialized journals, to a wider audience of interested readers. We wish to thank all contributors for their efforts to combine relevance with analytical rigour and to present an up-to-date and accessible picture of the exciting combination of game theory, oligopoly, and industrial organization known as 'the new industrial economics'. As editors, we should like to thank Edward Elgar for his constant encouragement and support and all the contributors for their willingness to cooperate in what turned out to be a quite laborious joint venture.

BK Title's

Introduction   eds.

What is new about the New Industrial Economics? In a sense each of the chapters in this volume provides its own answer; nevertheless, perhaps it may be useful to highlight some of the themes that run through the present book, thereby providing a perspective and a framework in which each contribution can be best understood.

Although the New Industrial Economics is quite radically different from the 'old', it is impossible to identify a single turning-point, a discrete breakthrough that separates the two approaches. Indeed, it is possible to see the new industrial economics as both a reaction against and a natural extension of the more traditional analysis.

STRUCTURE–CONDUCT–PERFORMANCE

The 'structure–conduct–performance' paradigm lies at the heart of the 'old', primarily empirically based, industrial economics analysis. In this paradigm it is suggested that a series of basic economic (and other) conditions determine market structure – factors such as the number of buyers and sellers, the degree of product differentiation that is likely to characterize a particular market, barriers to entry and so on. Structure in turn determines conduct – pricing behaviour, investment, research strategy and product innovation. Finally the two together determine the performance of the industry under investigation – in terms of measures such as economic efficiency, consumer welfare and factor employment.

Investigation of the working and relevance of this paradigm progressed either by case study or through large-scale cross-section econometric analysis. In its favour, there is no doubt that in the hands of competent investigators a series of insights were gained and a series of stylized facts identified. The structure–conduct–performance approach suffers, however, from a number of serious deficiencies. In particular, while it may be possible to identify a relationship between, for example, industry profitability and market concentration, there is no reason to believe that such a positive correlation tells us anything about causation. It is possible to construct models that have the direction of causation going in either direction, or in both simultaneously.

What this points to is a difficulty in the traditional approach in identifying which of the relevant economic phenomena are exogenous and which are endogenous. Developments in the new industrial economics suggest that most of the factors that enter into market structure, conduct and performance are endogenous. They are derived from the basic economic conditions that characterize the markets under investigation and the strategic interactions of the players in those markets. As a consequence, many of the factors that enter into the various parts of the structure–conduct–performance paradigm are simultaneously determined. Put another way, we can identify a series of feedback loops from performance to conduct and structure and from conduct to structure. It makes little sense, therefore, to think of the nice linear progression that characterizes the early analysis.

STRATEGIC BEHAVIOUR

The key distinctive feature of the New Industrial Economics is the appreciation of the strategic dimension of firms' decisions; firms do not merely react to given external conditions, but try to make their economic environment as beneficial to themselves as possible, taking into account that their competitors will do likewise. The wealth of possibilities arising from these interactions is both the promise and the curse of the New Industrial Economics. The final outcome of a typical game, in terms of firms' payoffs and welfare, will depend on the strategy space, the firms' beliefs, the possibility of commitments, the time-horizon and time preferences, and so on, with small changes in the assumptions leading to dramatic changes in the conclusions. The dual task of the 'new' industrial economist is, firstly, to restrict, as far as possible, the range of possible outcomes by ruling out 'unreasonable' and/or 'non-credible' behaviour and, secondly, to present the econometrician and the policy-maker with a menu of theoretical models, each suitable to analyse specific industries. The fact that in the New Industrial Economics there is no general theory encompassing the whole gamut of industrial behaviour should not be seen as a limitation, but rather as an achievement.

Some of these ideas will be expanded upon below but an example may serve at this stage to indicate their importance. Once we pay explicit attention to the idea that any threat from one player (a firm, say) to another (another firm) has to be credible, then some of the simpler ideas about, for example, limit pricing, turn out to be rather complex. Simply put, for a threat to be credible, the player issuing the threat should be willing to go through with the stated punishment even if its rival ignores the threat.

Consider, then, limit pricing. The idea here is that an incumbent firm aiming to maximize long-run profits departs from short-run profit maximization in which it equates marginal revenue and marginal cost since this would generate a price sufficiently high to attract new firms to enter the market. Rather, price is set at a level just low enough to prevent the potential entrants from breaking even (see Scherer and Ross, 1990, Chapter 10 for more details and suggested reading). The important question that is largely ignored in the limit pricing analysis is whether it is credible for the incumbent firm to stick to the limit price in the event that a potential entrant decides to enter despite the low price. In the majority of cases, it turns out that the limit price is not the price that the incumbent firm would choose *after* entry by a new firm. As a consequence, the potential entrant will pay no attention to the pre-entry pricing behaviour of the incumbent. Rather, the potential entrant will make its entry decision on the basis of the prices that are likely to apply after entry.

In these circumstances, if we are to continue to talk of limit pricing, we should probably do so in a dynamic sense. We should also relate it to the possibility that an incumbent firm may use its pricing policy to establish a reputation, for example, of aggressive reaction to new entrants. The resulting models will be more formally based on modern oligopoly theory while at the same time being consistent with the perceived behaviour of firms in 'live' markets.

NON-COOPERATIVE GAMES

The most obvious difference between the old and the new Industrial Economics is the latter's explicit formalization of the game-theoretic aspects of the problems under examination. Game theory has not merely provided a language and a body of techniques capable of articulating and analysing the interactions amongst economic agents. The more fundamental and far-reaching effect of game theory on Industrial Economics has been to disrupt the simplistic structure–conduct–performance paradigm to which we have already referred by breaking the unidirectional causality running from structure through conduct to performance. The neat, if over-simple, links between structure, conduct and performance of the old Industrial Economics have been superseded by a bewildering range of possible permutations of structure, conduct and performance. Thus, in the old Industrial Economics, super-normal profits (performance) in an industry would be associated with collusive behaviour (conduct) brought about by high concentration (structure) possibly due to exogenous barriers to entry. In the new Industrial Economics, the number of firms is determined endogenously and depends on the type of game being played by firms, defined in terms of choice variables (prices, outputs and so on), timing of decisions, number of replications of the game, and so on. As a result, structure, conduct and performance are simultaneously determined in terms of 'fundamentals', such as technology (or technological opportunities), demand conditions and information asymmetries. Factors such as barriers to entry, or specific advantages possessed by firms, now become decision variables that are endogenously determined by the strategic decisions of the firms.

TESTING

Of course, one of the immediate implications of the new Industrial Economics is that empirical testing is likely to be rather more complicated than before. It is unlikely in the world of strategic interaction within which the new Industrial Economics theorist works that there will be nice, unidirectional and unambiguous relationships to be sought through cross-section or case study work. Nevertheless, now that the complexities of 'real-world' interactions among firms are matched by a magnificent panoply of possible theoretical models, the stage is set for alternative theories to be submitted to the test of econometric analysis. Not surprisingly, the new Industrial Economics has paved the way for the new industrial econometrics (for an excellent example, see Chapter 9).

SOME ISSUES

It may be useful to anticipate some of the game-theoretic questions that will be asked (and sometimes answered) in this volume. Consider first the simplest case of a fixed number of firms setting a single choice variable. For the problem to be well defined, firms would have to be somehow interdependent, for example by selling a 'similar' product. It turns out that the type of demand interdependence (that is, whether goods are substitutes or complements) makes a great deal of difference to the resulting market equilibrium.

In some cases the relationship between products can fully determine the nature of the game being played. Suppose, realistically, that each firm can set either its price or its output level. Decisions are taken simultaneously by all firms. Would firms decide to compete on price, on quantity, or will they alternate randomly between the two? It turns out (see Singh and Vives, 1984) that game selection – whether to play Cournot (quantity-setting) or Bertrand (price-setting) – is fully determined by demand relationships: if goods are substitutes (complements) firms will always set output levels (prices).

This raises a number of other issues that we have not been able to consider to any great extent in this book, primarily because the theoretical issues involved are highly complex and still being worked out. It is well known that the nature of market equilibrium is crucially dependent upon the strategic variables chosen by the players. In particular, quantity-setting firms will generate a very different outcome from price-setting firms.

One of the reasons for this very large difference in the resulting equilibria lies in the extreme form that price competition is assumed to take in many of the models. Recent analysis suggests that these differences are considerably moderated when additional constraints are built in. For example, if firms have to pre-commit to capacity prior to competing in price then the outcome of the resulting price game will, in particular circumstances, approach the outcome of a quantity game (Kreps and Scheinkman, 1983). Specifically, the more expensive it is to change capacity the nearer will the equilibrium of the Bertrand (price) game approach to that of the Cournot (quantity) game (Vives, 1986).

What has yet to be worked out is how general these results are. Clearly, the more general they turn out to be, the more we can move to a single set of solution concepts rather than the variety with which we have to work currently.

TIME

Having established which game firms will be playing (either exogenously in an *ad hoc* manner or endogenously as the outcome of demand conditions), the new industrial economist has to consider the time horizon of each player. The simplest assumption, of course, is that the game is played *una tantum* (one-shot game). Such dramatic, once-and-for-all decisions, however, are quite rare in economic life and thus the new industrial economist may be reluctant to rely on the depressing implications of the one-shot game for purposes of industrial policy.

The disturbing feature of many of the cases in which we analyse the strategic interactions between firms is that the payoffs to the various players generate a prisoner's dilemma. Firms find themselves driven by the lure of ephemeral gains obtained by deviating from the joint-profit-maximizing strategy (see Chapters 1 and 2). More realistically we can assume that firms have to take decisions on a repetitive basis (for example, petrol stations, to take a much studied case, can set their prices with a daily frequency). It turns out, however, that so long as the number of times the game is replicated is finite, mere repetition of the game cannot alter the characteristics of the one-shot game. The reason for this is simple and the logic of the underlying argument powerful. Suppose the game is played T times ($T < \infty$) and consider the strategies for the 'last' round. As the previous $T - 1$ rounds are now history, the optimal strategies for the Tth round will be the same as for the one-shot version of the game. Having thus determined the strategies for the last round, we can repeat the same argument for the $(T - 1)$th round. As before the previous $T - 2$ rounds are bygones and optimal behaviour in the next round has already been determined. This turns the game in the $(T - 1)$th round into a one-shot game. Repeating the same argument for each round we obtain the result that, if a strategy s^* is optimal in the one-shot version of the game, it must also be optimal for each of the T replications of the game. In particular, if s^* is the outcome of a one-shot prisoner's dilemma game, it will also be the outcome of T repetitions of that game. Apparently we are still stuck in the same undesirable situation.

Fortunately the real-life resourcefulness displayed by large corporations in trying to attain much more desirable collusive outcomes without resorting to any explicit (and thus illegal) agreements is matched by the game theorists' ingenuity in devising ways out of Pareto-inferior outcomes of finitely-repeated games. Chapters 1 and 2 explore interesting ways out. The more obvious solution is to consider infinitely-repeated games, which by their very nature make the backward-induction argument ineffective: if there is no 'last' period (because either the players' time-horizon is infinite or there is always a positive probability that the game be repeated once more), the game cannot be unravelled anti-chronologically. The implications of these types of games are much more varied, almost to a disturbingly excessive degree. By a suitable choice of parameters (for example, the all-important discount factor) it is possible to generate equilibria ranging from full collusion to the one-shot outcome.

Another way out of the finitely-repeated game impasse is to enrich the structure of the game by allowing for intertemporal interactions, whence the large literature on multi-stage games (see Chapters 1–4 and 7). The distinguishing feature of multi-stage games is the recognition that the passage of time allows a game not only to be repeated but also to change in some crucial respects. In fact most of the economic activities closest to the hearts of industrial economists fall into the category of intertemporally related phenomena. By definition, all types of investment (whether in physical or human capital, in R&D and so on) bear fruit in future periods and thus belong to the realm of multi-stage games.

The difference between strategic and non-strategic behaviour in the context of multi-stage games can be appreciated with reference to the following simple example. Consider a duopoly and suppose that firm 1's profits can be written as:

$$\pi_1 \equiv \pi'_1 + \delta\,\pi''_1 \tag{1}$$

where

$$\pi'_1 \equiv f(q'_1, q'_2) \text{ and } \pi''_1 \equiv s(q'_1, q''_1, q''_2) \tag{2}$$

Equation (1) can be interpreted as saying that firm 1's profits are the sum of domestic profits (the 'dash' market) and foreign profits (the 'double dash' market), where δ is the exchange rate. Identities (2) say that, whereas firm 1's domestic profits depend on firms 1's and 2's domestic choice variables (that is, q'_1 and q'_2), firm 1's profits on the foreign market depend not only on the two firms' 'foreign' choice variables (q''_1 and q''_2), but also on firm 1's 'domestic' choice variable (q'_1).

The key feature of the interpretation of (2) is that the two markets are interrelated, but the two firms choose their control variables simultaneously. The solution, of course, is determined by four first-order conditions:

$$\frac{\partial\pi_i}{\partial q'_i} = 0; \quad \frac{\partial\pi_i}{\partial q''_i} = 0, \qquad i = 1,2 \tag{3}$$

Now let us change the interpretation of (2) and assume that the 'dash' and the 'double dash' superscripts refer to the *same* market at two different points in time, with δ now being a discount factor. The fact that choices of q' and q'' no longer need be simultaneous has far-reaching consequences for the notion of strategic behaviour and the very concept of equilibrium. As there are two stages, a valid notion of equilibrium will have to have the property, loosely speaking, that each firm at the time of choosing its second-stage variable(s) should not 'regret' its first-stage choice. This is the intuition behind the concept of a subgame perfect equilibrium (see Chapter 1 for a definition and Chapters 2–4 and 7 for applications). Strategic behaviour in this context means that firm 1 realises that firm 2's behaviour in the second stage is affected by firm 1's own behaviour in the first stage and that this strategic interaction ought to be taken into account in determining the optimal strategy. With reference to the above example, each firm will solve its profit maximization exercise anti-chronologically; that is, it will determine first its optimal strategy in the second stage:

$$\max_{q_i} \quad \pi''_i (q'_i, q''_i, q''_j) \qquad i \neq j = 1,2 \tag{4}$$

The first-order conditions for the above maximization yield

$$q''^*_i \equiv \sigma_i(q'_i, q'_j) \qquad i \neq j = 1,2 \tag{5}$$

As a result firm 1 will solve the following program:

$$\max_{q_l} \quad [\pi'_1(q'_1, q'_2) + \delta \, \pi''_1(q'_1, \sigma_1(q'_1, q'_2), \sigma_2(q'_1, q'_2))] \tag{6}$$

As is often the case in oligopoly theory, the generalized quest for competitive advantage may turn out to be self-defeating. Given the choice between strategic and naive behaviour, each individual firm may find strategic behaviour irresistibly alluring. Naive behaviour leads to sub-optimal profits if the firm's rivals behave strategically, whereas a switch to strategic behaviour leads to greater profits if the firm's competitors behave naively. However it is not difficult to envisage cases in which individual firms' profits under generalized strategic behaviour are in fact lower than under generalized naive behaviour. Game theorists may find themselves in a prisoner's dilemma of their own making.

CONNECTIONS WITH OTHER AREAS

One important consequence of developments in the New Industrial Economics is that some of the divisions that have emerged in the study of economics are now disappearing. In particular, undesirable divisions have grown between industrial economics, microeconomics and the study of international trade. To a large extent this can be blamed upon the microeconomic theorist's and trade theorist's concentration upon (obsession with?) models of perfect competition that have little relevance to the world of imperfect competition and partial monopoly power that is the concern of the industrial economist. Equally, however, the industrial economist could be accused of having spent far too little time thinking through the logical and formal foundations of the behaviour that is being investigated and 'explained'.

These divisions are now being broken down. As a simple example, this book and a number of other recent contributions to the theory of industrial economics would not be out of place on reading lists for intermediate and advanced microeconomics courses or courses in oligopoly. In addition many of the recent advances in international trade theory (and econometrics) are founded on models of imperfect competition that were first developed as part of the new industrial economics. Another indication is the types of economists who are currently contributing to the industrial economics literature. Most of the contributors to this volume and most of the authors whose work they cite would describe themselves as microeconomists first and industrial economics theorists second.

STRUCTURE OF THE BOOK

In Chapter 1 Forges and Thisse provide the reader with the basic tools for understanding strategic behaviour in those cases, of fundamental importance in industrial economics, in which firms behave non-cooperatively, that is cannot collude. The level of analysis is simple enough to entice the uninitiated student, and yet rich enough to captivate the sceptic, by providing examples, taken mainly from spatial competition, that show the power of the techniques used to pin down (or not, as the case may be) a 'reasonable' equilibrium.

Slade and Jacquemin (Chapter 2) provide both interesting applications of the theory of non-cooperative games introduced in Chapter 1 and a complementary analysis of cooperative behaviour by firms. The scope of their contribution ranges from *tacit collusion* (when self-interested firms independently maximize joint profits despite the obvious temptation of cheating on the resulting implicit cartel agreement) to the opposite case of *cut-throat competition* (where, in a simple but revealing example of a two-stage game, it is shown how two firms may end up producing more than a competitive industry) via the intermediate case of a cartel beset by *price wars*.

The subject-matter of Chapter 3 – barriers to entry – provides Ware with the perfect example to highlight the advances of the new industrial economics as compared with the structure–conduct–performance framework. The new industrial economist does not accept barriers to entry as given but instead attempts to explain market structure in terms of 'fundamentals' (such as preferences and technological opportunities). Starting with the grandfather of entry-deterrence models (the limit-price model of Bain, Sylos-Labini and Modigliani), Ware builds up an array of entry-deterrence models that satisfy the fundamental consistency requirement embodied in the notion of sub-game Nash perfectness, namely that threats aimed at repelling potential entrants must be credible. The natural framework to examine entry models is provided by two-stage games and Ware shows the richness of possibilities afforded by a simple leader–follower set-up.

Chapter 4 is concerned with one of the most resounding successes of the new industrial economics, namely the development of the theory of product differentiation. The observation that goods are not homogeneous, typical of many of the more traditional models, is trivial and banal – the challenge is to model differences among products and examine both the opportunities for strategic behaviour that product differentiation offers to firms and their welfare implications. Ireland explores the range of strategic possibilities and their welfare effects in the simple, but important, case in which consumers either buy one unit of one product or none at all. This is done to focus on the variable of interest, namely *product design*: strategic considerations may allow firms to obtain higher prices in equilibrium, but the very profitability of the resulting market segments may induce unwelcome entry by outsiders. Ireland quite rightly emphasizes the importance of the distribution of 'mismatch costs' (that is, the costs associated with less-than-ideal varieties) in driving the models.

Chapter 5 redresses a double imbalance found in most microeconomics textbooks, by highlighting the widespread application of discriminatory pricing practices and, above all, by showing how price discrimination is a natural outcome of *oligopolistic* markets. Norman shows how the strategic dimensions basic to the new industrial economics can be brought to bear to explain observed business practices. If price discrimination is feasible, attention must be paid to strategic behaviour not only by consumers (who must be encouraged to 'sort' themselves into appropriate groups), but also by firms which use prices as a strategic weapon. Using the spatial framework described in Chapter 4, Norman provides examples of pricing schedules that satisfy the criteria of incentive-compatibility and credibility (sub-game Nash perfectness). Moreover it is shown how price discrimination can lead to improved welfare.

Gaudet and Salant (Chapter 6) show (1) how a careful analysis of the comparative statics of standard oligopoly theory may yield interesting and counter-intuitive results in the area of horizontal mergers, and (2) how some of these results no longer hold when the decision to merge is endogenous. As they note, the economics of mergers is still in its infancy, and yet the policy implications of properly modelled mergers can be momentous, in so far as they may involve a radical change of attitude. In fact anti-trust agencies not only would have to retain the traditional 'reactive' role of trying to impede socially detrimental mergers, but would have to take a more activist stance involved in promoting socially beneficial mergers that may never occur under *laissez-faire*.

In Chapter 7, La Manna surveys recent developments in the modelling of patents. Here advances have been made both by enriching the very notion of patent – so as to encompass not only patent life, but also various types of patentability standards, as policy instruments – and, once again, by allowing for strategic behaviour, be it by inventors *vis-à-vis* regulators or by firms engaged in three-stage games.

The chapter by Casson differs from the others in so far as its contribution does not lie so much in the introduction of strategic elements in well-known cases, but rather in the 'annexation' to the camp of the New Industrial Economics of an altogether new, important area of potential applications. Building on the intuitions of Knight, Hayek and Schumpeter, Casson attempts to formalize the notion of *entrepreneurship*, by combining, and making precise, the elements of risk-bearing, innovative behaviour and leadership that characterize informal treatment of entrepreneurship. Particularly interesting, especially for those who wish to combine industrial economics with the theory of finance, is the attempt to consider the relationship between entrepreneurs and banks in the presence of capital constraints.

One need not be sold on Popperian falsificationism to believe that an important test for new theories is their ability to yield testable implications. In the present context this means that the New Industrial Economics should, in time, provide econometricians with a range of competing models to be tested against the data. The final chapter, by Domowitz, is an interesting attempt to accomplish just that. In addition, and in the best tradition of good econometric studies, it produces evidence of an empirical regularity unaccounted for by theoretical models. Domowitz considers the implications of three well-known models of oligopoly supergames in terms of cyclical behaviour of prices and price–cost margins. The idea that firms may use trigger strategies to sustain super-Cournot profit margins seems to find support in the data, although the study suggests that there are significant differences in behaviour depending on whether industries produce durables or non-durables: no existing theoretical supergame model can yet account for this finding.

1. Game Theory and Industrial Economics: An Introduction

Françoise Forges and Jacques-François Thisse

---

1 INTRODUCTION

In the *New Palgrave*, Robert Aumann defines game theory as the mathematical discipline concerned with 'the behaviour of decision makers (players) whose decisions affect each other' (vol. 2, p. 460). Stated so broadly, it would seem that most situations of interest to economists can be studied by means of game-theoretic tools. In particular it should be clear why economists have found game theory so appealing for the analysis of imperfectly competitive markets.

According to a well-established tradition, games are divided into two classes: cooperative and non-cooperative games. A game is said to be *cooperative* when players can make binding agreements; it is called *non-cooperative* when they cannot. Despite the considerable potential offered by cooperative games for the study of collusion among firms, most applications of game theory to industrial economics have been formulated as non-cooperative games. For this reason, we shall restrict ourselves to non-cooperative games only.

A non-cooperative game can be described in two different ways; that is, in strategic or extensive form. A non-cooperative game in *strategic* (or normal) *form* is a collection of strategies, describing the plans or actions that can be taken by players in all conceivable situations, and of payoff functions, specifying how the gains of each player depend on the strategies chosen by the players. A non-cooperative game in *extensive form* consists of a *tree* describing how the game has to be played. More precisely the tree specifies the possible events and their probabilities (notice that Nature is a non-player that takes random actions at specific points of the game), the player who has to move at a non-terminal node of the tree, the actions he can take, the information available to him when he must move (the nodes are partitioned into information sets representing the nodes that actual players cannot distinguish) and the payoffs (given at the terminal nodes) that each player can earn for all possible paths in the tree. (Notice that this definition assumes that the sets of actions available to players are finite. The infinite case is more complex.) For a long time, games in extensive form were mainly considered as a pedagogical device permitting one to describe in detail the course of the play. However, over the last decade, they have been used more and more, especially in cases where the lack of information of players is taken into account (we must stress here the eminent role of the pioneering contributions of Harsanyi and Selten). In particular, many applications of games in extensive form have been developed recently in industrial organization. Given the scope of this book, we shall deal mainly with games in strategic form. We shall limit ourselves to basic ideas about games in extensive form, referring the reader to the various references mentioned at the end of the chapter for further developments.

A fundamental concept in non-cooperative game theory is that of strategy. In a strategic form game, a *pure strategy* for a player is an action (or a plan of actions) that can be taken by this player, the specification of which depends on the game in question. This choice is made with certainty. In an extensive form game, a pure strategy is a collection of rules describing the choices of a player as a function of his information. It is a complete and deterministic plan of actions. A strategic form game can thus be associated with each extensive form game, by combining pure strategies of all players and computing the corresponding payoffs (expectation is taken when Nature is involved).

The notion of pure strategy can be extended to that of *mixed strategy*, which consists of a probability distribution defined over the pure strategies. Although this extension can prove to be very convenient from a mathematical point of view, it may seem quite artificial. In many situations, indeed, it is unreasonable that decisions should be made randomly. However some recent works show that such an objection results from too strict an interpretation of a mixed strategy. The players' behaviour which an observer (like an economist or a game theorist) perceives as mixed strategies can be justified in terms of the players' beliefs, reflecting the players' uncertainty about each other's moves.[1] In the context of this book we have nevertheless chosen to focus primarily on pure strategies.

Although the mathematical theory of games is often viewed as being rooted in the outstanding work of von Neumann and Morgenstern (1944), it is worth emphasizing here that game theory and industrial economics (or, more broadly speaking, the theory of imperfect competition) have been very much intertwined from the outset.[2] Oligopoly theory started with Cournot (1838) who introduced, for the first time, the fundamental concept of Nash equilibrium in the special case of quantity-setting firms. Much later, Bertrand (1883) objected that prices, and not quantities, would be the natural strategic variable in oligopoly situations. Bertrand's solution was dramatically different from Cournot's, thus showing the importance of the choice of specific strategies for oligopolistic firms. In turn, Edgeworth (1897) pointed to the possibility of the non-existence of an equilibrium in pure strategies when capacity constraints are added to the Bertrand model. In his celebrated 'Stability in Competition' Hotelling (1929) took a different route by recognizing the prevalence of product differentiation in many markets. In modelling price and product selection as a two-stage game, Hotelling suggested the idea of subgame perfection, a solution concept which became central in modern game theory. Industrial economics and game theory are now related so intimately that cross-fertilization should be obvious to anyone.

The remainder of the chapter is organized as follows. In the next section we discuss in detail the solution concept of a Nash equilibrium in one-shot games. In Section 3, we consider the Stackelberg equilibrium. The more general concept of subgame perfection for multi-stage games is taken up in Section 4. This type of game has been widely used in industrial economics. Most probably, the reason for this lies in the various situations that can be modelled in that way. In the subsequent section, we provide an introduction to the theory of repeated games. Finally, Section 6 describes briefly some recent developments of game theory relevant to the theory of industrial organization.[3]

2   NASH EQUILIBRIUM

In this section we consider non-cooperative games where players make a single move which they choose simultaneously.

2.1   Examples

As seen in the introduction, the basic feature of game-theoretic situations is that the outcome of the game for each player depends on the strategy chosen by all players. To make a decision a player must therefore take into account the behaviour of the others. However, in certain cases, a player can make his choice regardless of his opponents' decisions (even when his payoff is still influenced by those decisions). This occurs when the player has a dominant strategy. Specifically, a *dominant strategy* for a given player is a strategy that gives him a higher payoff than any other available strategy, whatever the others do. Under such circumstances, it seems natural to suppose that the player having a dominant strategy will select this particular strategy independently of the others' behaviour.

To illustrate this concept and subsequent ones, consider the following setting in which two players face a finite number of choices. The players are firms offering a homogeneous product to a very large number of consumers whose willingness to pay for the product is summarized in the inverse demand function $p = 12 - Q$, where Q is the sum of the firms' outputs and p the price that clears the market. A strategy for a firm is the quantity to be sold. For simplicity, we assume that quantities are produced at zero cost. Finally the payoff of a player is defined by his profit. More precisely, when firm i ($i = 1, 2$) chooses to sell the quantity q_i, its profit is equal to $q_i [12 - (q_i + q_j)]$ ECU, q_j being the quantity sold by the other firm.

Example 1

Suppose that each firm can produce either 4 or 6 units of the product. In other words, the strategy space of each player is given by the pair of outputs {4,6}. We are now equipped to construct the payoff matrix of the game. In each cell, the first (second) number gives the profit earned by firm 1 (2) when the strategies played by firms 1 and 2 are those specified in the corresponding row and column respectively. For example, when firm 1 chooses to sell 4 and firm 2 to sell 6, the former earns 8 ECU and the latter 12 ECU.

Table 1.1 shows that 4 is a dominant strategy for both players. Suppose indeed that firm 2 chooses to sell 4 units of the product. It is immediately evident that firm 1 makes a higher profit when it picks 4 instead of 6. Assume now that firm 2 chooses to sell 6 units. Again, 4 is more profitable than 6 for firm 1. Hence, whatever the strategy selected by firm 2, firm 1 is always better off when it chooses to sell 4 units; this is therefore a dominant strategy. Given the symmetry of the payoff matrix, the same argument applies to firm 2. Consequently both players choose strategy 4 and end up with a profit of 16 ECU each. Hence the pair (4, 4) appears as a reasonable solution of the game. Any combination of strategies of this kind is called an *equilibrium in dominant strategies*.

Table 1.1   Example 1

Player 1 \ Player 2	4	6
4	(16, 16)	(8, 12)
6	(12, 8)	(0, 0)

Furthermore the above game exhibits another interesting property: the payoffs gained by both players at (4, 4) Pareto-dominate those obtained for any other pair of strategies. In other words, by selling 4 units of the product each firm makes more profit than at any other possible configuration of outputs. Unfortunately the Pareto-dominance property does not characterize the equilibria in dominant strategies. To show this, consider the next example.

Example 2

We now assume that the strategy space of both players is {3, 4} instead of {4, 6}. The corresponding payoff matrix is shown in Table 1.2. It is readily verified from Table 1.2. that 4 is a dominant strategy for both players. Hence, as in the previous game, (4, 4) is an equilibrium in dominant strategies. However the corresponding payoffs are here Pareto-dominated by those obtained at (3, 3). So the following question suggests itself: why is it that (3, 3) is not chosen by the two players? The reason lies in the fact that, if player 1, say, anticipates that player 2 will choose 3, then it is more profitable for him to select 4, since he then earns 20 ECU instead of 18. Accordingly (3, 3) can hardly be viewed as a reasonable solution of the game (see, however, Section 5). On the other hand, the combination (4, 4), which is an equilibrium in dominant strategies, has the property of being self-enforcing. This kind of situation, where the pursuit of self-interest leads to a Pareto-inefficient solution for the players, was introduced in game theory in an example known as the *prisoner's dilemma*.[4]

In many games there exists no equilibrium in dominant strategies. This means that, to make an optimal decision, each player must foresee how his opponent will behave. In so doing, the most natural principle for the players is to disregard from the outset strategies which will never be picked by their opponents. Specifically, if one player's strategy is *dominated* in the sense that it gives him a lower payoff than another strategy, whatever the others do, then the others may assume that such a strategy will never be

Table 1.2   Example 2

Player 1 \ Player 2	3	4
3	(18, 18)	(15, 20)
4	(20, 15)	(16, 16)

chosen by that player. However the elimination of dominated strategies rarely suffices to yield a single solution to the game. Hence there is a need for a weaker solution concept. This is illustrated in the example below.

Example 3
Let us now suppose that the strategy spaces of players 1 and 2 are given by {2, 6}. The payoff matrix is then as shown in Table 1.3. Clearly, if firm 1 chooses to sell 2 units of the product, then firm 2 prefers 6; on the other hand, if firm 1 decides to sell 6 units, firm 2 prefers strategy 2. Thus firm 2's best action depends on the action picked by firm 1. And vice versa. In such cases the elimination of dominated strategies leaves us with an indeterminate outcome. Nevertheless, if each player is able to predict correctly the strategy chosen by his opponent, the pair (2,6) proves to be a reasonable solution to the game. Indeed it is immediately evident from Table 1.3 that no player can improve upon his payoff by changing his strategy unilaterally. This solution is called a *Nash equilibrium* in game theory and will be discussed extensively in 2.2. It is evident that an equilibrium in dominant strategies is a Nash equilibrium. In this sense the latter is a weaker solution concept than the former.

Furthermore we observe that, in this game, the Nash equilibrium is not unique. Indeed, through the symmetry of the payoff matrix, the pair (6, 2) is also a Nash equilibrium. Thus the game has two Nash equilibria : (2, 6) and (6, 2). Comparing the respective payoffs, we notice that no Nash equilibrium Pareto-dominates the other. Quite the contrary, the two equilibria lead to very different profit levels for the two firms : at (2, 6), firm 1 (2) earns 24 (8) ECU, while at (6, 2), the profit of firm 1 (2) is 8 (24) ECU. *A priori*, both equilibria are equally plausible. To predict which equilibrium will eventually emerge requires more information about the context in which the decisions are made. For example, if one firm has more 'power' than the other, then it may be assumed that this firm is able to enforce the equilibrium more favourable to itself.[5]

Table 1.3   Example 3

	Player 2	2	6
Player 1			
2		(16, 16)	(8, 24)
6		(24, 8)	(0, 0)

Another difficulty one encounters with the Nash equilibrium concept is that such an equilibrium may not exist (at least in pure strategies). To illustrate this point, we consider a completely different setting.[6]

Example 4

Let two population centres be situated at C_1 and C_2. Each centre has M identical consumers, with M large. Each consumer buys a single unit of homogeneous product supplied by two firms. Firm 1 is located at C_1 and firm 2 at C_2. The transport cost (borne by the consumers) between the two centres is equal to 3 ECU. Unlike the previous examples, we now assume that firm i's strategy is its price p_i, which is the same for all consumers at the firm's door. So consumers located at C_i and purchasing from the local firm pay p_i ECU, while they pay $p_j + 3$ ECU if they patronize the firm established in C_j ($j \neq i$). As the product is homogeneous, each consumer buys from the firm with the lower full price : min $\{p_i, p_j + 3\}$ for consumers at C_i and min $\{p_j, p_i + 3\}$ for consumers at C_j. The strategy space of each firm is $\{6, 8, 10\}$. Clearly, for any pair of prices such that $|p_i - p_j| < 3$, each firms supplies its local market, that is, M consumers. On the other hand, if $|p_i - p_j| > 3$ – which occurs when one firm chooses 6 and the other 10 – then the lower-price firm captures the $2M$ consumers and its competitor has a zero demand. Hence, the payoff matrix is as shown in Table 1.4.

It is easy to see that the game under consideration has no Nash equilibrium (in pure strategies). The intuition behind this result is as follows. Firstly, if one firm anticipates that its competitor will choose 6, then it can always secure its local market by charging a price of 8 ECU. Secondly, if one player anticipates that his opponent will pick 8, then he can maximize his payoff by choosing 10 and serving his local market. Finally, if one firm predicts that the other will choose 10, it will announce a price of 6 ECU, at which it captures the whole market. Hence no stable price constellation

Table 1.4   Example 4

Player 1 \ Player 2	6	8	10
6	$(6M, 6M)$	$(6M, 8M)$	$(12M, 0)$
8	$(8M, 6M)$	$(8M, 8M)$	$(8M, 10M)$
10	$(0, 12M)$	$(10M, 8M)$	$(10M, 10M)$

exists in this game since one firm never obtains its maximal payoff when facing the choice of its rival.[7] In 2.2, we will see how to extend the present framework so as to guarantee the existence of a Nash equilibrium; that is, by resorting to mixed strategies.

The preceding examples have allowed us to shed light on some of the major issues associated with the strategic interaction of players in a one-shot game. In the next sub-section, we focus on the Nash equilibrium and present some general results characterizing this particular solution concept.

2.2 Definition and Results

The basic elements of a non-cooperative game G in strategic form are as follows:

(1) $N = \{1, \ldots, n\}$ is the set of players.

In other words, we consider games with a finite and given number of players.

(2) s_i is a strategy of player $i \in N$.

A strategy specifies precisely what a player does. As explained in the introduction, we limit ourselves, unless explicitly stated otherwise, to pure strategies.

(3) S_i is the strategy space of player $i \in N$.

This set describes all the actions available to player i. We suppose that S_i is a subset of the Euclidean space $\mathbb{R}^m$. Thus a strategy is a m-vector of real numbers.

(4) $s = (s_1, \ldots, s_n) \in S \equiv S_1 \times \ldots \times S_n$ is a combination of strategies, one for each player.

Stated differently, s describes the choices made by the set of players in the game under consideration, while S is the set of feasible combinations. It will be convenient to have a notation standing for the choices made by all players but one: s_{-i} is a combination of strategies from which player i's strategy has been deleted.

(5) $P_i(s) \in \mathbb{R}$ is the payoff function of player $i \in N$.

This means that the 'objective function' of player i depends not only upon this player's choice but also upon the decisions made by the others. Once all players have chosen their actions ($s \in S$), the value of the payoff function of each player is determined exactly.

(6)   Each player knows all the strategy sets $S_j, j \in N$, and all the payoff functions $P_j, j \in N$, each player knows that each player knows this information, each player knows that each player knows it, . . .

In other words, everyone in the game knows everything. In the literature, this is referred to as a game of *complete information*.

It is clear that the examples discussed in 2.1 are special non-cooperative games in which there are two players, the strategy spaces are finite and the payoff functions are firms' profits. Hence, using the elements constitutive of a non-cooperative game just described, we can give a general definition of the concept of Nash equilibrium introduced in Example 3 : a Nash equilibrium is a feasible combination of strategies such that each player maximizes his payoff with respect to his own strategy conditionally on the choices made by the others. More formally:

Definition 1

A *Nash equilibrium* of a non-cooperative game G is a feasible combination of strategies s^* which satisfies $P_i (s^*) \geq P_i (s_i, s^*_{-i})$ for all $s_i \in S_i$ and all players $i \in N$.

This solution concept is due to Nash (1951), whence its name. The Cournot (1838) equilibrium in oligopoly theory is a special case of it in which strategies are quantities sold by firms (see Examples 1 to 3 and 2.3). The Bertrand (1883) equilibrium is another special case in which strategies are prices quoted by firms (see Example 4 and 2.3).

To justify the Nash equilibrium as a 'reasonable' solution for non-cooperative games, we find it useful to introduce the following additional concept.

Definition 2

A strategy which maximizes $P_i (s_i, s_{-i})$ over S_i is called a *best reply* of player $i \in N$ against the choices s_{-i} of the others.

Notice that a best reply against s_{-i} may not exist and need not be unique (see below for further details).

We now propose two intuitive interpretations of the Nash equilibrium. Firstly, we assume that, given (6), each player is able to duplicate the reasoning process of any other player. This implies a sort of symmetry : if a player can find that a certain action is the best one on his part, then other players can imagine themselves in his place and can reproduce his argument. In this context, consider a feasible combination $\bar{s} = (\bar{s}_1, \ldots, \bar{s}_n)$ which is not a Nash equilibrium. We claim that this combination of strategies will not be chosen by the players. Suppose indeed that they do choose $(\bar{s}_1, \ldots, \bar{s}_n)$. As $\bar{s}$ is not a Nash equilibrium, it must be that (at least) one of the strategies, $\bar{s}_j$ say, is not a best reply for player j against $\bar{s}_{-j}$. So why did player j select $\bar{s}_j$? This is because the belief of player j on some player k's behaviour was not $\bar{s}_k$ but rather $\hat{s}_k$ different from $\bar{s}_k$. But given that player k has chosen effectively $\bar{s}_k$ and not $\hat{s}_k$, this amounts to saying that player j has been mistaken in duplicating player k's reasoning, contrary to the above assumption.

A second possible interpretation is as follows. Suppose that each player goes separately to a consulting firm whose members have received a good training in game theory. As the firm deals with each player independently of the others, it will make a simultaneous recommendation to the players which has the property of a Nash equilibrium s^*. Since players do not make binding agreements – the non-cooperative hypothesis – each player may or may not follow the consulting firm's recommendation. However, given (6), everyone is aware of the fact that the recommendation s^* made to himself is a best reply against the recommendation s^*_{-i} made to the others. Consequently, in the absence of communication among themselves, players have a strong individual incentive to select the strategies proposed by the consulting firm. If they do so, once the game is over the players will notice that they have each made the best possible choice.

Whatever the interpretation retained, a Nash equilibrium can be viewed as a set of requirements guaranteeing that the players' decisions are globally consistent with the pursuit of self-interest. A Nash equilibrium, when it happens to occur, is therefore self-enforcing.

As seen in Example 4, a Nash equilibrium may fail to exist (at least when players limit themselves to pure strategies). For the setting described by (1)–(6), the following result provides the standard conditions guaranteeing the existence of such an equilibrium.

Theorem 1
If the strategy spaces S_i for all $i \in N$, are compact and convex and if the payoff functions P_i, for all $i \in N$, are continuous in s and quasi-concave in s_i, then there exists a Nash equilibrium (in pure strategies).

The proof follows Nash (1951) in using a fixed point argument. We provide here a sketch of the proof in the case where the payoff functions are strictly quasi-concave. For any given s_{-i}, the continuity of P_i with respect to s_i over the compact set S_i implies that P_i has a maximum, that is player i has a best reply against s_{-i}. Since P_i is also strictly quasi-concave in s_i, the best reply is unique and is denoted by $R_i(s_{-i}) \in S_i$. Furthermore, as P_i is continuous in s, the function $R_i(s_{-i})$ can be shown to be continuous with respect to s_{-i}. These properties hold for all $i \in N$. Hence the (vector valued) function $R(s) = [R_1(s_{-1}), \ldots, R_n(s_{-n})]$ from $S_1 \times \ldots \times S_n$ into itself satisfies all the assumptions of the Brouwer fixed point theorem. In other words, $s^* \in S_1 \times \ldots \times S_n$ exists such that $s_i^* = R_i(s_{-i}^*)$ for all $i \in N$. Given the definition of a best reply, it is then readily verified that s^* is a Nash equilibrium of the corresponding game.[8]

It must be stressed that the conditions of Theorem I are sufficient but not necessary for a Nash equilibrium to exist. We shall see in 2.3 that a game satisfying (1)–(6) but not the assumptions of Theorem 1 may have a Nash equilibrium.[9]

A major implication of Theorem 1 concerns games where each player has finitely many pure strategies (that is, S_i is a finite set as in the examples of 2.1). Let us extend such a game by considering as strategy spaces the sets $\Delta(S_i)$ of all probability vectors defined over S_i. An element of $\Delta(S_i)$ is a mixed strategy and can be interpreted as a lottery over pure strategies. The payoff function P_i can be extended to $\Delta(S_1) \times \ldots \times \Delta(S_n)$ by taking expectations with respect to the product probability distributions induced by mixed strategies. Theorem 1 then applies (since the strategy spaces $\Delta(S_i)$ are convex and the payoff functions multilinear) so that every game with finite strategy spaces has an equilibrium in mixed strategies.

In Example 3, we have seen that a game may have several Nash equilibria. Uniqueness may appear as a desirable property. Geometrically uniqueness occurs when the best reply is unique and when the corresponding curves intersect only once. There are different sets of conditions implying the existence of a unique Nash equilibrium. In the next result, we state a simple condition yielding uniqueness in the case where a strategy is given by a single instrument so that S_i is a compact interval $[l_i, u_i]$ of the real line.

Theorem 2
If the strategy spaces are given by $[l_i, u_i] \subset \mathbb{R}$, if P_i is continuous over S and strictly concave in s_i over $[l_i, u_i]$, if P_i is twice continuously differentiable on S, if the first and second right (left)-derivative of P_i at u_i (l_i) exist, and if

$$\frac{\partial^2 P_i}{\partial s_i^2} + \sum_{\substack{j \in N \\ j \neq i}} \left| \frac{\partial^2 P_i}{\partial s_i \partial s_j} \right| < 0 \tag{D}$$

whatever $s \in S$, for all $i \in N$, then there exists a unique Nash equilibrium.

Basically the condition (D) implies that the strategic interdependence among players is relatively weak in the sense that a change in s_i affects player i more than the others together.[10]

2.3 The Cournot and Hotelling Models

To illustrate the applicability and the relevance of the results presented in the previous sub-section, we study here two well-known duopoly models.

In the Cournot (1838) model, it is assumed that two firms producing a homogeneous product at a constant marginal production cost, $c > 0$, face an inverse demand function given by $p = \max\{a - bQ, 0\}$, where a and b are two positive constants. In order to avoid corner solutions, we suppose that $a > c$. The strategy of a firm is the *quantity* of product sold by this firm. The strategy spaces are identical and given by the compact interval $[0, a - c/b]$. Finally, the profit function of firm i is equal to

$$P_i(q_i, q_j) = \begin{cases} [a - b(q_i + q_j) - c]q_i & \text{if } 0 \leq q_i \leq \frac{a-c}{b} - q_j \\ 0 & \text{if } \frac{a-c}{b} - q_j \leq q_i \leq \frac{a-c}{b} \end{cases}$$

with $i, j = 1, 2$ and $i \neq j$. Clearly P_i is continuous in (q_i, q_j). Moreover P_j is non-negative and strictly concave when $q_i \geq (a - c)/b - q_j$ and zero otherwise so that P_i is quasi-concave on $[0, (a - c)/b]$. Consequently the assumptions of Theorem 1 are satisfied and the Cournot duopoly game has a Nash equilibrium. Furthermore P_i is twice continuously differentiable and $\partial^2 P_i/\partial q^2_i + |\partial^2 P_i/\partial q_i \partial q_i| = -b < 0$. Hence Theorem 2 also holds and the Cournot duopoly model has a unique Nash equilibrium.

We know that this equilibrium is a fixed point of the best reply function $R_1(s_2) \times R_2(s_1)$. Therefore it must lie at the intersection of the two corresponding curves $s_1 = R_1(s_2)$ and $s_2 = R_2(s_1)$. In other words, the Nash equilibrium (q^*_1, q^*_2) is the solution of the first-order conditions

$$\frac{\partial P_1}{\partial q_1} = a - 2bq_1 - bq_2 - c = 0 \tag{1.1}$$

$$\frac{\partial P_2}{\partial q_2} = a - bq_1 - 2bq_2 - c = 0. \tag{1.2}$$

Given the symmetry of (1.1) and (1.2), it is immediately evident that $q^*_1 = q^*_2 = (a - c)/3b$. This equilibrium can be interpreted as follows (see the above discussion in 2.2). It is clear that the first-order conditions (1.1) and (1.2) are both necessary and sufficient for each firm to maximize its profit with respect to its own strategy. Thus, as each player knows the profit function and the strategy set of the other, he can duplicate his opponent's choice process by differentiating this one's profit function with respect to his quantity. In so doing, each player faces the same system of equations (1.1)–(1.2), the solution of which is unique. Given that each firm knows that its rival aims at maximizing its own profit, it can 'reasonably' anticipate that its rival will select the solution of its first-order condition. Consequently, by choosing the solution to its first-order condition, each firm does the best for itself. Indeed, once the firms have chosen their quantities according to this procedure, each one observes that its anticipations have been fulfilled and has, therefore, made the decision which gives it the highest profit. Such a behaviour is quite sophisticated in the sense that the firms are aware of and take into account the interdependence in which they are involved. This is to be contrasted with the usual textbook interpretation of the Cournot model according to which each firm behaves 'as if' the choice made by the other firm was given and uninfluenced by its own action (the 'zero conjectural variation' hypothesis).[11]

We now consider the Hotelling (1929) model. Two firms producing a homogeneous product are located symmetrically on a bounded line of length l at distance $a \in [0, l/2]$ from the endpoints of this line. The marginal production cost, $c > 0$, is constant and the same for both firms. Transport costs are linear in distance and borne by the consumers; let t be the transport rate. Consumers are uniformly distributed along the same line; without loss of generality the density is set equal to one. Each consumer buys exactly one unit of the product irrespective of its price. Since the product is homogeneous, a consumer will patronize the firm with the lower full price; that is, the mill price plus the transport cost. The strategy of a firm is the *mill price* quoted by this firm. The strategy spaces are identical and given by the interval $[c, \infty]$. Finally the profit function of firm i is defined by

$$
P_i(p_i, p_j) = \begin{cases} (p_i - c)l & \text{if } c < p_i \leq p_j - t(l - 2a) \\[2ex] (p_i - c)[a + \dfrac{p_j - p_i + t(l - 2a)}{2t}] & \text{if } p_j - t(l - 2a) < p_i < p_j + t(l - 2a), \\[2ex] 0 & \text{if } p_j + t(l - 2a) \leq p_i, \end{cases}
$$

with $i, j = 1, 2$ and $i \neq j$. The function P_i is depicted in Figure 1.1.

We notice immediately that P_i exhibits two discontinuities at $p_i = p_j - t(l - 2a)$ and $p_i = p_j + t(l - 2a)$. Furthermore $P_i(p_i, p_j)$ is not quasi-concave in p_i. Consequently the assumptions of Theorem 1 (and therefore of Theorem 2) are not satisfied. This does not mean, however, that there exists no Nash equilibrium (in pure strategies). Thus, if $a = l/2$, the model is equivalent to the standard Bertrand model and there is a unique equilibrium given by $p^*_1 = p^*_2 = c$. Let us now suppose that $a \in [0, l/2]$. If a Nash equilibrium exists it must be such that $|p^*_i - p^*_j| < t(l - 2a)$. Suppose on the contrary that (p^*_1, p^*_2) is a Nash equilibrium but that $|p^*_i - p^*_j| \geq t(l - 2a)$. If the inequality is strict and if p^*_i is the higher price, then $P_i(p^*_i, p^*_j) = 0$. As firm i can always secure a positive profit by charging $p_i \in]0, t(l - 2a)[$, this contradicts the fact that (p^*_1, p^*_2) is an equilibrium. If the equality holds and if p^*_i is the higher price, firm j serves the whole market. Two cases may then arise. First, when $p^*_j = 0$ firm j has zero profit and would gain by charging a positive price less than $p^*_i + t(l - 2a)$. Second, when $p^*_j > 0$ firm i, which sets a positive price, can make a positive profit by choosing $p_i = p^*_j$. In both cases, we arrive at a contradiction. Hence we must have $|p^*_i - p^*_j| < t(l - 2a)$. As a consequence, p^*_i must maximize $P_i(p_i, p^*_j) = (p_i - c)[a + (p^*_j - p_i + t(l - 2a))/2t]$ for $i = 1, 2$ and $i \neq j$. Taking the first-order conditions $\partial P_1/\partial p_1 = 0$ and $\partial P_2/\partial p_2 = 0$ yields the candidate equilibrium prices $p^*_1 = p^*_2 = c + tl$. We have now to verify whether or not these prices form a Nash equilibrium. For that, p^*_i must be a best reply against p^*_j over the whole interval $[c, \infty[$, $i = 1, 2$ and $i \neq j$. This amounts to saying that $P_i(p^*_i, p^*_j) = tl/2$ must be larger than or equal to the profit earned by firm i when this firm undercuts its rival; that is, when it sets a price equal to $p^*_j - t(l - 2a) = c + 2ta$ and gains a profit equal to $2tla$.

Figure 1.1   Profits in the Hotelling game

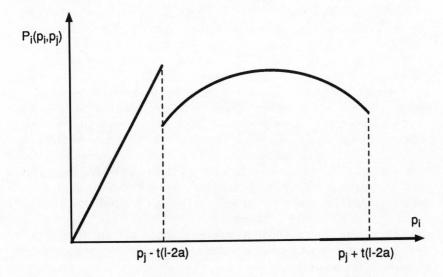

Comparing these two expressions, we see that $P_i(p^*_i, p^*_j) \geq P_i[p^*_j - t(l - 2a), p^*_j]$ if and only if $0 \leq a \leq l/4$. In other words, there exists a unique Nash equilibrium if the two firms are not located inside the first and third quartiles. On the other hand, if the firms are established inside the quartiles but separated, there is no Nash equilibrium (in pure strategies). When firms are close enough to each other, undercutting is a profitable strategy which, in turn, implies equilibrium does not exist.[12]

3 STACKELBERG EQUILIBRIUM

In this section we deal with non-cooperative games where players make a single move which they choose sequentially (or, put in another way, at different stages of the games). It is worth noting here that the order in which players move is part of the description of these games. For simplicity we limit ourselves to the case of two players (the extension to $n \geq 3$ players poses no specific problem). Hence a game is called an *i-Stackelberg game* ($i = 1, 2$) when i is the player moving first.

3.1 Definitions and Results

In a game where they move simultaneously (as in Section 2), players lie in a situation of symmetry in that none of them is able to observe the choice made by the other. Here, on the contrary, we consider a situation of asymmetry in which one player can observe the choice made by its opponent before making his own decision.

To illustrate, let us return for a moment to the payoff matrix 3 and assume that player 1 moves in stage 1 and player 2 in stage 2 (that is, we consider a 1-Stackelberg game). We may expect this game to be played as follows. By assumption, player 2 knows player 1's decision when he takes his action. If firm 1 has chosen 6, then firm 2 maximizes its profit by picking 2. If firm 1 has chosen 2, then firm 2 selects 6. Consider now the problem faced by firm 1. By assumption, player 1 is aware of the fact that player 2 moves after him and takes the best possible action, given the choice he has made. Consequently, in choosing his action, player 1 will anticipate player 2's reaction to his own decision and will select the action maximizing the resulting payoff. This means that firm 1 picks 6 while firm 2 chooses 2. This solution is called a 1-Stackelberg equilibrium and will be discussed in detail below. Let us now change the game by reversing the distribution of roles and suppose that player 2 moves first and player 1 second (that is, we consider a 2-Stackelberg game). An argument similar to that just developed leads to a different solution (firm 1 selects 2 and firm 2 picks 6) called a 2-Stackelberg equilibrium.

In view of this example, the following comments are in order. Firstly, the distinctive feature of the Stackelberg game is the asymmetry between players. This asymmetry is reflected in the way the strategies are defined. If player i moves first, then a strategy for player i is just an *action*. On the other hand, a strategy for player j, with $j \neq i$, is a *function* that maps an action for player i into an action for player j. In the above example, this means that player i's strategy space is given by $\{2, 6\}$, whereas player j's strategy space is $\{(2, 2),(2, 6),(6, 2),(6, 6)\}$, where a strategy such as $(2,6)$ means 'choose 2 if player i has chosen 2, choose 6 otherwise'. Secondly, the equilibrium payoffs of a 1-Stackelberg game are in general different from those of a 2-Stackelberg game. This raises the problem of determining who moves first and why. We shall return to this issue in 3.2. Finally, establishing the existence of an i-Stackelberg equilibrium can be proved under rather weak conditions. In finite two-person games, it can be shown indeed that there exists a unique i-Stackelberg equilibrium, for $i = 1$ and 2, when the payoff functions are one-to-one (see, for example, Moulin, 1982, p. 71). It is readily verified that this property holds for the payoff matrix 4 of 2.1.

We keep the notation introduced in assumptions (1) to (6) stated in 2.2, but we now interpret s_i as an action of player i and S_i as his action space. The strategies of the players will be specified in the definition below. Formally, we have :

Definition 3
Suppose that the game has two stages and that player i (j) takes his action in stage 1(2). Then an *i-Stackelberg equilibrium* is a Nash equilibrium of the non-cooperative game in which

1. S_i is the strategy space of player i;
2. player j's strategy space is the set of functions that map a strategy $s_i \in S_i$ of player i into an action $s_j \in S_j$ of player j.

Player i is called the leader and player j the follower of the corresponding Stackelberg game.

Intuitively, the follower reacts optimally to the choice made by the leader while the latter makes his decision in anticipating the former's reaction. By moving first, player i reveals his choice to player j whose decision problem reduces to an optimization problem defined by player i's equilibrium strategy. In turn, player i faces an optimization problem in which player j's equilibrium strategy (that is, a best reply function) is nested.

As seen above in the case of finite games, the conditions for a Stackelberg equilibrium to exist are much weaker than those imposed by the

Nash equilibrium in simultaneous games. In particular, the following existence property holds. [13]

Theorem 3
If the action spaces S_1 and S_2 are compact and if the payoff functions P_1 and P_2 are continuous on $S_1 \times S_2$, then there exists an i-Stackelberg equilibrium for $i = 1$ and 2.

Thus an *i*-Stackelberg equilibrium always exists without imposing concavity/convexity assumptions on the constituent elements of the game. The standard conditions of optimization theory – compactness of the action spaces and continuity of the payoffs – are sufficient. However, as in Theorem 1, these conditions are not necessary.

3.2 Stackelberg Duopoly and Sequential Entry

Von Stackelberg (1934) is mainly remembered for his reformulation of the Cournot duopoly (see 2.3). Assume that firm 1 is the leader and firm 2 the follower. The best reply function of firm 2 is unique and can be obtained from (1.2) as

$$q^*_2(q_1) = \frac{a - bq_1 - c}{2b}. \tag{1.3}$$

Replacing q_2 by $q^*_2(q_1)$ given by (1.3) in firm 1's profit function yields

$$P_1[q_1, q^*_2(q_1)] = \frac{a - bq_1 - c}{2} q_1.$$

Maximizing this expression with respect to q_1 leads to the solution

$$\bar{q}_1 = \frac{a - c}{2b}.$$

Introducing $\bar{q}_1$ in (1.3) gives the optimal decision for firm 2, that is,

$$\bar{q}_2 = \frac{a - c}{4b}.$$

Some simple calculations show that the profits earned by firms 1 and 2 at the 1-Stackelberg equilibrium are respectively equal to $(a-c)^2/8b$ and $(a-c)^2/16b$. Hence firm 1 makes higher profits than firm 2, and, therefore, enjoys being the leader of the game.[14]

In the above game, the order of moving was given *a priori*. Recently it has been recognized that the distribution of roles (being the leader or the follower, or playing simultaneously) should not be exogenous but should result from the firm's decisions. Along these lines, one possible approach is to embed simultaneous and sequential play into an extended game where players first select the timing of choosing actions in the basic game. Sequential playing then emerges as an equilibrium of the extended game if and only if one player prefers leading to simultaneous play to following and the other prefers following to simultaneous play (see Hamilton and Slutsky, 1990, p.37). Note that this condition is not satisfied in the Cournot duopoly since the equilibrium profit at the simultaneous game is $(a-c)^2/9b$, which exceeds the follower's profit $(a-c)^2/16b$.

However, in some cases, because of context-specific considerations, the distribution of roles comes naturally.[15] To make clear this idea, consider the following model of entry. The demand side of the model is similar to that of the Hotelling model (see 2.3). On the supply side, it is assumed that firms enter sequentially and locate once and for all. Hence it seems reasonable to expect that, at each stage of the entry process, the entrant will consider as given the locations of firms entered at earlier stages but will treat the locations of firms entering at later stages as conditional upon his own choice. In other words, the entrant is a follower with respect to the incumbents, and a leader with respect to future competitors. The location chosen by each entrant is then obtained by backward induction, from the optimal solution of the location problem faced by the ultimate entrant, to the entrant himself.[16]

4 SUBGAME PERFECT NASH EQUILIBRIUM

We now consider non-cooperative *multi-stage* games where players may choose simultaneously an action at each stage of the game and know the actions taken by the others in previous stages. In a certain sense, the equilibrium concept discussed in this section aims at combining the basic ideas of the preceding two sections.

4.1 Subgame Perfection

The fact that the game is played over several stages and that players are able to observe the actions previously taken has some important implications. First, the division into stages is often motivated by the fact that, in practice, the choice of some actions is prior to the choice of others. Accordingly, if decisions made in early stages are relatively less flexible than decisions made in later stages, players will try to anticipate the consequences of the former upon the latter. In other words, in picking their actions at any stage, players will look ahead to their implications for the next stages. Hence, as in the preceding section, players will solve the game by backward induction. We shall study an example in 4.2.

Second, in some games, certain Nash equilibria appear as implausible once the underpinning division into stages of these games is uncovered. To illustrate this idea, consider the following two-stage, two-person game. Player 1 is an established firm and player 2 a potential entrant. Furthermore the entrant must incur a sunk cost of 10 ECU. Finally, if player 2 chooses to enter in stage 1, the resulting game in stage 2 is identical to that of Example 1. In stage 1, player 2 faces two actions: enter (E) or stay out (S). In stage 2, player 1 (and player 2 if he chooses to enter) has two actions, producing 4 or 6. Therefore player 1 has four strategies ((4(E), 4(S)), (4(E), 6(S)), (6(E), 4(S)) and (6(E), 6(S)) whereas player 2 has three strategies (given by (E, 4(E)), (E, 6(E)) and (S). The corresponding game in extensive form is represented in Figure 1.2 (the information set of player 2 contains two nodes in the game induced by E because the players move simultaneously at the output stage. We leave to the reader the description of the game in strategic form (that is, the payoff matrix).

It is readily verified that this game has two Nash equilibria (in pure strategies). At the first equilibrium, the second firm enters the market and then sells 4 ; the incumbent also sells 4. At the second one, firm 2 stays out and the incumbent sells 6 . In this case, firm 1's output is so large that firm 2 can never earn positive profits if it enters. Stated differently, the output of the incumbent is large enough to prevent entry. However one should not forget that firm 2 decides to enter or not in the first stage. Once firm 2 has chosen to enter, then it never pays for the incumbent to sell 6. Indeed the game is now reduced to the game described in Example 1, so that {4(E), 4(E)} emerges as an equilibrium in which both firms gain positive profits. Hence the second equilibrium proves to be unreasonable since the potential entrant, when facing the entry decision, correctly anticipates that the incumbent will not choose 6 . In other words, {(6(E), 6(S)), S} is sustained by an 'incredible threat' of firm 1.

Selten (1965, 1975) is given credit for having introduced into game theory the idea of subgame perfection that makes it possible to cope with the foregoing problem. To describe Selten's equilibrium concept, we suppose that, *after each stage*, the players are fully informed of the past so that the remainder of the game is itself a game called *subgame* of the original game. Selten then requires that *the equilibrium strategies of the players are best replies to one another for each subgame of the game* (that is, whatever the previous 'history' of the game, even when that history does not occur under the equilibrium strategies). In other words, in order to be subgame perfect, a Nash equilibrium must induce an equilibrium in every subgame. In this way, the strategies selected by the players are such that each player anticipates the impact of his current decision upon the subsequent ones and such that incredible threats are eliminated. Given the discussion of the above example, it is clear that {(4(E), 6(S)), (E, 4(E))} is subgame perfect, but {(6(E), 6(S)), S} is not.

The above definition of subgame applies to games in extensive form (with finite strategy space), where the notion of subgame is transparent and corresponds to that of subtree of the original tree. However there are cases where subgames may not exist (the players may never know at which node of the tree they are) and, consequently, the concept of subgame-perfect Nash equilibrium becomes meaningless. To make this point clear, consider a two-person game where players have to choose between *L* (left)

Figure 1.2   Entry game in extensive form

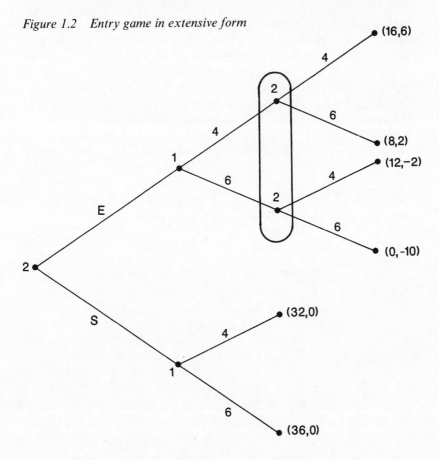

and *R* (right) at each stage of the game. The first stage of the (extensive form) game of complete information is depicted in Figure 1.3. Players 1 and 2 take an action simultaneously. This is expressed in Figure 1.3 by the fact that the information set of player 2, say, contains two nodes. In other words, all player 2 knows is that the game has reached some node within the information set defined by the solid line. When players 1 and 2 have taken their action in stage 1, they know where they are in the tree and the play proceeds at one of the four possible subgames, starting at the node indexed by I.

Assume now that Nature makes an initial move unobserved by the players. In Figure 1.4, player 1's information set contains two nodes (instead of one, as in Figure 1.3). It is then clear that no subgame appears after both players have moved because they are unable to know with certainty at which node of the tree they are. This difficulty has motivated the development of more sophisticated approaches which are beyond the scope of this chapter.[17] It is worth noting that the need for a refinement of the Nash equilibrium concept appears in strategic form games too where sub-game perfection is of no use. Here also a lot of work has been done recently.[18]

Before turning to an application of subgame perfection to a location–price model, we present a result for a special class of multi-stage games which sets up links between this section and the previous one. A multi-

Figure 1.3   Simultaneous game with complete information

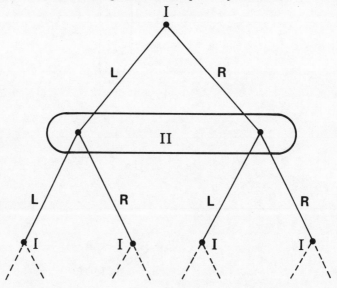

stage game in extensive form is called a game with *perfect information* if, each time a player has to move, he knows all the decisions made in the previous stages and is the only player who moves at this stage (more formally, all the information sets contain a single node). It should be clear that such games can always be solved by a backward induction procedure which is similar to what is done in dynamic programming. Accordingly, for games with perfect information, we obtain automatically the existence of subgame-perfect Nash equilibria in pure strategies.[19] The Stackelberg game studied in Section 3 enters naturally into that category since it assumes a two-stage game with perfect information where the leader plays only in stage 1 and the follower only in stage 2.

4.2 The Location–Price Model

Consider the Hotelling model (see 2.3) in which firms are now assumed to choose first their locations and then their prices. In the present context, the concept of subgame perfection captures the idea that, when firms select their locations, they both anticipate the consequences of their choice on price competition. In particular, they should be aware that this

Figure 1.4   Simultaneous game with incomplete information

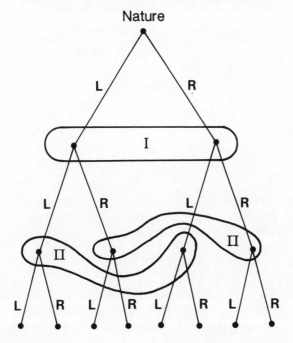

competition will be more severe if they locate close to each other. On the other hand, if they move far apart from each other, they weaken their ability to encroach on their rival's market territory. The solution to this trade-off is given by the Nash equilibrium of the first-stage game.

We have seen in 2.3 that a Nash equilibrium (in pure strategies) may not exist for some location pairs.[20] To obviate this difficulty (see below), we suppose from now on that transport costs are quadratic in distance (tx^2).

In the first stage, firms 1 and 2 choose locations in the interval $[0,l]$ at distances a and b from the left and right endpoints of $[0,l]$, respectively. With any location pair (a,b) such that $a + b \leq 1$ is associated a (continuous) subgame, the strategies of which are the firms' prices and the payoff functions, their profit functions given by:[21]

$$P_1(p_1, p_2; a, b) = \begin{cases} (p_1-c)l & \text{if } l < a + \dfrac{p_2-p_1}{2t(l-a-b)} + \dfrac{l-a-b}{2}, \\[2ex] (p_1-c)\left(a + \dfrac{p_2-p_1}{2t(l-a-b)} + \dfrac{l-a-b}{2}\right) \\[2ex] \qquad \text{if } 0 \leq a + \dfrac{p_2-p_1}{2t(l-a-b)} + \dfrac{l-a-b}{2} \leq l, \\[2ex] 0 & \text{if } a + \dfrac{p_2-p_1}{2t(l-a-b)} + \dfrac{l-a-b}{2} < 0, \end{cases}$$

and

$$P_2(p_1, p_2; a, b) = \begin{cases} (p_2-c)l & \text{if } l < b + \dfrac{p_2-p_1}{2t(l-a-b)} + \dfrac{l-a-b}{2}, \\[2ex] (p_2-c)\left(b + \dfrac{p_2-p_1}{2t(l-a-b)} + \dfrac{l-a-b}{2}\right) \\[2ex] \qquad \text{if } 0 \leq b + \dfrac{p_2-p_1}{2t(l-a-b)} + \dfrac{l-a-b}{2} \leq l, \\[2ex] 0 & \text{if } b + \dfrac{p_2-p_1}{2t(l-a-b)} + \dfrac{l-a-b}{2} < 0. \end{cases}$$

It is readily verified that Theorem 1 applies so that there exists a Nash equilibrium in prices. Furthermore, as the best reply curves intersect only once, this equilibrium is unique and given by

$$p^*_1(a, b) = c + t(l - a - b)\left(l + \frac{a - b}{3}\right), \tag{1.4}$$

$$p^*_2(a, b) = c + t(l - a - b)\left(l + \frac{b - a}{3}\right). \tag{1.5}$$

The functions (1.4) and (1.5) describe the *choice rules* of players 1 and 2 for any price subgame. They are defined conditionally upon the locations selected in the first stage. Substituting (1.4) and (1.5) in the above profit functions, we obtain the payoff functions $P^*_1(a, b)$ and $P^*_2(a, b)$ of the first-stage game. It can be shown that $\partial P^*_1/\partial a < 0$ and $\partial P^*_2/\partial b > 0.$[22] Hence, $a^* = b^* = 0$ is the unique Nash equilibrium of the location game. Consequently the Hotelling model with quadratic transport costs has a subgame perfect Nash equilibrium given by $a^* = b^* = 0$ and by the choice rules (1.4) and (1.5). Put into words, the equilibrium path is such that firms 1 and 2 locate at the endpoints of the market and charge a price equal to $c + tl^2$.

5 REPEATED GAMES

The games introduced in Section 2 – where players make simultaneous and single moves – have been modified gradually in Sections 3 and 4 so as to investigate multi-stage interactive decision processes. Here we advance one step further with repeated games where the *same game is played repetitively* and the players are interested in their *long-run payoffs*. By allowing repetition, these games turn out to be appropriate for scenarios involving threat and revenge. The main result is that repetition *enables cooperation*. Specifically, outcomes requiring cooperation (that is, collusion with binding agreements) in a one-shot game can emerge as (non-cooperative) Nash equilibria of the repeated game.

5.1 Repeated Prisoner's Dilemma

Let us consider Example 2 (see 2.1) and suppose that the two firms have to play this game a large, unknown number of times (which can be idealized by assuming an infinite sequence of rounds). It will emerge from the discussion below that this game is different from the one-shot game analysed in 2.1.

Assume that each player is able to observe the move of his opponent after each stage (or period) $t = 1, 2, \ldots$ (this assumption is called *full monitoring*). Then, the ability to condition choices in stage t on the observed actions of previous stages allows firms 1 and 2 to achieve in a non-cooperative way an outcome normally associated with cooperation; that is, (3, 3). More precisely, each player can adopt the following strategy: choose 3 at stage t when (3, 3) has been played at every previous stage; otherwise select 4 . If both players start with (3, 3) at stage 1 and follow the above strategy in the subsequent stages, the players' profit at each stage is equal to 18 ECU, so that their average payoff is also 18 ECU. (In the present model, we evaluate the long-run payoffs by the limits of the average profits. Notice, however, that the cooperative outcome (3, 3) can also be obtained when the long-run payoffs are the discounted profit streams and when the discount factor is sufficiently close to one. These notions will be made more precise in (5.2.) A deviator would get a payoff of 16 ECU, since his profit at each stage after he has deviated is now 16 ECU. Consequently deviation is not profitable. If each player presumes that the other will have the good sense to behave according to the above-mentioned strategy, their presumptions will be correct, and the cooperative solution (3, 3) at each stage will be sustained as a Nash equilibrium of the repeated game since no firm can earn a higher average profit. Furthermore our argument uses the fact that the game continues after each stage, so that the threat of punishment (moving to choice 4) is a real one. Because it involves playing the Nash equilibrium of the one-shot game, the threat is credible. Indeed, if one firm announces that it will choose 4, then the other cannot do better than choosing 4 too. Thus, it should be clear that the above-described strategies, called *trigger strategies*, are subgame-perfect.[23]

In summary, the properties of the trigger strategies are twofold : (1) players expect the cooperative solution to be repeated as long as both of them have, in previous stages, chosen them; (2) the players' strategies incorporate a possibility to punish a deviator. The punishment is to choose the Nash equilibrium strategy of the one-shot game. This punishment affects both players, but the deterrent effect of the punishment is large enough for no one to deviate.

Obviously, as seen above, playing 4 at each stage of the repeated game independently of the past history, is also a subgame-perfect Nash equilibrium of the infinite game. Hence repetition enables cooperation but does not force it.

If we now suppose that the game is played a known, finite number T of times, the trigger strategies no longer constitute a subgame-perfect equilibrium of the finitely repeated game. Indeed, at the last stage T, any player can gain from deviating since no punishment can take place in the future. Stage T is just similar to a one-shot game so that firms will choose (4, 4). Consider now what happens at stage $T - 1$. One may expect firms to anticipate the situation arising in stage T. Consequently they lie in a situation similar to that of stage T and, therefore, choose (4, 4). By using such a backward induction argument, it is readily verified that playing (4, 4) at each stage $t = 1 \ldots T$ is the only subgame-perfect Nash equilibrium of the finitely repeated game. More generally, the non-cooperative solution (4, 4) is here the only Nash equilibrium of the game (see, however, Section 6).[24,25]

Before generalizing the above results, consider the infinite repetition of the game described in Example 3. As in Example 2, playing 2 as long as all past moves are 2, and 6 otherwise, is a Nash equilibrium with average payoffs of 16 ECU. But this equilibrium is not subgame-perfect because it involves irrational behaviour outside the equilibrium path. This is the case in each subgame following a history which involves choice 6. Indeed, at this Nash equilibrium, firm 1, say, makes the threat of switching to 6 forever if firm 2 ever chooses 6. But this threat is not credible : once firm 2 selects 6, firm 1 does better by choosing 2, which gives it a positive profit.

Nevertheless the solution (2,2) can be sustained as a subgame-perfect Nash equilibrium when more sophisticated strategies are used. They involve punishment for a finite number of stages, followed by a return to the strategies (2,2). In this case, deviation turns out also to be worthless, but now punishment does not harm the non-deviating player.[26]

5.2 The Folk Theorem

For simplicity we consider a two-person game G with finite action spaces S_1 and S_2. For the rest, we use the notation introduced in 2.2.

To begin with, consider the game G_T, consisting of playing G for T times. The first stage $(t=1)$ is played exactly as G: the two players make simultaneous moves. Their moves are then revealed to the players before stage 2 has to be played. Given this information, players make simultaneous moves in stage $t=2$. In the next stages $(t=3 \ldots T)$, players proceed similarly. In so doing, player i $(i=1, 2)$ at stage t chooses an action in S_i on the basis of the information revealed in the previous stages $(\tau = 1 \ldots, t - 1)$; that is, the past history of the game. Thus a (pure) *strategy* σ_i for player i in G_T is a *finite* sequence of mappings,

$$\sigma_i^t : S^{t-1} \rightarrow S_i, t = 1 \ldots T,$$

where S^0 is a given singleton and S^{t-1} the Cartesian product of $S(t-1)$ times. The mapping σ_i^t expresses the fact that player i bases his choice in stage t on the previous observations belonging to S^{t-1}. Let $\sigma = (\sigma_1, \sigma_2)$ be a pair of strategies chosen by players 1 and 2. The payoff functions of G_T are defined by the average (short-run) payoffs:

$$H_i^T (\sigma) = \frac{1}{T} \sum_{t=1}^{T} P_i (s^t (\sigma)), \ i = 1, 2,$$

where the history of the game $s^t (\sigma) = (s_1^t (\sigma), s_2^t (\sigma))$ at stage t can be expressed in a natural way as

$$s^1(\sigma) = (\sigma_1^1, \sigma_2^1)$$
$$s^2(\sigma) = (\sigma_1^2(s^1(\sigma)), \sigma_2^2(s^1(\sigma)))$$

$$s^3(\sigma) = (\sigma_1^3(s^1(\sigma), s^2(\sigma)), \sigma_2^3(s^1(\sigma), s^2(\sigma)))$$
etc.,

$s^t (\sigma)$ denoting the actions chosen at stage t when the strategies σ_1 and σ_2 are played. G_T is then a well-defined game which can be analysed by the methods developed above.

Consider now the case where the game G is repeated an infinite number of times. The notion of strategy is easy to generalize : a strategy becomes an *infinite* sequence of mappings $\sigma_i = (\sigma_i^t)_{t \geq 1}$ which is obtained for $T \to \infty$; let $\sum_i$ denote the corresponding strategy space of player i. However the description of the payoff functions in the infinitely repeated game is somewhat more delicate. There are two standard ways of proceeding.

In the first one, a discount factor δ $(0 < \delta < 1)$ is introduced to account for some impatience of the players. Given that $(1 - \delta) \sum_{t=1}^{\infty} \delta^{t-1} = 1$, the δ-*discounted game* G_δ has the following payoff functions:

$$H_i^\delta (\sigma) = (1 - \delta) \sum_{t=1}^{\infty} \delta^{t-1} P_i(s^t(\sigma)), \quad i = 1, 2.$$

As with G_T, G_δ is a well-defined game.

In practice, G_T and G_δ may not be very tractable for values of T and δ far from their limit. Hence it is useful to analyse an idealized version, corresponding to the second approach, where agents are completely patient: the infinite game G_∞. In this game, the definition of the payoffs may pose problems because the limits of the average short-run payoffs do not necessarily exist. However, as seen below, the definition of a Nash equilibrium for G_∞ does not require the specification of the payoff functions for all pairs of strategies.

Definition 4

A pair of strategies (σ_1^*, σ_2^*) is a Nash equilibrium of the game G_∞ if the following two conditions hold:

1. $H_i^\infty (\sigma^*) = \lim_{T \to \infty} H_i^T (\sigma^*)$ exists for $i = 1, 2$;

2. $\limsup_{T \to \infty} H_i^T(\sigma_i, \sigma_j^*) \leq H_i^\infty (\sigma^*)$ for all $\sigma_i \in \sum_i$, $i, j = 1, 2$ and $j \neq i$.

Thus it is required that the payoffs converge along the equilibrium path when $T \to \infty$ (condition (1)). The worth of the deviation is evaluated through a strong criterion; that is, the upper limit of the sequence $(H_i^T(\sigma_i, \sigma_j^*))_{T \geq 1}$ (condition (2)).

The most famous result on repeated games is the 'Folk Theorem', so denominated because its authorship is not clear.[27] Its statement, in the present context, consists of a characterization of the set E_∞ of the equilibrium payoffs of G_∞. To this end, we introduce the following two concepts. First, the set of feasible payoffs in the game G is the largest set of expected payoffs which can be generated in a play of G, assuming that players can use a joint lottery to select an outcome. Formally this set is defined as the convex hull of $\{P_1(s), P_2(s); s \in S\}$. In Example 2 (see 2.1 and 5.1), this set is the convex polygon with vertices (16, 16), (20, 15), (18, 18) and (15, 20) represented in Figure 1.5. Let us illustrate how in the infinite repetition of Example 2 the two players can obtain a convex combination of the vertices such as

$$(17.5, 17.5) = \frac{1}{4}(16, 16) + \frac{3}{4}(18, 18).$$

For that, they just have to play (4, 4) once every four times and (3, 3) the rest of the time (for example, play (4, 4) at stage 1 and (3, 3) in the next three stages, then again (4, 4) and so on). This is easily generalized.

Figure 1.5   Feasible payoffs of game G

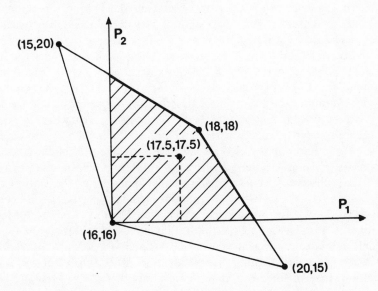

Second, the individually rational level v_i of player i in G is defined as the lowest payoff at which his opponent can hold him down. A payoff for G is then said to be *individually rational for player i* if it is at least as large as v_i. In Example 2, the individually rational level of each player is 16 because, by selecting 4, a player is sure that the payoff of his opponent cannot exceed 16, and this is the lowest level with this property. We can now state a version of the Folk Theorem.[28]

Theorem 4
The set E_∞ of Nash equilibrium payoffs of G_∞ coincides with the set of feasible and individually rational payoffs of G.

Applied to Example 2, this theorem says that all the payoffs in the shaded area of Figure 5 are Nash equilibrium payoffs of the infinitely repeated game. In particular we see that both the Nash equilibrium payoffs (16,16) of the one-shot game G and the cooperative payoffs (18,18) belong to this area.

One of the nice aspects of Theorem 4 is that it allows one to characterize precisely the equilibrium payoffs of G_∞ in terms of the game G. The feasible individually rational payoffs of G can be interpreted as the acceptable outcomes that could result from a contract passed between the two players; that is if G were played cooperatively.

A much less attractive feature of the Folk Theorem is that almost any outcome of the game G can be an equilibrium of the infinitely repeated game. In general, unlike what we observe in the infinite repetition of Example 2, the set E_∞ may even contain payoffs which do not weakly Pareto-dominate Nash equilibrium payoffs of G (to see this, apply Theorem 4 to Example 1 of 2.1). Does one get a smaller set by restricting oneself to subgame-perfect Nash equilibria? The answer is no: Theorem 4 still holds for subgame-perfect Nash equilibria. (Notice that the proof of this result requires some care in the description of the punishment strategies, so as to avoid incredible threats.) In particular, it is easy to prove that any feasible and individually rational payoffs of G which Pareto-dominate Nash equilibrium payoffs of G (if any) are subgame-perfect equilibrium payoffs of G_∞ (as in Example 2 where (18,18) Pareto-dominates (16,16)).

Finally, observe that a complementary approach to large horizon games is to study the set E_δ (E_T) of (possibly subgame-perfect) equilibrium payoffs of G_δ (G_T) for δ approaching one (for T going to infinity). Most results state that Theorem 4 still holds; that is, E_δ (E_T) is close to the set of feasible individually rational payoffs of G when $\delta \rightarrow 1$ (when $T \rightarrow \infty$).[29] In this respect, it is worth noting that the repetition of Example 2 provides an exception. Indeed, for every finite T, we know that $E_T = \{(16,16)\}$. The non-convergence is due to the fact that G has a single pair of equilibrium payoffs.

5.3   The Repeated Cournot Duopoly

Consider the Cournot duopoly described in 2.3 but which is now repeated infinitely many times. The single Nash equilibrium of the one-shot game is $q_1^* = q_2^* = (a-c)/3b$ with payoffs $P_1^* = P_2^* = (a-c)^2/9b$. Clearly the individually rational level v_i of firm i is $v_i = 0$, while the upper frontier of the feasible payoff area is obtained by taking all the convex combinations $\theta P_1^* + (1-\theta)P_2^*$ with $\theta \in [0, 1]$. The corresponding set of feasible individually rational payoffs for the Cournot game is represented by the shaded area in Figure 1.6. The Folk Theorem remains applicable in that any outcome belonging to this area can be supported as a Nash equilibrium of the repeated Cournot game G_δ if players discount the future sufficiently little.

In particular, for supporting cooperative outcomes, the trigger strategies still have the undeniable advantage of simplicity. For example, Friedman (1971) has proposed the following particular strategies for G_δ. He

Figure 1.6   Feasible payoffs for the repeated Cournot game

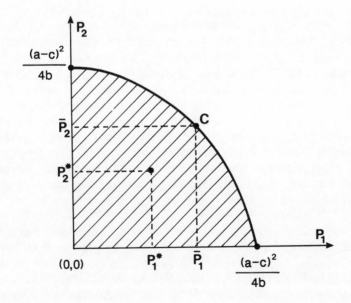

first restricts his analysis to payoffs which are not Pareto-dominated by others; they are represented in Figure 1.6 by the solid curve C. This leaves us with a continuum of possible solutions. Assume that $(\bar{q}_1, \bar{q}_2) \in C$ has been chosen and let $\tilde{q}_i = \text{argmax } P_i(q_i, \bar{q}_j)$ for $i = 1, 2$ and $i \neq j$. Then each firm is 'tempted' to move to $\tilde{q}_i$, which gives it a higher short-run profit. Friedman proposes choosing $(\bar{q}_1, \bar{q}_2)$ according to the *balanced temptation rule*, defined as follows:

$$\frac{P_i(\tilde{q}_i, \bar{q}_j) - P_i(q^*_i, q^*_j)}{P_i(\bar{q}_i, \bar{q}_j) - P_i(q^*_i, q^*_j)} = \frac{P_j(\tilde{q}_j, \bar{q}_i) - P_i(q^*_j, q^*_i)}{P_j(\bar{q}_i, \bar{q}_j) - P_j(q^*_i, q^*_j)}$$

for $i = 1, 2$ and $i \neq j$. This rule leaves each firm equally tempted to deviate and, for this reason, appears as intuitively appealing. Given the symmetry of the game, $(\bar{q}_1, \bar{q}_2)$ is uniquely determined by $\bar{q}_1 = \bar{q}_2 = (a - c)/4b$ with profits $\bar{P}_1 = \bar{P}_2 = (a - c)^2/8b$. The corresponding trigger strategies form a subgame-perfect Nash equilibrium of G_δ if the discount factor δ is large enough; that is, $\delta > 0.47$.[30]

6 NEW PERSPECTIVES IN NON-COOPERATIVE GAME THEORY

During the 1980s non-cooperative game theory became the main tool for modelling problems in industrial organization, thus modifying drastically the development of this field. To the different reasons discussed in the foregoing sections, we must also add the success of *games of incomplete information* in explaining several phenomena that have so far received limited theoretical justification (such as limit pricing, advertising, product quality and reputation effects, to mention a few).[31] In this chapter, owing to the lack of space, we have chosen to concentrate on games of complete information. Nevertheless the reader should be equipped for the study of games of incomplete information. Indeed, once an appropriate formalism for these games has been developed, they can be analysed just as the games considered here, using for example the solution concept of Nash equilibrium.[32]

Several generalizations of the models introduced in Section 5 have been worked out. Firstly, the repeated games with incomplete information turn out to be quite appropriate for the study of the strategic use of information. The repetition of the game becomes a 'signalling mechanism', besides being an 'enforcement mechanism', as discussed in Section 5.[33] Secondly, another major extension concerns the games with partial monitoring, where the actions of the players are not completely observable at the end of each stage (recall that, in Section 5, full information was a crucial assumption for the cooperative payoffs to be sustainable by threats of retaliation).[34] Thirdly, a rather new avenue for research deals with bounded rationality in players' behaviour. The motivation here is to justify cooperation in finite repetitions of games similar to our Example 2 (observed in experimental plays)[35] or, even more, to design a framework in which repetition forces cooperation.[36]

Another promising line of research is constituted by the recent development of non-cooperative bargaining games.[37] Clearly, potential applications of these games to industrial economics are many. For example, unlike what is assumed in standard oligopoly theory, we may suppose that buyers do not behave like price-takers but haggle with sellers on prices.[38]

We could not end this (unavoidably incomplete) review of topics of interest without mentioning some work relative to the foundations of the main solution concepts used in non-cooperative game theory. This, in turn, may lead to the development of new solution concepts like, for example, the correlated equilibrium.[39]

NOTES

The authors thank C. d'Aspremont and J. Friedman for very stimulating comments.

1. See, for example, Aumann (1987).
2. For a historical overview of game theory prior to the work of von Neumann and Morgenstern, the reader is referred to Rives (1975).
3. The basic concepts and results of game theory are presented in detail in Luce and Raiffa (1957), Moulin (1982), Friedman (1990) and the forthcoming *Handbook of Game Theory with Economic Applications*, edited by Aumann and Hart. For specific presentations of non-cooperative game theory in the light of oligopoly theory and industrial economics, see Friedman (1977), Fudenberg and Tirole (1989), Rasmusen (1989) and Kreps (1990, Chapters 11 to 15). Finally the articles of the *New Palgrave* devoted to game theory have been gathered into a separate volume edited by Eatwell, Milgate and Newman (1989).
4. This terminology derives from the problem of two prisoners, interrogated separately, who may confess to a minor crime in common or accuse each other of a major crime. An accuser is free unless he is himself accused; the accused one or ones receive a heavy sentence. This story was first told by A. Tucker in a seminar held in 1950 at the Psychology Department of Stanford University. The prisoner's dilemma has a payoff matrix similar to Table 1.2. See, for example, Luce and Raiffa (1957, pp. 94 ff) for further details about this game.
5. A similar problem arises in the following game known as the *battle of the sexes*. A man (player 1) and a woman (player 2) have to decide on an evening entertainment. Each can go either to a football match (F) or to a ballet (B). Unlike standard stereotypes, we assume that the woman prefers the football match and the man prefers the ballet. However the two players always prefer going somewhere together to going anywhere alone. The corresponding payoff matrix can then be written as follows:

Player 1 \ Player 2	F	B
F	(2, 3)	(1, 1)
B	(1, 1)	(3, 2)

Clearly this game has two Nash equilibria, given by (F, F) and (B, B). Which activity (F or B) will be chosen depends on the ability of a player to enforce his more preferred choice (for example if this player has the reputation of being inflexible) or on some particular social inᶜtitution (patriarchal or matriarchal society) which gives the man or the woman the power to decide on the activity to be chosen. Notice that there is a slight difference between the battle of the sexes and the game described in Example 3. The two equilibria are on the main diagonal of the payoff matrix in the former but not in the latter. Example 3 has the same structure as a game known under the name of *chicken* (see for example, Rasmusen (1989, pp. 73 ff)).

6. Surprisingly, for *any* (positive) demand function $p(\cdot)$, *any* 2×2 game with payoff matrix given by

Player 1 \ Player 2	y_1	y_2
x_1	$x_1 p (x_1+y_1), y_1 p (x_1+y_1)$	$x_1 p (x_1+y_2), y_2 p (x_1+y_2)$
x_2	$x_2 p (x_2+y_1), y_1 p (x_2+y_1)$	$x_2 p (x_2+y_2), y_2 p (x_2+y_2)$

has a Nash equilibrium in pure strategies. To show this, it suffices to verify that the existence of a cycle leads to a contradiction.

7. To further illustrate this problem, consider the following two-person game known in game theory as *matching pennies*. In this game, players choose heads (H) or tails (T). If the choices match, player 1 receives 1 penny from player 2; and vice versa when they do not match. The corresponding payoff matrix is therefore given by

Player 1 \ Player 2	H	T
H	(1, −1)	(−1, 1)
T	(−1, 1)	(1, −1)

It is readily verified that this game has no Nash equilibrium in pure strategies.

8. In the case of quasi-concave payoff functions, the best reply functions become point-to-set mappings. For a general proof, see Moulin (1982, pp. 104 ff) or Friedman (1990, pp. 68 ff).

9. More general existence theorems – allowing for jumps in the best replies – relevant to oligopoly theory can be found in Vives (1990).

10. Theorem 2 is a special case of a result due to Rosen (1965). Friedman (1990, pp. 48 ff) provides a survey of the main uniqueness theorems.

11. Most of the main papers devoted to the Cournot model have been collected by Daughety (1988).

12. See Gabszewicz and Thisse (1989) for a survey of Hotelling-type models.

13. The proof is contained in Siemaan and Cruz (1973, p. 540).

14. Notice that the leader does not always gain more than the follower. In particular, when the two players are identical, Gal-Or (1985) shows that the leader obtains higher (lower) payoffs than the follower when the best reply functions of the players are downwards- (upwards-) sloping, respectively. In the Cournot duopoly the best reply functions slope down (see, for example, (1.3)).

15. See Boyer and Moreaux (1989) for a survey of the main contributions where the distribution of roles between leader and follower is endogenous.

16. The reader interested in the details of this model is referred to Prescott and Visscher (1977).

17. See Rasmusen (1989, Chapter 5) for an elementary presentation of those concepts and Fudenberg and Tirole (1989) for further developments.

18. A good introduction to these refinement concepts is contained in van Damme (1987, Chapter 1).

19. This result is due to Kuhn (1953).

20. Despite the discontinuities in the profit functions, there exists an equilibrium in mixed strategies; see Dasgupta and Maskin (1986).

21. When $a + b > l$, the profit functions of firms 1 and 2 are given by $P_2(p_2, p_1; l - b, l - a)$ and $P_1(p_2, p_1; l - b, l - a)$, respectively.

22. The same inequalities hold, *mutatis mutandis*, when $a + b > l$.

23. These strategies have been known since Luce and Raiffa (1957, pp. 97 ff) discussed them. They have been named by Radner (1980).

24. This kind of argument may yield surprising results. To illustrate, consider the following example, due to Selten (1978) and known as the *chain store paradox*. There is one firm (player 1) operating 20 branches in 20 identical (but geographically separated) markets. In each market there is another (single-branch) firm which considers the possibility of entering this market. It is assumed that the game is played over a sequence of 20 consecutive stages. In each stage $k = 1 \ldots 20$, player $k + 1$ must choose to enter (IN) or to use his capital in some other business (OUT). The incumbent can behave in two ways: he decides either to cooperate (C); that is, to share the local market (with payoffs C^I and C^E), or to be aggressive (A); that is, to prey on the entrant (with payoffs A^I and A^E). For this model to yield the desired result, we need $P^M > C^I > A^I$ (where P^M stands for the monopoly profits) and $C^E > 0 > A^E$ (so that player $k + 1$ wishes to enter if and only if he is not preyed upon). Using an argument similar to the one developed above shows that the only subgame perfect Nash equilibrium is given by (C, IN) repeated 20 times. In other words, all the potential entrants come into business; the incumbent shares each market with his local competitor and earns rather low profits. Clearly this solution hinges on the assumption of complete information. Allowing for some lack of information (possibly because the incumbent has a 'bounded rationality' behaviour) may lead to a completely different picture. In particular, by deterring entry over the first stages, the incumbent can build the reputation of being aggressive which, in turn, has the effect of convincing the subsequent players to stay out. In each of the remaining stages, the incumbent then reaps the monopoly profits; that is P^M. Hence, by clouding the issue, player 1 can guarantee to himself higher payoffs (see, for example Phlips, 1988, Chapter 7 and the references given therein for detailed discussions of the paradox).

25. See Friedman (1990, Chapter 4) and Sorin (1988) for further details. Notice that Friedman (1985) and others have shown that this result does not necessarily hold when the one-shot game has multiple Nash equilibria: a credible threat consists of playing the

Nash equilibrium which is the least favourable one to the opponent. See Fraysse and Moreaux (1985) for an application to oligopoly theory.

26. See Friedman (1990, Chapter 4), Sorin (1988) and references contained therein.
27. It seems that the Folk Theorem was mentioned for the first time in a series of papers by Aumann published in the late 1950s and early 1960s.
28. See, for example, Aumann (1985, pp. 230 ff) for a proof.
29. A very nice introduction to the literature on repeated games can be found in Friedman (1990, Chapter 4). A detailed survey of the main versions of the Folk Theorem for games of complete information is provided by Sorin (1988).
30. See Friedman (1971, Proposition 4).
31. A good introduction to those applications can be found in Milgrom and Roberts (1987) and Rasmusen (1989, Chapter 12 and 13).
32. The appropriate model for games of incomplete information has been conceived by Harsanyi (1967–8).
33. A recent survey has been given by Forges (1988).
34. See again Sorin (1988) for an overview and references.
35. See Axelrod (1984) for a review of experimental games, and Kreps, Milgrom, Roberts and Wilson (1982) for a justification of cooperation in finitely repeated prisoner's dilemma using bounded rationality.
36. See Aumann and Sorin (1989).
37. The basic reference is Rubinstein (1982). A good introduction to that theory is contained in Sutton (1986).
38. For an application to the Hotelling model, see Bester (1989).
39. The concept of correlated equilibrium is due to Aumann (1974). See also Bernheim (1986) for an overview of different solution concepts.

2.   Strategic Behaviour and Collusion

Margaret E. Slade and Alexis Jacquemin

1   INTRODUCTION

The traditional structure–conduct–performance paradigm of industrial economics, in which exogenous market structure determines endogenous conduct and the two jointly determine economic performance, has lost ground in recent years. Most 'new industrial economics' analyses begin with assumptions concerning behaviour or conduct.[1] The implications of these assumptions for both market structure and economic performance are then derived.

If we think of participants in a market as being engaged in a game, then the choice of the rules of the game and the strategy space is crucial. For example, first we must decide if the game is cooperative or non-cooperative. Next, is the game static (one-shot) or is it repeated many times? If the game is repeated, can players condition their choices or strategies in any period on the choices made by others in the past? And then, do early-period choices affect later-period payoffs or are payoffs time-independent? And finally, are there spillovers between firms or are the effects of their actions purely private?

The answers to these questions about conduct are all important in determining the equilibrium outcome of the game – the market structure and economic performance. Indeed a clever choice of assumptions can yield virtually any desired market configuration. In this chapter we attempt to highlight the role of assumptions in determining outcomes. We present several stylized classes of games that we feel capture many real-world situations. The models are very simple. Nevertheless we believe that an understanding of these simple models yields insights into the complex mix of cooperation and rivalry that characterizes most markets. Clearly such an understanding is a prerequisite for intelligent public policy towards modern industry.

In this chapter we address only a few topics that have recently engaged our attention. We do not attempt to survey the entire field or to mention all relevant contributions. The next section is an informal discussion of firms' incentives to collude and the problems which they encounter in the process. Section three introduces repeated games with stationary payoffs. In this context, we first consider formal models of successful tacit collusion and then discuss cartel instability and breakdown. Sections four and five, in contrast, introduce two-stage games in which first-period choices alter continuation-game payoffs. Here we look at both rivalry and cooperation. The final section contains a brief discussion of the policy implications that can be drawn from the earlier analysis.

2   FACTORS THAT FACILITATE OR HINDER COLLUSION[2]

Whether firms collude tacitly or overtly, legally or illegally, they face many problems. First, an agreement must be reached. Second, as soon as price is above the non-cooperative level, firms have an incentive to cheat on their collusive arrangement. If the arrangement is to persist, therefore, methods of detecting cheating must be devised. And finally, once cheating is detected, it must be punished. Each stage in this process has its own peculiar problems. Nevertheless we do observe successful collusion. This section highlights the factors that facilitate or hinder success or failure.

Sellers who recognize their mutual dependence will have an incentive to cooperate as long as the profit that each can obtain when acting jointly is higher than when they act independently. In a static world with costless collusion, the non-cooperative outcome is always a feasible cooperative alternative. Under these circumstances, therefore, firms can always do at least as well when colluding as when each acts on its own behalf.

Successful collusion means locating on the profit-possibility frontier (PPF). In the case of duopolists, this frontier is delineated by the maximum profit for firm i, given any feasible profit for firm j. Suppose, for example, that firm i chooses output q^i as its strategic variable and that the inverse demand facing each firm is $h^i(q^i, q^j)$, $i = 1, 2\ j \neq i$. If each firm's cost function is $C^i(q^i)$, then its profits are

$$\pi^i(q^i, q^j) = h^i(q^i, q^j)q^i - C^i(q^i), i = 1, 2, \ j = 2, 1. \tag{2.1}$$

Figure 2.1 shows the set of feasible collusive outcomes in π^1–π^2 space. The PPF is the dashed curve Π^*–Π^*, the boundary of the feasible region.

Choosing a point on this frontier is relatively easy when firms are symmetric. In this case, their joint output will equal the monopoly-industry output Q^M and Q^M will be split equally between the two firms, with each producing $q^M = Q^M/2$. Finally, they will jointly earn the monopoly-industry profit Π^M, and each, moreover, will obtain $\pi^M = \Pi^M/2$ privately.

In other cases, however, joint-profit maximization may not be a reasonable goal and reaching an agreement can be more difficult. This will be true when firm heterogeneities are introduced. Let us first consider the asymmetries already incorporated into equation (2.1), product and cost differences.

With product heterogeneity, each firm will charge a different price and quantities sold will be measured in diverse units. Instead of agreeing on a single price or industry output, therefore, it becomes necessary to determine a whole schedule of prices or quantities, thus multiplying the possible points of disagreement. Negotiations can be simplified, however, by tying all product prices to the price of a single pre-specified product.

With cost heterogeneity, difficulties with the division of profits arise. Maximization of industry profit requires that industry marginal revenue be equated to each firm's marginal cost. With differences in marginal costs, therefore, joint-profit maximization means that firms produce unequal output, earn unequal profit, and may even require that some plants close down altogether.

Although often difficult to administer and sometimes illegal, side payments can be the most effective way to obtain an agreement in a situation of product and cost heterogeneity. This can be illustrated with the help of Figure 2.1. In Figure 2.1, M is the point of joint-profit maximization. M dominates all points within the rectangle $0 - \pi^{2M} - M - \pi^{1M}$ but not all feasible alternatives.

Indeed suppose that firms do not collude but adopt Cournot–Nash behaviour. Let point C represent the Cournot–Nash equilibrium with $\pi^{1C} + \pi^{2C} < \pi^{1M} + \pi^{2M}$. Without side payments, firm 2 will not accept the outcome M, given that it would lose $\pi^{2C} - \pi^{2M} > 0$. It is possible, however, for both firms to increase their profits simultaneously by agreeing to produce q^{1M} and q^{2M}, so that industry profit is Π^M, and to divide the fruits of their joint action in such a way that firm 2, as well as firm 1, gains relative to its non-cooperative prospect. This requires a side payment $S > 0$ from 1 to 2.

Let $\hat{\pi}^i$ denote the profit received by i, inclusive of side payments. The set of possible side payments S from 1 to 2 defines a linear relationship $\hat{\pi}^1 = \Pi^M - \hat{\pi}^2$, which is represented in Figure 2.1 by the solid line $\Pi^M - \Pi^M$, the PPF with side payments. On this line, only the set of points on the segment AB is acceptable to both firms. The exact point on this segment that will be chosen depends on the relative bargaining strengths of the two players.[3]

The problem of reaching an agreement is still more delicate when one considers other types of asymmetry such as differences in preferences. In a dynamic context, for example, firms may have different discount rates. In

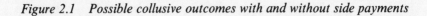

Figure 2.1   Possible collusive outcomes with and without side payments

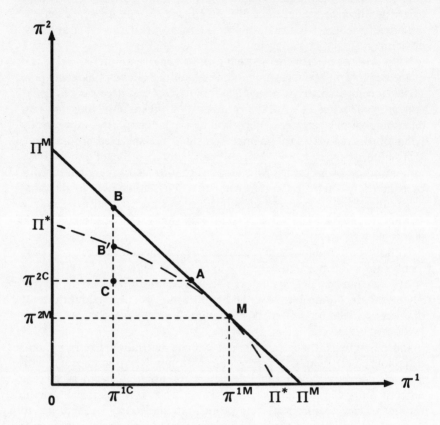

this case, they will disagree about the weights to be given to current and future profits. One firm may want to charge a high price, for example, even though entry is thereby encouraged, whereas the other may take a longer-run view. Preferences can also differ concerning means of coordinating. One seller may be willing to resort to illegal devices, for example, whereas the other may only be willing to collude tacitly.

The introduction of uncertainty can also complicate a collusive arrangement. With randomly changing conditions, agreements must be reached more often, thereby increasing negotiation costs. In addition, divergence of opinion about future conditions becomes more likely. Most important, uncertainty about demand or cost can make it impossible to locate the

PPF, a prerequisite for choosing a point on this frontier. For these reasons, industries that are subject to rapid technical change find it particularly difficult to collude.

When agreements cannot be overt, because of legal restrictions for example, firms must devise ways to signal the need to change price or output. In the case of price-setting firms, a recognized price leader can be agreed upon or the price of a major input can be used as a focal point. These schemes might not lead firms to the PPF but they can enable prices to remain above non-cooperative levels for considerable periods of time.

Reaching an agreement is only the beginning of the process. When a collusive arrangement has been consummated, the mere fact that price is above the non-cooperative level and that marginal revenue for each firm is greater than its marginal cost gives that firm an incentive to cheat. And, the more profitable the cartel, the greater the temptation to defect. A cartel therefore contains the seeds of its own undoing.

The incentive to increase output or to cut price will not be the same for all firms in an industry or for all industries. The elasticity of individual-firm demand is an important factor affecting incentives – the greater this elasticity, the greater the incentive to cut price and increase sales. Firm-specific elasticities are affected both by the industry-wide elasticity and by the number and size distribution of firms within the industry. Very small firms are most apt to take price as parametric and to expect large profits as a result of defection.[4]

Both marginal and fixed costs affect the profitability of cheating. When marginal cost is fairly flat in the neighbourhood of the collusive output, price cutting is more profitable. And when fixed costs are a high fraction of total costs, restricting output may result in excess capacity and therefore a temptation to cut price and increase market share. Finally, if sales are large or infrequent or if detection lags are long, cheating is encouraged. Each of these factors implies that substantial increases in sales can result from a single price cut and makes cheating more desirable.

Because incentives to cheat are pervasive, firms that enter into a collusive agreement must be able to detect secret price cuts or output increases. Suppose that price is the strategic variable. When rival prices are unobservable, firms may have to rely on the behaviour of their own sales for detection purposes. With few firms in a market, a secret cut by one firm results in large decreases in the sales of its rivals and is thus more noticeable. We therefore expect collusion to be more successful when sellers are few.

Collusion should also be more successful when buyers are many. For example, if the probability of detecting a single price cut, ρ, is independent of the number of cuts given and if n cuts are given, the probability that cheating will be detected is $1 - (1 - \rho)^n$. This number approaches one as n increases.

Detection is also facilitated when sellers have more information about rival behaviour. Market information can be increased if firms pool their private information. This practice, however, may be frowned upon by anti-trust authorities. As a response, market participants might form a trade association with a mandate to gather and disseminate information concerning industry conditions.

Buyers can also convey private information. When prices are not public knowledge, however, buyers must be provided with incentives to reveal their offers from rival sellers. One method of accomplishing this task is to promise to match the secret price cuts given by others. Finally temporal patterns of sales are more revealing than single-period information. That is to say, an event that could happen by chance once is much less likely to be random if repeated. When sales are frequent, therefore, detection is facilitated.

Unfortunately for the participants, detection by itself is insufficient to deter cheating. The offender must also be punished. Various forms of punishment strategies are discussed in the next section, where we introduce the notion of tacit collusion in a repeated-game context. We should note first, however, that our discussion has centred on firms that collude on price or output. In reality, firms can choose from a rich set of non-price instruments of rivalry such as advertising, product quality, R&D expenditure, or productive capacity. Some of these alternatives are illustrated in later sections.

Several authors have attempted to investigate the determinants of cartel stability empirically (Hay and Kelly, 1974; Fraas and Greer, 1977; Jacquemin, Nambu and Dewez, 1981; and Suslow, 1988, for example). The findings of these more rigorous investigations tend to confirm the more intuitive notions discussed here.

3 TACIT COLLUSION

We have seen that firms would like to collude but they face many obstacles to accomplishing their objective. This section presents a formal model of tacit collusion based on the notion of a repeated game. The game described is non-cooperative. This means that players never meet to communicate their strategies or to correlate their moves. Nevertheless, in the Nash equilibrium of the repeated game, each firm is better off in every period than in the Nash equilibrium of the one-shot game. We call such outcomes tacitly collusive.

Collusive agreements have a very long history, perhaps thousands of years.[5] The notion that firms might consummate collusive arrangements without meeting or communicating, although not as old, dates at least back to Chamberlin (1929) who coined the phrase 'conscious parallelism'. He noted that, when firms are few and their objectives are similar, they can calculate and move to the cooperative equilibrium without formal communication. We will see how this is accomplished in a game-theoretic setting.

For illustrative purposes, we make simplifying assumptions concerning functional forms. The flavour of our conclusions, however, is not specific to our examples and is in fact characteristic of a much more general class of games. We begin with a model where symmetric oligopolists choose quantity as a strategic variable and produce under conditions of linear demand and cost. Industry-inverse demand and firm costs and profits are respectively

$$P = h(Q) = a - Q, \qquad Q = q^i + q^j \tag{2.2}$$

$$C^i = c\,q^i, \qquad c < a, \tag{2.3}$$

and

$$\pi^i(q^i, q^j) = (a - Q - c)q^i. \tag{2.4}$$

The Cournot-Nash equilibrium of the one-shot game is the solution to

$$\max_{q^i} \pi^i(q^i, q^j), \quad i = 1, 2, \ j = 2, 1. \tag{2.5}$$

First-order conditions for this maximization are

$$a - 2q^i - q^j - c = 0 \tag{2.6}$$

or

$$q^i = R(q^j) = (a - c - q^j)/2, \tag{2.7}$$

where $R(q^j)$ is i's best-reply function. That is, given that j has chosen q^j, i's profit-maximizing or best reply is to produce $R(q^j)$. The intersection of the two best-reply functions yields the Nash equilibrium of the game.

It is straightforward to show that the Cournot–Nash, monopoly,[6] and competitive equilibria of this game are respectively characterized by

$$q^N = (a - c)/3, \ p^N = (a + 2c)/3, \ \pi^N = (a - c)^2/9, \tag{2.8}$$

$$q^M = (a - c)/4, \ p^M = (a + c)/2, \ \pi^M = (a - c)^2/8, \tag{2.9}$$

and

$$q^C = (a - c)/2, \ p^C = c, \ \pi^C = 0. \tag{2.10}$$

In each case, the equilibrium is unique because the firm profit functions are strictly concave and it is symmetric because the game is symmetric.

Now suppose that the one-shot game is repeated a finite number of times, $T < \infty$. In the repeated game, each firm seeks to

$$\max_{\{q_t^i\}} \sum_{t=1}^{T} \delta^t \, \pi^i(q_t^i, q_t^j), \qquad \delta = 1/(1 + r), \tag{2.11}$$

where δ is the discount factor (r is the discount rate), q_t^i is firm i's output in period t, and $\{q_t^i\}$ is i's sequence of choices ($q_1^i, q_2^i, \ldots, q_T^i$). A player's choice q_t^i can depend on the history of play.

We seek a subgame-perfect equilibrium of the repeated game.[7] Given that strategies can depend on the history of the game, we hope that tacitly collusive outcomes can be sustained as non-cooperative equilibria. That is to say, we hope that by threatening to punish a rival for deviations from cooperation, collusion can be supported. As is customary, we begin by considering the last period.

In the last period, as there is no future, the game is equivalent to a one-shot game whose unique equilibrium is (q^N, q^N). Each firm will therefore choose $q_T^i = q^N$, regardless of the history of play. Now stepping back one period, each firm will realize that q^N will be chosen in the last period, no matter what happens in the current period. Again, as there is no future to influence, the game is equivalent to a one-shot game and each player will produce q^N. Stepping back to period $T - 2$, it is possible to use the same reasoning to show that q^N will again be chosen by both players. In fact the entire game unravels and we see that $\{q_t^i\} = (q^N, q^N, \ldots, q^N)$, $i = 1, 2$, is the unique subgame-perfect equilibrium of the finitely repeated game.

This result is very disappointing. We had hoped to sustain cooperation but find that no new equilibria emerge when the stage game is repeated finitely often.[8] The situation is very different, however, when the game is repeated infinitely often.

In the infinitely repeated game each firm seeks to maximize its discounted-profit stream, which is given by (2.11) with $T = \infty$. We make use of the notion of a trigger strategy introduced by Friedman (1971). Let q^*

with $q^N \geq q^* \geq q^M$ be an agreed-upon collusive output. A trigger strategy consists of playing q^* in the first period and in each subsequent period until some player defects. After the first defection, both firms revert to Nash behaviour for the one-shot game and produce q^N in every subsequent period. Formally a trigger strategy is defined by

$$q_0^i = q^*, \quad i = 1, 2 \text{ and} \tag{2.12}$$

$$q_t^i = \begin{cases} q^* \text{ if } q_\tau^j = q^*, \ 0 \leq \tau \leq t-1, \ j = 1, 2 \\ q^N \text{ otherwise.} \end{cases}$$

To see if the trigger strategy is credible, we must calculate the gains from adhering to this strategy and compare them to the gains from defection. A cooperative firm receives.

$$\Gamma^c = \sum_t \delta^t \pi^i(q^*, q^*) \equiv \sum_t \delta^t \pi^* = \pi^*/(1-\delta). \tag{2.13}$$

To calculate the gains from defection, we use the best-reply function $R(q)$ introduced earlier. A defecting firm receives $\pi^1(R(q^*), q^*)$ for one period and π^N thereafter, implying that

$$\Gamma^d = \pi^1(R(q^*), q^*) + \delta\pi^N/(1-\delta). \tag{2.14}$$

Let δ^* be the discount factor that equates (2.13) and (2.14). Then for all δ such that $\delta^* \leq \delta < 1$, q^* can be sustained as a stationary-Nash equilibrium of the repeated game. Manipulation of (2.13) and (2.14) yields

$$\delta^* = \frac{\pi^1(R(q^*), q^*) - \pi^*}{\pi^1(R(q^*), q^*) - \pi^N}. \tag{2.15}$$

Equation (2.15) tells us that collusion is easier to sustain when the punishment is severe (π^N is small), when the collusive outcome is desirable (π^* is large), when the one-shot gain from defection is not too tempting ($\pi^1(R(q^*), q^*)$ is not too large), and when the reaction time is short (the discount factor is close to one).[9]

In our example with $q^* = q^M$,

$$\delta^* = \frac{[3(a-c)/8]^2 - (a-c)^2/8}{[3(a-c)/8]^2 - (a-c)^2/9} = 0.53. \tag{2.16}$$

Equation (2.16) shows that the joint-profit-maximizing outcome is sustainable even when the future is heavily discounted. That is to say, $\delta = 0.53$ corresponds to a discount rate of $r = 0.89$.

Many other classes of repeated-game strategies can sustain tacit collusion. For example, Friedman (1968), Kalai and Stanford (1985), and Samuelson (1987) consider games where period-t choices are determined by continuous functions of the choices made in period $t-1$ (continuous intertemporal-reaction-function strategies), and Abreu (1986) looks at single-period punishments that are more severe than Nash reversion (carrot-and-stick strategies). The flavour of the results, however, is unchanged and most of the conclusions remain the same.

Turning from theory to practice, many economists have attempted to measure equilibrium outcomes in markets that might be susceptible to tacit collusion (Roberts, 1984 – coffee roasting; Spiller and Favaro, 1984 – banks; Suslow, 1986 – aluminium; Slade, 1986 – retail gasoline; and Bresnahan, 1987 – automobiles, for example). The general conclusion is that most outcomes lie in the region A-B'-C of Figure 2.1, which is consistent with our model. For an overview of this literature, see Geroski (1988) and Bresnahan (1989).

Moreover, many industries have been accused of 'conscious parallelism'. These include cement, drugs, dyes, lumber, theatres and tobacco. All are industries that are dominated by a few large firms. Our analysis, however, might lead one to conclude that almost all industries should be almost perfectly collusive almost all of the time. In reality, the situation can be very different. One fundamental reason is uncertainty.

In a world of perfect information – the assumptions underlying the previous model – it is possible to fine tune. For example, exact conditions for cartel sustainability can be calculated. When uncertainty is introduced, in contrast, matters become more complex. Not only is breakdown possible, in many cases it is inevitable. The breakdown of tacitly collusive arrangements, a pervasive phenomenon, is illustrated by the US producers of lead-based anti-knocks (gasoline additives). No cheating occurred in this industry until demand fell drastically as a result of government intervention in the form of environmental regulation. At this point, however, firms began to offer secret discounts off the tacitly agreed-upon price, causing strife in the industry (US Federal Trade Commission, 1981).

This problem can be illustrated formally with a game-theoretic model of cartel breakdown and price wars. Most price-war models rely on three ingredients – a collusive output q^* and a punishment strategy, a random variable θ that can affect either demand or cost, and a specification of which participants can observe the variables of interest. In these models, what seems to be disequilibrium behaviour is in fact part of an equilibrium repeated-game strategy.

For example, in the model of Green and Porter (1984) uncertainty affects the demand equation (2.2), which is modified as follows

$$P_t = h(Q_t)\theta_t = (a - Q_t)\theta_t, \tag{2.17}$$

where θ_t is an identically and independently-distributed random variable with cumulative-density function $F(\theta)$. Firm i can observe P_t and q_t^i but cannot observe q_t^j, $j \neq i$, or θ_t. This means that firms confronted with a price decrease cannot distinguish between the effects of a bad demand shock (low θ_t) and a rival defection ($q_t^j > q^*$).

Strategies in this model are modified-trigger-price strategies. Price in (2.17) is a random variable, implying that it is not possible to fine tune. Instead a trigger-price $\tilde{P}$ is specified. When P_t drops below $\tilde{P}$, punishment (reversion to q^N) is triggered for T periods.[10] The details of the model are presented in the appendix. An implication of the model is that for many distributions $F(\theta)$, price will periodically drop below $\tilde{P}$ and trigger the punishment. Breakdown (Nash reversion) occurs in spite of that fact that no one has deviated and increased output. If, for example, θ is normally distributed, no matter how $\tilde{P}$ is chosen there will be periodic price wars.

Other price-war models rely on different assumptions concerning strategies, uncertainty, and observability. For example, the model of Rotemberg and Saloner (1986) is very similar to that of Green and Porter. The principal modification is that both rival output and the random variable θ_t can be observed. Haltiwanger and Harrington (1991) allow θ_t to be serially correlated, which makes the observability assumption more plausible.

The Slade (1989a) price-war model, in contrast, makes use of continuous intertemporal-reaction-function strategies. In this model, rival output is observable but the demand shocks θ_t are not. Firms use the price wars to learn about changed conditions in the market, and learning is modelled in a Bayesian fashion via the Kalman filter.

Econometric tests of these price-war models have been undertaken. For example, Porter (1983) used weekly data on the Joint Executive Committee, a price-setting cartel that controlled eastbound rail transport from Chicago to the eastern seaboard, to test the Green and Porter model. And Slade (1987a and b) used daily data on retail gasoline sales in Vancouver, BC to test the Slade model. Both of these markets are subject to periodic breakdowns.[11]

These studies conclude that repeated play enables firms to enhance their profit position *vis-à-vis* the non-cooperative outcome of the one-shot game. Nevertheless industry profit is far short of the monopoly level. In both industries, pricing decisions are made at frequent intervals. It therefore seems unlikely that high discount rates are responsible for failure to achieve near-monopoly profit. Instead, coordination and communication difficulties (and their costs) are probably greater than assumed in most theoretical analyses.

4 RIVALRY

With the help of repeated games, we saw how firms could earn collusive profits without formal communication. These collusive outcomes lie in the area A-B'-C in Figure 2.1. Even the punishments in many repeated-game models are no worse than the point C. One might therefore be tempted to conjecture that oligopoly profits that lie outside this region are never observed. This conjecture, however, is false. In some industries oligopolistic rivalry is very intense and leads to outcomes that fall in the rectangle $0 - \pi^{2C} - C - \pi^{1C}$.

Intense rivalry is often denoted 'cut-throat' competition.[12] Industries that have experienced this phenomenon include railroads, coal (up to the 1950s in the USA and up to the 1970s in Europe), rayon, hotels in older US cities, Belgian and British steel, and textile manufacturing (Scherer, 1980). Most of these industries were secularly declining. Intense competition, however, is not confined to old or sick sectors. Indeed we shall see that it can occur in a growing market.

It is convenient to model rivalry in the context of a two-stage game. With the repeated games of the previous section, payoffs are stationary. *Strategies*, on the other hand, depend on the history of play. With a two-stage-game, in contrast, *payoffs* in the second period are altered by first-period moves. Typically, in the first stage a tangible asset is chosen, whereas in the second stage price or quantity is the strategic variable.

Two-stage games have many applications in the strategic-investment literature. These include investment in productive capacity (Spence, 1977b; Dixit, 1980), cost-reducing R&D (Brander and Spencer, 1983), advertising expenditure (Schmalensee, 1983) and the choice of financial structure for the firm (Brander and Lewis, 1986). For an overview of two-stage games, see Shapiro (1989b).

Our illustration, which is taken from Slade (1989b), involves learning by doing, where each firm's cost falls with its cumulative production. Unit cost in this model varies by firm and by period. Profits are therefore

$$\pi_t^i = (a - Q_t - c_t^i)\, q_t^i \qquad i = 1, 2, \ t = 1, 2. \tag{2.18}$$

In period one, each firm's marginal cost is the same constant c_1. The two periods are linked through second-period costs, which are

$$c_2^i = \alpha - \beta \, q_1^i, \qquad a > \alpha > 0, \, \beta > 0. \tag{2.19}$$

(2.19) indicates that i's period-two cost falls as its period-one output increases. Finally firms seek to maximize the present value of their payoff streams,

$$\Gamma^i(q_1^i, q_1^j, q_2^i, q_2^j) \equiv \pi_1^i(q_1^i, q_1^j) + \delta \, \pi_2^i(q_1^i, q_2^i, q_2^j). \tag{2.20}$$

It is useful to begin with an analysis of the first-order condition for the maximization of Γ^i with respect to q_1^i,

$$\partial(\pi_1^i + \delta \, \pi_2^i)/\partial q_1^i = \partial \pi_1^i/\partial q_1^i + \delta \, \{\partial \pi_2^i/\partial q_1^i + (\partial \pi_2^i/\partial q_2^i)(\partial q_2^i/\partial q_1^i) \\ + (\partial \pi_2^i/\partial q_2^j)(\partial q_2^j/\partial q_1^i)\}. \tag{2.21}$$

The first expression on the right-hand-side of (2.21) is the static effect. The Nash equilibrium of the one-shot game is obtained by setting this expression equal to zero. The second expression on the right-hand-side is the pure-intertemporal effect. This effect, which is due to the cost reduction associated with higher q_1^i, would be recognized by a forward-looking but non-strategic player such as a monopolist who controls both firms' assets. The third expression equals zero by the first-order conditions for the period-two maximization.

It is the final expression that is of particular interest. This effect, which we denote dynamic-strategic, is recognized in the calculation of the subgame-perfect equilibrium. Dynamically strategic players, who anticipate how their period-one choices will alter rival behaviour in the continuation game, take this alteration into account in making their moves.

In our example, clearly the pure-intertemporal effect, $\partial \pi_2^i/\partial q_1^i = \beta \, q_2^i$, is positive. This means that the cost reduction associated with period-one output leads firms to produce at higher levels in the initial stage. At this point, however, we cannot sign the dynamic-strategic effect.

We begin the calculation of the subgame-perfect equilibrium, starting with period two. In this period, firm i chooses q_2^i to maximize π_2^i, conditional on q_2^j and both period-one outputs. First-order conditions for this maximization are

$$a - 2q_2^i - q_2^j - c_2^i = 0. \tag{2.22}$$

Solving the two first-order conditions (2.22), we obtain

$$q_2^{i*} = (a - 2c_2^i + c_2^j)/3 = (a - \alpha + 2\beta q_1^i - \beta q_1^j)/3 \tag{2.23}$$

which, when substituted into (2.18), yields

$$\pi_2^{i*} = (a - 2c_2^i + c_2^j)^2/9 = (a - \alpha + 2\beta q_1^i - \beta q_1^j)^2/9. \tag{2.24}$$

Anticipating the outcome (2.24), in the first-period firm i chooses q_1^i to maximize $\pi_1^i (q_1^i, q_1^j) + \delta \pi_2^{i*}(q_1^i, q_1^j)$, which is a function solely of period-one outputs.

We can now use equations (2.18) and (2.23) to sign the dynamic-strategic effect. These equations show that

$$(\partial \pi_2^i/\partial q_2^j)(\partial q_2^j/\partial q_1^i) = (- q_2^j)(- \beta/3) > 0. \tag{2.25}$$

The two dynamic effects therefore reinforce one another with both leading to larger production and to lower prices in the first period. Indeed it is even possible for dynamically strategic firms to produce at higher rates than the rates that would be chosen by firms in a competitive industry.

This model can be modified in many ways. For example, the first-period choice variable can be interpreted as cost-reducing-R&D expenditure without changing the flavour of the results.[13]

Empirical investigations have uncovered evidence of fierce competition in industries that are obvious oligopolies. For example, McNicol (1975), McKinnon and Olewiler (1980), and Slade (1991b) have investigated the situation in North-American primary metals and have found not only low prices but evidence that metal firms ration their customers in an effort to keep the price down.

At this point, however, a note of caution is in order. Two-stage games do not always lead to intense competition in the first period. Whether competition is fierce depends on the answers to several questions, including:

1. Does investment make a firm tough or soft (does it shift the period-two reaction functions out or in)?
2. Do the period-two reaction functions slope up (strategic substitutes) or down (strategic complements)?[14]
3. Are the products produced by the two firms' (ordinary) substitutes or complements?[15]

5 COOPERATION

With the example of the previous section, both the costs and the benefits of investment (in q_1^i) are private. In other words, q_1^i does not enter firm i's period-one cost function or its period-two profit function. Under these circumstances, it is straightforward to show that a monopolist or two cooperating firms will produce less in both periods than two non-cooperating players. An interesting question, however, is what happens when there are spillovers.

For example, if q_1^i is interpreted as cost-reducing R&D, investment by one firm might reduce the costs of the other. A similar situation arises with advertising, where expenditures by one firm can increase the demand for a second firm's product. In the presence of spillovers, cooperative arrangements can be preferred to Nash non-cooperative behaviour.

In the case of R&D, Jacquemin (1988) identifies three potential benefits to cooperative agreements. First, cooperation at only one stage of the firms' operations (R&D) is more flexible than a merger. At the same time, such an arrangement can be more long-lasting than arms' length transactions in a market. Second, cooperative arrangements can lead to synergistic effects that accelerate the speed of invention and innovation with less risk and duplication of effort. And third, with imperfect capital markets, pooling complementary resources can provide financial capital at more advantageous terms.[16]

We can investigate these issues using a slight modification of the model of the last section. The modified model is taken from d'Aspremont and Jacquemin (1988). Suppose that players choose R&D expenditures (x_1^i) in stage one and compete in output (q_2^i) in stage two. We use a different symbol for R&D expenditures to emphasize the different nature of the two choices. In the first stage, there are costs but no benefits. Firms' period-one profits are therefore

$$\pi_1^i = -\frac{c_1}{2}(x_1^i)^2, \tag{2.26}$$

where we have assumed a quadratic-cost function for R&D.

Expenditures in the first period by one firm reduce period-two costs of *both* firms. We therefore modify the cost function (2.19) as follows:

$$c_2^i = \alpha - \beta x_1^i - \gamma x_1^j, \qquad 0 < \gamma < \beta. \tag{2.27}$$

We can substitute our modified cost function into equation (2.23) to obtain

$$q_2^{i*} = (a - 2c_2^i + c_2^j)/3 = [a - \alpha + (2\beta - \gamma)x_1^i + (2\gamma - \beta)x_1^j]/3 \tag{2.28}$$

which, when substituted into (2.24), yields

$$\pi_2^{i*} = (a - 2c_2^i + c_2^j)^2/9 = [a - \alpha + (2\beta - \gamma)x_1^i + (2\gamma - \beta)x_1^j]^2/9. \tag{2.29}$$

Anticipating the outcome (2.29), in the first-period firm i chooses x_1^i to maximize $\pi_1^i(x_1^i, x_1^j) + \delta \pi_2^{i*}(x_1^i, x_1^j)$, which becomes

$$\Gamma^i = \pi_1^i(x_1^i, x_1^j) + \delta\,\pi_2^i{}^*(x_1^i, x_1^j) =$$
$$- \frac{c_1}{2}(x_1^i)^2 + [a - \alpha + (2\beta - \gamma)x_1^i + (2\gamma - \beta)x_1^j]^2/9. \qquad (2.30)$$

Without loss of generality, we have set $\delta = 1$.

The first-order conditions for the maximization of (2.30) can be solved for the non-cooperative-equilibrium R&D expenditures. This process yields

$$x_1^i{}^* = \frac{(2\beta - \gamma)(a - \alpha)}{4.5c_1 - (2\beta - \gamma)(\beta + \gamma)}. \qquad (2.31)$$

Substituting (2.31) into (2.28), we obtain industry non-cooperative-equilibrium output,

$$Q_2^* \equiv q_2^i{}^* + q_2^j{}^* = \left[\frac{2(a - \alpha)}{3}\right]\left[\frac{4.5c_1}{4.5c_1 - (2\beta - \gamma)(\beta + \gamma)}\right]. \qquad (2.32)$$

So far we have assumed non-cooperative behaviour at both stages. Suppose, in contrast, we allow the firms to cooperate in R&D while maintaining Cournot–Nash competition in the product market. Under these circumstances, firm i will choose x_1^i to maximize $\Gamma^i + \Gamma^j$, where Γ^i is given by equation (2.30). The first-order conditions for this alternative maximization can be solved for the symmetric cooperative-equilibrium-R&D expenditures and the non-cooperative-equilibrium-output choices

$$x_1^i{}^\bullet = \frac{(\beta + \gamma)(a - \alpha)}{4.5c_1 - (\beta + \gamma)^2} \qquad (2.33)$$

and

$$Q_2^\bullet \equiv q_2^i{}^\bullet + q_2^j{}^\bullet = \left[\frac{2(a - \alpha)}{3}\right]\left[\frac{4.5c_1}{4.5c_1 - (\beta + \gamma)^2}\right], \qquad (2.34)$$

respectively.

An examination of equations (2.31)–(2.34) shows that

$$x_1^i{}^* < x_1^i{}^\bullet \text{ and } Q_2^* < Q_2^\bullet \Leftrightarrow 2\beta - \gamma < \beta + \gamma \Leftrightarrow \gamma > \beta/2. \qquad (2.35)$$

Equation (2.35) demonstrates that, when spillovers are important (γ is large), cooperation at the R&D stage results in both higher expenditures on R&D and higher industry-wide output. The ultimate result is lower product prices.

In practice, public bodies have become more lenient towards research joint ventures and cooperative efforts. For example, article 85 of the Treaty of Rome contains a broad prohibition of explicit and tacit collusion where it is likely to affect trade between member states and has as its purpose or results in prevention, distortion or restriction of competition within the Common Market. Nevertheless group or block exemptions can be granted. The regulation of R&D which came into force in 1985 kept intact the exemption of cooperative agreements relating only to R&D. Moreover it extended this favourable treatment to agreements which also provide for joint exploitation of the results.

Blanket exemptions, in that they eliminate the need for detailed analysis of each case, are an effective method of cutting enforcement costs. Nevertheless one must bear in mind the caveats of Section 4. Here again our results are not general but are sensitive to the answers to the questions posed earlier. We must now add an additional query – is the externality positive or negative (is γ greater than or less than zero)?

6 POLICY

In recent years, economic thought concerning collusive practices has changed profoundly, mainly as a result of game-theoretic analysis. Unfortunately, this change has not led to more robust conclusions. On the contrary, it is the source of a more fragmented view. The diversity of models and results, which are very sensitive to the assumptions selected, suggests a case-by-case approach to policy where insights into the ways in which firms acquire and maintain positions of market power become essential.

New theories of industrial economics have shown that simple formulas for efficiency can be deceptive and misleading. They suggest that the assumptions underlying the fundamental theorems of welfare economics are ill suited to deal with many of the problems to which competition policy is applied. The industrial sectors of modern economies are characterized by non-convexities, non-price competition, rapid technical change, imperfect information and an incomplete set of markets. Most often a delicate appreciation of complex tradeoffs is required for policy purposes.

We have attempted to bring to light a typology of situations and practices for which recent developments in economic analysis offer sounder theoretical characterizations than in the past. We offer no definitive answers. Instead we hope that an understanding of simple models that attempt to capture complex ideas will lead to increased comprehension of the tradeoffs that must be made. Such an understanding is a prerequisite for intelligent public-policy decisions.

NOTES

The authors would like to thank Hugh Neary for thoughtful comments on an earlier draft.

1. An overview of this literature can be found in Stiglitz and Mathewson (eds) (1986).
2. This section draws on Jacquemin and Slade (1989), Scherer (1980), Gravelle and Rees (1980) and Stigler (1964).
3. There are various possible solutions to this problem, the most famous one being the Nash bargaining solution (Nash, 1950). In Figure 2.1, C is the threat point – the payoff that each player expects to receive if agreement cannot be reached. With the axioms proposed by Nash, the unique outcome of the bargaining process is the (feasible) point that maximizes the product of gains from agreement, $(\pi^1 - \pi^{1C})(\pi^2 - \pi^{2C})$.
4. D'Aspremont *et al.* (1983), in the context of a model of a dominant cartel and price-taking fringe, show that, with a continuum of firms, as each player can ignore the effect of its entry into and exit from the cartel, there can be no stable cartel. In contrast, with a finite number of firms, there is always a stable cartel. It can also be shown that the size of the cartel is a decreasing function of the industry elasticity of demand.
5. For example, Cordero and Tarring (1960) state that 'Pliny, writing perhaps in AD 70, mentions a decree which limited the output of British lead. It is suggested that a quota system was imposed at the request of owners of lead mines in Spain when the export of British lead began to result in severe international competition.'
6. By monopoly, we mean the symmetric outcome of joint-profit maximization.
7. See Chapter 1 for a definition of subgame perfection.
8. When there are multiple equilibria of the one-shot game, however, the situation is very different and many tacitly collusive outcomes are possible (see Benoit and Krishna, 1985; Friedman, 1985).
9. To see this, note that, if the annual discount rate is r and the game is played n times a year, then $\delta = 1/(1 + r/n)$, which approaches one as n increases.
10. Abreu, Pearce and Stacchetti (1986) show that in this model a one-period reversion to an output greater than Cournot-Nash is the most effective way of policing the cartel.
11. Geroski, Ulph and Ulph (1986) estimate a dynamic model of the oil industry. Their estimation, however, is not based on a specific price-war model.
12. Cut-throat competition can lead to predatory pricing, the best-known example being the Standard Oil Company, which was accused of using price warfare to drive rivals out of the market. Recent models which analyse this practice rely on some form of asymmetric information. For example, with reputation and other signalling models, the incumbent's motive is to deter entry or to induce exit by persuading entrants that their competition is tough. Non-price instruments can also be used to achieve the same ends (product innovation, vertical restraints and so on). For a survey of these practices, see Ordover and Saloner (1989).
13. With this modification, period one revenues (but not costs) are zero.
14. Typically, reaction functions slope down in Cournot or quantity competition and slope up in Bertrand or price competition.
15. For a more complete analysis of this typology, see Fudenberg and Tirole (1984).
16. For additional analyses of cooperative R&D, see Ordover and Willig (1985), Katz (1986) and Jacquemin (1987).

APPENDIX: THE GREEN AND PORTER PRICE-WAR MODEL

A strategy consists of a collusive output q^*, a trigger price $\tilde{P}$, and a punishment period T. For given $\tilde{P}$, T, and distribution of the random variable $F(.)$, if no one has defected, the probability that punishment occurs is

$$\text{prob}\{P_t < \tilde{P}\} = \text{prob}\{h(Q^*)\theta_t < \tilde{P}\} = \text{prob}\{\theta_t < \tilde{P}/h(Q^*)\}$$
$$= F(\tilde{P}/h(Q^*) \equiv \alpha^*, \tag{2A1}$$

where $Q^* \equiv 2q^*$.

Let $\hat{\pi}^*$ and $\hat{\pi}^N$ be the expected values of π^* and π^N, respectively, and let $\hat{\pi}^d$ be the expected value of $\pi^1(R(q^*), q^*)$, where expectations are taken over θ. Then a cooperative firm expects to receive

$$\hat{\Gamma}^c = \hat{\pi}^* + (1-\alpha^*)\delta\hat{\Gamma}^c + \alpha^*[\sum_{t=1}^{T} \delta^t\hat{\pi}^N + \delta^{T+1}\hat{\Gamma}^c], \tag{2A2}$$

which can be solved for $\hat{\Gamma}^c$. A defecting firm, in contrast, expects to receive

$$\hat{\Gamma}^d = \hat{\pi}^d + \sum_{t=1}^{T}\delta^t\hat{\pi}^N + \delta^{T+1}\hat{\Gamma}^c, \tag{2A3}$$

which can be solved for $\hat{\Gamma}^d$.

Firms will adhere to their agreed-upon strategies and produce q^* in every period as long as $\hat{\Gamma}^d \leq \hat{\Gamma}^c$. Periodically, however, price can drop below $\tilde{P}$ and trigger a price war. For example, if θ is normally distributed, no matter how $\tilde{P}$ is chosen, there will be periodic wars. This is true because the normal distribution has infinite tails and thus α^* is strictly positive.

3. Entry Deterrence

Roger Ware

INTRODUCTION

A traditional textbook on industrial economics would list 'entry barriers' as a structural variable and a major determinant of the ability of industry incumbents to earn supernormal profits. An achievement of the past two decades of research in the field is a solid recognition of the fact that entry barriers, and other industry characteristics such as technology, are not exogenous, but rather the endogenous result of competition in, and for, the industry. Entry barriers can be created strategically to maintain the profits of a monopoly incumbent. In a similar way the struggle for cost-reducing innovations clearly determines the configuration of industry technology. Both of these examples involve aspects of industry conduct feeding back on, and determining, the structure of the industry. The ultimate goal of this research agenda is a theory of industry performance in which only tastes, behaviour and some basic conditions of the industry are exogenous: market structure is to be explained as an outcome of more primitive conditions.

Fundamental to the notion of a conduct-driven theory of industrial economics is a theory of strategic behaviour. My goal in this chapter is to survey the study of strategic behaviour in one important area: that of strategic behaviour towards entry. The idea that incumbent firms may attempt to restrict access to their markets is certainly not new, and of course it extends widely to many labour markets as well as to those for consumer goods. Nevertheless important new insights have been gained from work on strategic behaviour in the past decade and a half, and it is on these insights that this chapter focuses.

Several other recently published and excellent surveys overlap with the subject matter of this chapter. In particular Gilbert (1989a) and Tirole (1988) discuss many of the issues covered below. Space limitations have prevented discussion of empirical investigations of the ideas which are surveyed here: the reader is referred to Geroski, Gilbert and Jacquemin (1990) for an excellent survey.

1.1 Limit Pricing

The origins of modern approaches to the analysis of entry deterrence are to be found in the theory of limit pricing. This concept originated in the work of Bain (1956), Sylos-Labini (1962) and Modigliani (1958). The essence of the argument is as follows. Given a technology with increasing returns to scale, an incumbent monopolist can deter entry by lowering price below the monopoly price so as to reduce the market available to the entrant; a sufficiently low price will deter entry altogether. More precisely, the incumbent monopolist chooses a quantity sufficiently large for a potential entrant, computing potential profits from the residual demand, to be unable to earn positive profits. Formally we can define the limit output (*LO*) as follows. Let $\hat{x}_e$ = argmax $\pi(x_e, x_i)$, where π ($\cdot$) is the entrant's profit function, and x_e, x_i are the outputs produced by entrant and incumbent respectively. Then *LO* is the solution to $\pi(\hat{x}(LO), LO) = 0$. The limit price (*LP*) is given by $LP = f(LO)$ where $f(\cdot)$ is the inverse demand function.

1.2 Dynamic Limit Pricing: the Gaskins Model

Gaskins' (1971) model has also had a significant impact on the development of ideas about strategic entry deterrence and limit pricing. A dominant firm chooses an intertemporal price path (p_t) to maximize

$$\pi(t_0) = \int_{t_0}^{\infty} (p_t - c)(D(p_t) - x_t) e^{-r(t-t_0)} dt \tag{3.1}$$

where $D(p_t)$ is total demand at price p_t, x_t is the total supply from competing firms, c is the dominant firm's average cost of production (taken to be constant), and r is the discount rate. It is assumed that the rate of entry, $\partial x/\partial t$, is an increasing function of the price set by the dominant firm. In the absence of cost advantages in favour of the dominant firm, the only equilibrium limit price is the price that is equal to average (and marginal) cost. It follows, from the formal solution to the model, that the dominant firm must disappear; that is, its limiting market share as t approaches infinity is zero.

There are obvious problems with the specification of dynamic limit pricing. First, it is not clear why the dominant firm should be a price leader, particularly after its share of the market has been significantly eroded by entry. Second, the dynamics of the entry process are specified exogenously, rather than derived from the optimizing behaviour of entrants. In particular, the dominant firm and entrants do not engage in the kind of strategic interaction which we review in this chapter.

1.3   Lack of Credibility (Perfection) in the Static Limit Pricing Model

The static limit pricing model has rightly been criticized on the grounds that the monopolist's implied threat to continue producing the pre-entry quantity *after* entry is not credible; with most specifications of demand and costs, the incumbent monopolist would have an incentive to reduce output in response to entry. In the language of dynamic games, the original limit pricing solution is not a subgame-perfect equilibrium. This point can be illustrated simply with the aid of the game tree shown in Figure 3.1. In this 'generic' entry game the entrant chooses either to enter or to stay out, and the incumbent responds to entry either by accommodating the entrant, 'the share strategy' or by being aggressive, 'the fight strategy'. There are two Nash equilibria to the game: 'Fight, if entry; Stay out' and 'Share, if entry; Enter'. Only the latter is subgame-perfect, however. The former equilibrium is sustained by an incredible threat: faced with the *fact* of entry, the incumbent would benefit from sharing the market. In game-theoretic terms, the threat to fight by the incumbent is not a Nash equilibrium strategy to the entry subgame.

Figure 3.1   The 'generic' entry game payoffs (incumbent, entrant) where $P_M > P_D > 0 > P_W$

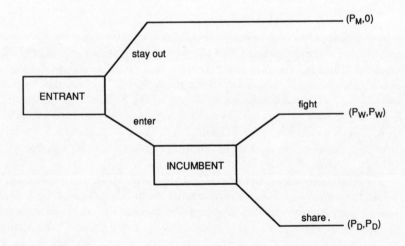

2 ENTRY DETERRENCE IN THE TWO-STAGE FRAMEWORK

The development of models of credible threats to deter entry owes much to the work of Thomas Schelling. In his *The Strategy of Conflict* (1960) Schelling defines a strategic move as 'one that influences the other person's choice in a manner favourable to oneself by affecting the other person's expectations of how oneself will behave'. More recently strategic behaviour has been modelled within the framework of two-stage and multi-stage games. All of these models conform to the following general structure. In the initial period, one or more of the firms has the opportunity to take some action that will have real economic consequences for the state of competition in the second period. The first period may consist of sequential moves of perfect information by all the agents, for example, such as investments in capacity, or in a production technology. These first period actions are the 'strategic' ones. In the second period, some simple Nash equilibrium emerges, given the conditions inherited from the initial period. Subgame perfection requires that these second-period actions form a (static) Nash equilibrium in the second period subgame.

It is important to realize the essential role of sunk costs in a dynamic, strategic environment. The essence of these entry deterrence models is that firms can make commitments at early dates that influence the competition to follow. But no action is a commitment if it is swiftly and costlessly reversible. It is the sunkness – at least the partial sunkness – of investments that qualifies them as strategic decisions.

The entry process is an intrinsically asymmetrical one, in that incumbent firms already have their capital in place before entry, whereas the entrant must sink capital on *entering*. Although two-period models can be symmetric (for example, Brander and Spencer, 1983) the asymmetric two-period game in which incumbent firms make sunk investments before entry has proved very fruitful in its application to the analysis of strategic entry deterrence.

2.1 The Basic Two-firm Two-stage Entry Game

An important analysis of the two-period entry game is Dixit (1980). The following exposition follows Ware (1984) more closely, because the treatment of sunk investments is more satisfactory in the latter model. In Dixit's model, only the incumbent is able to commit sunk investment before the production period. However, since this investment takes the form of capacity which is necessary for production, then production by the entrant must also be preceded by investment in sunk capacity. The entrant's ability to commit, albeit after the incumbent but before production, is a valuable asset that has a significant impact on the equilibrium to the entry game. Moreover the entrant has no choice: if he is to enter, he has to make an investment in sunk capacity in exactly the same way as the incumbent.

Both incumbent monopolist and the potential entrant produce with a technology described by the cost function:

$$C^i(q_i, k_i) = (1 - \alpha)q_i + \alpha k_i + F_i$$

where q_i is quantity produced, k_i is investment in capacity with $q_i < k_i$ and f_i is the fixed cost of entering the industry. Thus the production technology is Leontief. Further, the parameter α, where $0 < \alpha < 1$, measures the proportion of unit costs (whose total is set equal to one), which takes the form of sunk capacity.[1] Each firm is capable of producing an undifferentiated product with inverse demand given by $p = f(X)$, where X is aggregate output. The function $f(X)$ is twice differentiable and for $f(X) > 0$, $f'(X) < 0$. Further, assume that demand satisfies the Hahn–Novshek condition: $f'(X) + x_i f''(X) < 0$, for all $x_i < X$, where x_i is the output of firm i.[2] This condition ensures that reaction functions are downward-sloping. In the model under review, the significance of the Hahn–Novshek condition is that the response of an incumbent firm to entry can never be to increase output. The incumbent firm would never hold excess capacity as a barrier to entry, because it follows that none of this excess capacity would be used after entry. At a more formal level, it can be shown that perfect equilibria to this game, and all games with this structure, will not involve excess capacity (see Eaton and Ware, 1987).

The structure of the game is as follows: firm 1 chooses a level k_1 of investment in sunk capacity. Firm 2 then makes an entry decision which, if positive, also involves a choice of level k_2 of investment in sunk capacity. In the second period of the game either one or both firms produce quantities so as to maximize profits, conditioned by their investments in period one. The game is thus a dynamic game of almost perfect information, and the appropriate equilibrium concept is that of the perfect Nash equilibrium. Effectively the incumbent firm, as first mover, computes the equilibrium response to his actions, and makes an investment choice with foresight about the final-period equilibrium.

The entry game is perhaps best analysed by first describing the final-period equilibrium. Equilibrium can be thought of as 'constrained Cournot', in that $x_i = \min(k_i, Z(x_j))$, $i, j = 1, 2$, where

$$Z(x_j) \equiv \operatorname*{argmax}_{x_i} x_i f(x_i + x_j) - (1 - \alpha)x_i,$$

Figure 3.2   The four phases of constrained Cournot equilibrium for duopoly

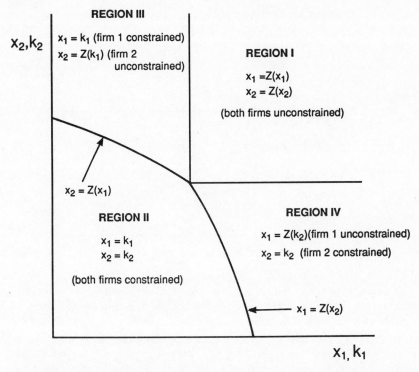

that is, the Cournot reaction function. If firm 2 stays out, then, of course, its second period output is zero.

Figure 3.2 illustrates the solution to the quantity game. There are four regions in the figure: in I, both firms are unconstrained by their capacities; in II both are constrained; in III(IV), one (two) is constrained and two (one) is unconstrained. The boundary between regions II and IV is $Z(x_2)$ and the boundary between II and III is $Z(x_1)$.

To understand firm 1's period-one investment choice, it is useful to construct firm 2's reaction function in k_1, k_2 space. This is illustrated in Figure 3.3. To the left of point A, 2's response to 1's investment is given by its full cost reaction function, defined as $\overset{\text{argmax}}{k_2} \{k_2 f(k_1 + k_2) - k_2\}$. At point A, firm 2 is indifferent between the choice given by the above equation $\bar{k}_2$ and $\bar{k}_2$, in which it exercises a kind of limited Stackelberg leadership by picking the best point T along firm 1's variable cost reaction function, implying excess capacity for firm 1. For all capacity choices $k_1 > \bar{k}_1$, firm 2 will make the same choice $\bar{k}_2$, since increasing capacity only adds to excess capacity for firm 1, but has no effect on the second-period equilibrium.

Figure 3.3   Firm 2's reaction correspondence

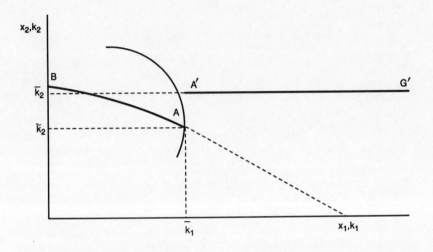

It is clear that firm 1 would not invest $k_1 > \overline{k}^1$ in the perfect equilibrium. Its choice will be dictated by a comparison of the best choice given entry of 2, with a choice of k_1 which deters entry, if deterrence is possible. Whether deterrence is possible depends on firm 2's profits at point A – if they are positive, then firm 1 is unable to deter entry, and the perfect equilibrium will involve entry with quantities given by the best point for firm 1 on BA.

Given entry, the perfect equilibrium choice of k_1 is min $(k_1^s, \overline{k}_1)$, where k_1^s is the Stackelberg choice of capacity for 1, defined by $k_1^s = \frac{\text{argmax}}{k_1}$ $\{k_1 f(k_1 + Z(k_2)) - k_1\}$ and k_2 in perfect equilibrium is given by the corresponding point on BA, firm 2's reaction function.

Let x_1^D denote the quantity produced by firm 1, which would just drive firm 2's profits to zero in a post-entry game, and deter entry. Also let k_1^M denote the monopoly choice of k_1, unconstrained by threat of entry. Then four qualitatively different perfect equilibria to the entry game are possible.

1. *blockaded entry* $(k_1^M > k_1^D)$ The incumbent firm does not face a credible threat of entry at all because, simply by investing in its profit maximizing choice of capacity, unconstrained by entry, entry will be rendered unprofitable.
2. *strategic deterrence* $(k_1^M < k_1^D)$ The incumbent is able to deter, and

deterrence is more profitable than a strategy of accommodation towards the entrant.

3. *strategic accommodation* $(k^M_1 < k^D_1)$. The same conditions as above hold, but in this case a strategy of allowing entry is more profitable for firm 1 than that of deterrence.

4. *unimpeded entry* $(k^D_1 > \bar{k}_1)$. Firm 1 is unable credibly to install sufficient capacity to deter the entrant, and so must be content with choosing its best point on BA, as described above.

Several broad conclusions can be drawn from the above two-firm entry game.

(1) Limit pricing can be resurrected in a game theoretic framework, and may be an important feature of entry deterrence models. The original limit output model suffered from the defect that the threat to produce the limit output *after entry* was not credible. In the above model, by sinking part of his costs prior to entry, the incumbent is sometimes able to make the limit output credible, and thus deter entry. Exactly as Schelling described, the sinking of part of the incumbent's costs prior to the production period lowers his avoidable costs and gives him an incentive to produce a larger quantity in response to any quantity produced by an entrant. Knowing this, the entrant may choose not to enter.

(2) Excess capacity is not a barrier to entry in this model. Wenders (1971) and Spence (1977b) argued that incumbent firms would hold excess capacity as a threat to expand output in the event of entry. Such a threat to expand output, however, is generally not credible in the actual event of entry. This might be regarded as a disturbing feature of these models, because there is some evidence that excess capacity is used as a barrier to entry by incumbent firms. A model which does exhibit excess capacity in equilibrium is Barham and Ware (1990).

(3) Strategic entry deterrence may be welfare-improving. The market described by the model of this section is a natural monopoly. To the extent that strategic entry deterrence leads to an outcome with larger output and lower price than, say, a monopoly unthreatened by potential entrants, aggregate net surplus is increased.

(4) The greater the proportion of costs which can be sunk by the first mover, the greater is the strategic advantage enjoyed. In this model the advantage is only apparent when entry is accommodated. If entry is accommodated, strategic advantage takes the form of higher profits for the first mover relative to the second mover. The incumbent firm obtains its strategic advantage from incurring production costs before its rival(s), so that in the final period when production and sales take place

variable costs per unit of production are low, and the incumbent will be guaranteed a large market share in the final equilibrium.

2.2 Other Examples in a Similar Framework

Strategic holding of inventory by incumbents

Sinking costs 'up front' is embodied in its purest form by production for inventory, to be stockpiled until a later period. Rival firms who hold no inventory and who must produce for sale must incur the full production costs for each unit, whereas sales of inventory incur no variable costs. If the stockpile of inventory is sufficiently large, entry may be deterred and the threat to 'dump' the stockpiled inventory on the market is never exercised. The strategic advantage embodied in inventory in this way is discussed in Ware (1985) and Arvan (1986).

Raising rivals' costs

Salop and Scheffman (1983, 1986) argue that an established firm may be able to invest to raise industry costs, either for new entrants alone or for the whole industry. If costs are raised sufficiently, entry will be deterred. Two examples are the buying up of low extraction cost resource deposits, which raises extraction costs for new entrants (the classic example is the allegation against the Alcoa Corporation); and Williamson's (1968) observation that efforts to increase union wages in coal mining could benefit incumbent firms by making entry more difficult.

To demonstrate this argument requires no more than a presentation of the *basic preemption paradigm*, a result which demonstrates that any incumbent monopolist will be willing to outbid a potential entrant for a scarce industry resource, whether it is ore deposits, an industry patent, or unionized labour. The result depends only on industry profits declining as a result of entry, which would occur with any post-entry game short of perfect collusion. Suppose that an entrant were prepared to bid for the resource up to a price w which would just drive its post-entry profits to zero. Post entry profits would then be

$$\pi_i(w) + \pi_e(w) < \pi_i(w+\varepsilon),$$

where a wage of $w+\varepsilon$ on the right-hand side implies that the incumbent has pre-empted the resource and entry has been deterred. Given that $\pi_e(w)=0$ it follows that:

$$\pi_i(w) < \pi_i(w+\varepsilon)$$

and the incumbent monopolist will prefer to deter entry. In words, given that its monopoly profits will always exceed total industry profits after entry, the incumbent will always be prepared to bid a little more than w, and the entrant will be excluded.

The pre-emption paradigm crops up repeatedly in the entry deterrence literature. Eaton and Lipsey (1979) in an early formalization of the issue argued that an incentive exists for *spatial pre-emption*; that is, for a monopolist to build plants in new locations (in a growing market) just before it would be profitable for a rival firm to enter those same markets. West (1982) found weak evidence to support the existence of spatial pre-emption in supermarket locations. Gilbert and Newbery (1982) show that for the same reason an incumbent monopolist has an incentive to acquire an industry patent before a new entrant, thus preserving the monopoly.

Learning economies

There is considerable evidence that cumulative experience in a given production process lowers unit costs. The strategic implication of this is clear: an early entrant can gain an advantage over future rivals by pushing down the learning curve with high levels of production. Production today (prior to entry) has two benefits: profits are created today, but also future costs are lowered and hence the incumbent's market share in any future post-entry game will be increased. If early, pre-entry production is large enough, entry may be made unattractive. The properties of strategic investment in learning are thus very similar to those of strategic investment in a cost-reducing technology.

The foregoing assumes that the benefits of learning by a pioneer firm do not diffuse to rival firms, without their having to undertake the same production levels. Lieberman (1984) found that the diffusion of learning is fairly common. However, to the extent that firms are able to retain some of the cost advantages of experience, strategic learning effects will still occur.

Competition between networks

Networks are goods with demand-side complementarities. These can be direct, as in the case of telephone services (each person added to the network increases the value to existing subscribers) or indirect, as for example in the case of home video movies, where the larger selection available in a compatible format increases the value of VCRs. The work of Farrell and Saloner (1985, 1986a, 1986b) and Katz and Shapiro (1985, 1986) has considerably advanced the understanding of network phenomena, and their implications for entry deterrence.

One effect of network externalities is similar to that of learning, or any other cost-reducing sunk investment. Early investment by incumbents to build up the network can increase market share in any post-entry game with rivals (for the same *current period* production); a sufficiently large expansion of the network prior to entry may deter entry altogether.

A second feature of networks is novel, however. Today's consumers form expectations about *future* adoption of the technology. A consumer will be more willing to invest in a particular standard today the larger he expects the network to become in the future. The worst outcome would be the possibility of 'stranding', where a new standard is adopted, and 'software' for the old standard will not be provided in future. Owners of Betamax VCRs, and of eight-track tape players, are examples of stranded consumers. With the possibility of competing standards, anything the incumbent can do to convince current consumers to stay on his network, rather than defect to another, will make entry more difficult. Farrell and Saloner (1986b) show that a product pre-announcement by an incumbent may prevent consumers from making a switch to a socially desirable competing technology.

Strategic investment and the durability of capital
We have emphasized that the commitment value of capital depends on the sunk nature of the investment. It is important to investigate how this strategic interaction depends on the *durability* of the capital, and whether the strategic advantage of first movers can be expected to persist over the long term. Eaton and Lipsey (1980, 1981) investigated the effect of depreciating capital on simple two-stage capital commitment models of entry deterrence and found that, while in general a recognition that capital depreciates tends to reduce the advantage of the first mover, more general conclusions were difficult to draw. To quote their conclusion,

> This review demonstrates that the properties of entry equilibrium are dependent upon the nature of Product Specific Capital and apparently minor changes in the nature of Product Specific Capital can produce dramatic changes in the properties of equilibrium. As a corollary, knowledge of the nature of Product Specific Capital is necessary to determine whether entry deterrence is possible, is profitable, and is socially wasteful. (Eaton and Lipsey, 1980)

2.3   Top Dogs, the Fat Cat Effect, the Puppy Dog Ploy and the Lean and Hungry Look: ᴀ More General Framework for Analysing Two-stage Competition

The above title is drawn from Fudenberg and Tirole (1984), who proposed a framework for analysing two-stage competition which helps to draw together much of the earlier work, including that on two-stage models of entry deterrence.

Consider a general model of two-stage competition with two firms. Firm 1 has the opportunity to make a sunk investment K in the first period, which alters the costs (or demand) faced by firm 1 during the second period, but does not affect firm 2's costs (or demand). In the second period a non-cooperative equilibrium is reached, $x_1(K)$, $x_2(K)$. Firm 1's profits can thus be written $\pi^1(x_1(K), x_2(K), K)$, and the profit-maximizing choice of capital is obtained by differentiating:

$$\frac{d\pi^1}{dK} = \frac{\partial\pi^1 dx_1}{\partial x_1 dK} + \frac{\partial\pi^1 dx_2}{\partial x_2 dK} + \frac{\partial\pi^1}{\partial K} = 0. \tag{3.2}$$

Equation (3.2) may be called the fundamental equation of strategic two-stage competition. The first term vanishes by the envelope theorem (x_1 is optimally chosen in period two). The second term captures the *strategic effect* of marginal investment. The final term is simply the direct or non-strategic effect of marginal investment on profits. In a non-strategic, or open-loop, problem, only this last term would appear. Thus the sign of the second term (together with the concavity of π^1 in K) determines whether firm 1 will over-invest or under-invest relative to a non-strategic equilibrium. By working through the comparative statics, the strategic term can be evaluated as:

$$\frac{\partial\pi^1 dx_2}{\partial x_2 dK} = \frac{\pi^1_{x_2} \pi^2_{x_2 x_1} \pi^1_{x_1 K}}{|M|} \tag{3.3}$$

The second derivatives on the right-hand side are to be interpreted in the obvious way, and $|M|$ is the determinant of the matrix of second derivatives. Consider a standard entry deterrence game of the sort discussed in Section 2.1. If, in the equilibrium, firm 1 chooses to (or has no choice but to) accommodate entry, then an equation with the structure of equation (3.2) determines the equilibrium choice of investment. The Fudenberg and Tirole classification combines the first and third terms on the right-hand side of (3.2) in the following way.

$\pi^1_{x_2}\pi^1_{x_1 K} < 0$: investment makes you 'tough'. The effect of marginal investment by firm 1 is to lower the rival firm's profits by inducing firm 1 to be more aggressive in the second-period game.

$\pi^1_{x_2}\pi^1_{x_1 K} > 0$: investment makes you 'soft'. The effect of marginal investment by firm 1 increases the rival firm's profits, by

Table 3.1   Investment strategies under two-stage competition where entry
            accommodation is optimal

	'Tough'	'Soft'
Strategic	Under-investment	Over-investment
complements	*puppy dog*	*fat cat*
Strategic	Over-investment	Under-investment
substitutes	*top dog*	*lean and hungry look*

inducing firm 1 to be less aggressive in the second-period game.

Finally the centre term $\pi^2_{x_2 x_1}$ determines whether the strategy choices x_1 and x_2 are strategic complements or strategic substitutes.

$\pi^2_{x_2 x_1} > 0$: strategic complements;
$\pi^2_{x_1 x_2} < 0$: strategic substitutes.

A classification of the possibilities for equilibrium investment is given in Table 3.1 above. If firm 1 is able to deter the entry of firm 2, and finds this more profitable than the strategy of accommodation, the analysis is slightly different. Firm 1 now chooses K to maximize profits, subject to the constraint of keeping the *post-entry* profits of firm 2 non-positive. The constrained optimization can thus be written:

$$\max_{K}\ \pi^1(x_1, K) + \lambda \pi^2(x_1(K), x_2(K)),$$

where λ is a Lagrange multiplier. The first-order condition is:

$$\frac{\partial \pi_1}{\partial K} + \lambda \left[\frac{\partial \pi_2 dx_1}{\partial x_1 dK} + \frac{\partial \pi_2 dx_2}{\partial x_2 dK} \right] = 0 \tag{3.4}$$

The last term vanishes by the envelope theorem. The first term inside the brackets is now the strategic term, that is the term capturing the strategic impact of investment, as compared to the non-strategic effect of investment, captured by the first term. By working through the comparative statics once again, the second term can be rewritten:

$$-\lambda \pi^2_{x_1} \pi^2_{x_2 x_1} \pi^1_{x_1 K}.$$

Table 3.2   Investment strategies under two-stage competition where entry deterrence is optimal

	'Tough'	'Soft'
Strategic complements	Over-investment *top dog*	Under-investment *lean and hungry look*
Strategic substitutes	Over-investment *top dog*	Under-investment *lean and hungry look*

The first and third terms in the above expression are the same as in the accommodation case, but the second term is always negative. We can now classify outcomes in terms of investment in the deterrence case in Table 3.2.

The advantage of the Fudenberg–Tirole framework is that most of the simple two-stage models of entry deterrence can be accommodated into it. For example, the capital commitment models of Dixit (1980) and Ware (1984), and the inventory model of Ware (1985) are all examples of top dog games (for equilibria involving both deterrence and accommodation). However, suppose that investment lowers *marginal costs* and second-period competition is in prices (which are strategic complements); the type of equilibrium strategy depends on whether accommodation or deterrence is optimal. Deterrence still calls for the 'top dog' strategy, because investment makes deterrence easier. If firm 2 is to be accommodated, however, firm 1 should under-invest (play a 'puppy dog' strategy) because investment leads to a lower price for firm 1, and a response of a lower price from firm 2, which hurts firm 1.

Tirole presents several interesting applications.[3] For example, a simple model of entry in a differentiated market modelled on a line can be thought of as a 'puppy dog' game. Firms choose to locate as far apart as possible (this is under-investment in location relative to locating at the centre of the product space) because this reduces the severity of price competition between them.

2.4   Entry Deterrence in Models with Incomplete Information

In the models we have described, sunk capital creates a link between the current actions of the incumbent and future actions in response to entry. That is, sunk capital solves the Sylos paradox of why pre-entry choices should mean anything to the entrant, and hence the incumbent, unable to influence the entrant's choice, will pursue short-run profit maximization until entry actually occurs.

A second way of creating the link between today's actions and the profitability of entry is through *incomplete information*. The basic idea here is that the entrant may be less well informed than the incumbent about the industry environment, in some way which would influence the entrant's calculation of post-entry profits. Examples would be the incumbent's costs, the level of demand, even the elasticity of demand. The entrant may, however, attempt to infer the incumbent's cost level from his *pre-entry price*. This is the environment of a signalling model, where the incumbent knows that his pre-entry price will be a signal of his true costs, and hence of the profitability of entry. The natural equilibrium concept to use here is that of Bayesian Equilibrium, in which players update their prior beliefs according to Bayes' Law, and in equilibrium beliefs have to be consistent.

The classic paper here is Milgrom and Roberts (1982). In it they show that a monopolist facing the threat of entry, where both firm's costs are private information, will choose a price below the monopoly price corresponding to his actual costs. In effect the monopolist attempts to signal a lower level of costs than he actually possesses, to encourage the entrant to revise downwards his estimate of post-entry profits. In a sense, the Milgrom–Roberts model, like the capital commitment-style models, reintroduces a kind of limit pricing behaviour by the incumbent, in a rigorously specified model of equilibrium behaviour. To see that the full information monopoly price cannot be an equilibrium for the monopolist, consider a choice of p just below the monopoly price; that is, the monopolist chooses $M(p) - \varepsilon$. From the envelope theorem we know that this will have no first-order effect on the incumbent's profits, but the entrant will revise down his assessment of the incumbent's costs, which in turn will lower the probability of entry and the incumbent's profits by an amount which does not vanish to first order. Hence the incumbent will always pick a price below the monopoly price, which demonstrates, heuristically, the limit price result.[4]

Note also that, under some circumstances, the incumbent may wish to signal by raising price. Two examples that have been examined are the case where a high elasticity of demand encourages entry, so that the incumbent will signal a low elasticity by raising price (Salop and Scheffman, 1983), and the case where the entrant does not know his own costs, in which case the incumbent will signal high costs with a high price.

3   MULTIPLE ENTRANTS, MODELS OF ENDOGENOUS MARKET STRUCTURE

The goal of a theory of entry deterrence is to increase our understanding of market structure. That is, strategic entry deterrence is an aspect of industry conduct which may be a determinant of market structure. The models of entry deterrence which we have discussed above restricted attention to the strategic interaction between a monopoly incumbent (or at least a collusive oligopoly) and a single entrant. Although this literature has generated considerable insight into strategic behaviour towards entry, the framework is very restrictive as a theory of market structure. First, the methodology is applicable only to markets containing at most two firms. Second, the assumption of a single potential entrant is quite artificial, and gives rise to misleading results. While a monopolist may choose to accommodate a single entrant rather than incur the costs of deterrence, accommodation is much less likely if further entry is possible. A principle similar to the pre-emption principle (discussed in Section 2.2) is at work here. If allowing entry simply leads to an equilibrium in which the former monopolist shares the market with one or more entrants, but the equilibrium price is the same as if the monopolist had deterred all entry, then the latter strategy is likely to be more profitable. Only if entry deterrence is costly, and the costs can be shared with other entrants, will a monopolist voluntarily accommodate entry when it could be deterred.

In a framework of possible multiple entry, *market structure* becomes an endogenous property of the model, determined by interaction of strategic behaviour with the basic conditions of demand and technology. An interesting feature of equilibria with multiple entrants is that they tend to exhibit a *limit pricing* property not unlike the Bain–Sylos–Modigliani (BSM) model. To see this, consider a model in which firms enter in some arbitrary sequence and commit to quantities. Any configuration of entry production which deters further entry must involve a total production by the industry no smaller than the BSM limit output, otherwise entry would continue to occur. Thus the equilibrium price can be no larger than the BSM limit price.

The sequential entry models offer some insight into market structure. In Eaton and Ware (1987) the equilibrium number of firms is the smallest number that can deter the entry of an additional firm. While this is a fairly compelling idea, the result is driven by the assumption of Leontief costs, which implies that entry deterrence is not costly. In the models of Schwartz and Baumann (1988) and McLean and Riordan (1989), entry deterrence is costly, and the equilibrium may involve more than the minimum number of firms. Essentially, earlier entrants prefer to *delegate* the costs of entry deterrence to later entrants, even to the point of allowing more entry than is strictly necessary. In all of these models, profits typically decline with the order of entry; that is, the early entrants capture rents.[5]

In contrast to the two-firm game, investment in entry deterrence has a public good aspect in a multiple-firm framework. Each firm's investment in entry deterrence will benefit all incumbent firms equally, but the costs must be incurred privately. Two features of this non-cooperative nature of investment in entry deterrence which have been discussed in other work are *delegation* and *under-investment*.[6] Delegation refers to the incentive of early entrants in the sequence of investment not to do their full share of entry deterrence in the knowledge that later entrants will be forced to pick up the slack, because these later entrants have a strong incentive to deter further entry. Under-investment occurs when this process of coordination breaks down, in a classic prisoner's dilemma fashion. As a result the collective entry deterrence efforts of the incumbent firms, acting individually and non-cooperatively, amount to less than a jointly optimal amount of investment, based on cooperative investment decisions. Gilbert and Vives (1986) and Waldman (1987) have shown that whether or not under-investment occurs depends on the discrete nature of the investment requirement for entry deterrence, as well as on the importance of the positioning aspect of investment.

4   CONTRACTS AS A BARRIER TO ENTRY

Not all entry deterrence requires a real investment to make it credible. The signing of a *long-term contract* can have the effect of excluding entry. Aghion and Bolton (1987) offer an interesting example of a contract between a monopoly supplier and a single customer, which excludes a low-cost entrant in a way which is socially inefficient. The incumbent's costs equal $\frac{1}{2}$, whereas the entrant's are unknown to the consumer and supplier at the time of contract signing, but both have a common prior distribution which is uniform on [0,1]. Clearly efficiency requires that the entrant produce whenever its realized costs are less than $\frac{1}{2}$. Aghion and Bolton show that it is in the interest of the incumbent and customer to sign a contract of the form (P, P_0), where P is the price if the customer buys, and P_0 is a penalty for breach, if the customer chooses to buy from the entrant. Suppose $(P, P_0) = (\frac{3}{4}, \frac{1}{2})$. The entrant can only compete with a cost realization less than $1/4$, but it is easy to show that the incumbent is better off, and the customer no worse off, with this contract than with no contract, in which case the entrant would enter with costs less than or equal to $\frac{1}{2}$, but Bertrand pricing would keep the price equal to $\frac{1}{2}$.

Aghion and Bolton refer to the Brown Shoe case in US anti-trust law, and the commentary of Bork (1978), who argued that customers would never sign contracts which excluded low-cost entry if it were not in their own interest. Although this model does have a somewhat contrived structure (negotiation between the entrant and customer is precluded, for example) it does serve as a reminder that, with imperfect competition, there is no particular reason to expect private contracts to be socially efficient.

5 CONCLUSIONS

Parallel to the development of more sophisticated theories of strategic behaviour and market performance over the past two decades has been a lively debate about the meaning and importance of the concept of entry barriers. The debate has ranged from a somewhat semantic discussion of the appropriate definition of entry barriers (Bain, 1968; Stigler, 1968; von Weizsäcker, 1980) to a more fundamental debate as to whether the concept is useful at all (Demsetz, 1982; Gilbert, 1989a; Dick and Lott, 1990).

At the risk of misinterpretation, the extreme Chicago position (which is held vociferously, perhaps only by scholars at UCLA) seems to be that the only entry barriers are those that are created by government regulation. The total costs of any firm in an industry, including those with unique *production* advantages, are the same if the asset which confers the advantage is properly capitalized into costs. These costs are also shared identically by any potential entrant who can always contemplate purchasing an incumbent firm.

While this debate is important, it deflects attention from the issues which are most relevant for policy. In short, when is market structure efficient, and when is it inefficient? None of the protagonists in these definitional debates would deny that strategic behaviour could have adverse efficiency consequences (although they would differ widely as to the magnitude of the effects). An answer to this question requires a positive analysis of the development of market structure, together with a normative interpretation, and a further analysis of the scope for policy. The study of strategic entry deterrence, which has been surveyed in this chapter, is an important plank in this research agenda.

NOTES

1. Note that the meaning of α here is equivalent to $1 - \alpha$ in Ware (1984).
2. Roughly, this requires that demand be not too convex, and is satisfied by linear demand, but not by constant elasticity demand.
3. Tirole (1988), pp. 328–36
4. Note that the equilibrium price in this model is not the Bain–Sylos–Modigliani Limit Price.
5. Although Eaton and Ware show that exceptions are possible, because the last entrant can credibly threaten earlier entrants with a sharply lower price if they try to increase their market share (Eaton and Ware, 1987, pp. 12–13).
6. See Gilbert and Vives (1986), McLean and Riordan (1989), Waldman (1987) and Tirole (1988).

L / 3

4. Product Differentiation and Quality

. **Norman J. Ireland**

---

1 INTRODUCTION

Any two brands of the same basic product are likely to be different in some respects. Varieties of cars, washing machines, insurance policies or retail services all offer a choice to consumers. Product specifications, brand reputation, after-sales service and ease of availability are just some of the ways in which one variety of product may differ from another. Some consumers, taking the prices of the available varieties into account, will arrive at a different purchase decision from other consumers. That different products appeal to different consumers leads to the conclusion that product differentiation allows markets to be segmented; markets are divided up and less inter-variety competition takes place. Thus more monopoly power is able to persist. On the other hand more choice in product varieties might be welcomed by consumers. Product selection has both strategic possibilities for firms and welfare consequences for consumers.

In order to investigate the welfare and production consequences of product differentiation, one particular simplifying assumption is often made. This is that each consumer unit (an individual, a household, or more generally any economic decision-making agent) buys at most one unit of at most one variety of product supplied to the market. In many cases this accords with practice. Sometimes, however, products can be mixed to obtain any combination of varieties for the consumer. A number of foodstuffs are of this kind. A further example is that of the market for stocks, shares or unit trusts, where combinations can be found to approximately replicate any desired portfolio. However indivisibilities (buying half an orange?) or transactions costs (minimum agents' fees for stock purchase) have to be taken into account. Taking a single-unit-of-product-per-consumer approach avoids these complications, but of course limits the generality of the analysis.

One of the key questions that should be asked of any analysis of product differentiation within a market concerns the kind of market segmentation involved. Which consumers buy which variety? It is on the boundaries between market segments that competition for marginal consumers takes place. A common distinction is that of horizontal, compared to vertical, product differentiation. With the former, if two product varieties were offered at the same price, some consumers would choose each variety. With vertical product differentiation, on the other hand, all consumers would prefer the same variety, that of higher quality, and only if the other variety was offered at a lower price would it achieve positive sales. The willingness to pay extra for extra quality may be associated with the level of consumer income.

In order to be able to describe equilibrium market structure, including segmentation and welfare issues, our approach will involve defining costs of 'mismatch' for consumers having to choose from a finite set of available product varieties. This approach is described in Section 2. The classical Hotelling model of horizontal product differentiation is also discussed in this section. In Section 3 a more robust model of horizontal product differentiation due to Salop (1979) is considered and questions are raised concerning strategic product design, the extent of variety available to consumers and general welfare levels. In Section 4 a model of vertical product differentiation of the genre of Jaskold Gabszewicz and Thisse (1979, 1980) and Shaked and Sutton (1982, 1983) is outlined, and it is shown how markets may be restricted quite naturally to a very few participating firms. Conclusions and some likely directions for future research are contained in a final section.

Some simplifying assumptions have been made in order to concentrate on the main points of issue. Thus variable costs of production are assumed zero for all products so that cost-related effects are ignored. Firms are assumed each to produce only one variety for any market and to act as Nash players in any subgame. For the most part, consumers are assumed to have full information and each only purchases a single unit. Within the confines of these assumptions, a common approach is taken to issues of both horizontal and vertical product differentiation.

2   ADDRESS MODELS AND THE HOTELLING DEBATE

2.1   Mismatch Costs and Address Models

Consider two differentiated products, perhaps two models of cars or two insurance policies, which are available at given prices. We will label the products a and b and denote their prices p_a and p_b respectively. Within the single period of our analysis, each household will buy at most one unit of product: either one unit of product *a* or one unit of product *b*, or neither. Our view of households and products reflects an approach to the analysis of differentiated products contained within 'address' models. Each product is conceived as being fully described by the list of quantities of characteristics vested in it. Furthermore one household differs from another in its ideal or reference product which it would prefer to all others. Each household has its own view as to the perfect combination of characteristics which define this ideal product. The difference between the ideal product and any actual available product (such as product *a* or *b*) represents the amount of 'mismatch' of the available from the ideal.

That products can be described by their inherent characteristics and that households can be described by the characteristics content of their ideal products allow both existing products and households to be located in a space of characteristics. Hence the term 'address' model. The simplest address model is one often used in the product differentiation and spatial pricing literature. This is where the space of characteristics is viewed as a line between two points; for example, a road between two shops, with houses all along the road. Each household and each shop can be identified by its distance from the westerly end of the line. The household would ideally like to consume shop services at its own location. Instead it has to send to one of the existing shops. The further away a shop is, the greater the difference between the ideal and the actual situations. More generally, the product characteristic approach to consumer choice has become familiar from the work of Lancaster (for example, Lancaster, 1966, 1979).

Provided it is possible to measure the difference between the ideal and any available product for a particular household in a logical way it is also possible to measure the difference between any two available products. If one shop is two miles away and the other is one mile away then the latter shop is one mile nearer. Of course, being one mile nearer may not be the only difference between the shops; the road may have steep hills in one direction, or the shops may stock different brands of goods. What we need to do is to measure the total utility loss from consuming each product rather than the ideal product. To do this it is generally assumed that the marginal utility of income is (virtually) constant, so that an income or monetary measure of the mismatch cost can be obtained. Thus the time taken to get to each shop could be a more appropriate measure of distance than mere mileage; then the opportunity value of time for the household member could be used to convert this to a monetary equivalent. More generally the mismatch cost is just the gross (ignoring prices) utility loss from consuming a particular available product rather than the consumer's ideal product.

Figure 4.1   Linear locations of products

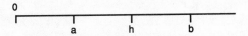

Suppose that, for the household located at h between a and b in Figure 4.1, $m(h - a)$ and $m(b - h)$ are the mismatch costs relating to products a and b. Thus m is the constant cost per unit of distance between the household's location and the available products. Then

$$v_h = m(a + b - 2h) \tag{4.1}$$

is the net advantage of product a over product b for this household. Now given the nature of the two products, v_h will vary with the location h (that is, the location of the household's ideal product in characteristic space). It may be that for some households v_h is large and positive (those located near to a's location); for others v_h is large and negative (those located near to product b), while for some v_h is near zero, indicating nearly equal mismatch costs.

2.2   Horizontal and Vertical Product Differentiation

The relative frequencies of v_h will of course depend on the relative densities of households at different addresses and the relationship of disutility to distance. Three examples of horizontal product differentiation are given in Figure 4.2a, assuming a constant and common mismatch cost per unit distance. If households are evenly (uniformly) distributed as suggested by distribution g^1, then the density of v is represented by f^1. If households are clustered towards the ends of the road (g^2) then the density of v is shown by f^2. The third case, f^3, is where households are mainly sited in the middle section of the road (as depicted by g^3). These three cases are given because it will be shown below that they imply very different competition effects and equilibrium prices in a duopoly.

In Figure 4.2b, some examples of very asymmetric distributions of households are given. With f^4, most consumers are situated near to a's location; with f^5, most are near to b's location. These distributions of customers obviously give advantage to one of the products over the other. Notice that, in the case of f^4, as the price difference $p_a - p_b$ becomes more positive, so the number of consumers choosing product b will become positive and then continue to grow; the price advantage for b outweighs the extra mismatch cost of b for more and more consumers. A

Figure 4.2   *The distributions of consumers' locations and consumers' mismatch costs*

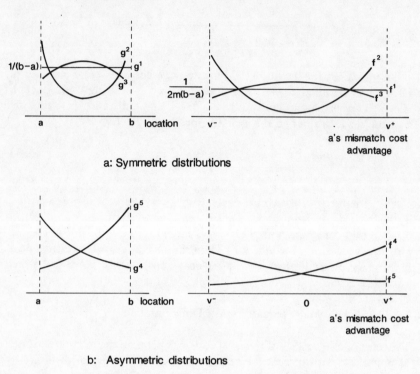

a: Symmetric distributions

b: Asymmetric distributions

$$v^- = -m(b-a)$$
$$v^+ = m(b-a)$$

downward-sloping demand curve for either product exists while $p_a > p_b$, since some consumers are willing to pay a greater premium than others for the commonly-agreed better product. In any equilibrium those consumers purchasing the better product are those willing to pay the greater premium: an example of vertical product differentiation. An alternative way of modelling this kind of market segmentation would be to view all consumers as being at the same location, but having different valuations of the quality difference. The situation could then be depicted as in Figure 4.3, with consumers' ideal product being an imaginary variety of arbitrarily high quality q, so that the location or address density is a spike at q, while products are located at the lower qualities a and b. The distribution of mismatch cost differences results from individuals' differing valuations

Figure 4.3 Locations as quality levels

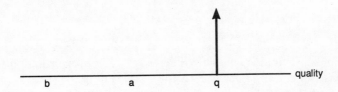

of the quality difference $b-a$. It is plausible to take the willingness to pay for higher quality as depending on income, such that the highest income consumers are willing to pay most for the better good since they have the highest cost of mismatch. We will return to such a model of vertical product differentiation in section 2.4.

For now, let us consider the various symmetric distributions of consumers in Figure 4.2a, leading to market segmentation by horizontal product differentiation. We will derive a Nash equilibrium where each firm chooses the price of its product under the assumption that its rival's price is given.

2.3 Horizontal Product Differentiation and the Extent of Price Competition

Let the cumulative density $F(v)$ be the proportion of households where $v_h \leq v$, and, as the density $f(v)$ is symmetric about $v = 0$, it is clear that exactly half the households have $v_h \leq 0$ and half have $v_h \geq 0$. Now a household at location h will buy product a rather than b if v_h is at least equal to the extra cost of product a, $p_a - p_b$. Therefore sales of product a are $1 - F(p_a - p_b)$ and if variable production costs are zero, the firm producing product a has revenue (and also profit) of

$$\pi_a = p_a\{1 - F(p_a - p_b)\}. \tag{4.2a}$$

Similarly the profit from selling product b is

$$\pi_b = p_b F(p_a - p_b). \tag{4.2b}$$

Of course (4.2a) and (4.2b) assume that no households choose the 'no-buy' option. This assumption will only hold to the extent that p_a and p_b are sufficiently low in equilibrium. If they are not then equations (4.2a) and (4.2b) have to be restated (see Section 3.3). For now, consider that each firm sets its price to maximize profits, given the Nash assumption that the other firm's price will not be affected. First-order conditions are:

$$d\pi_a/dp_a = 1 - F(p_a - p_b) - p_a F'(p_a - p_b) = 0 \qquad (4.3a)$$

$$d\pi_b/dp_b = F(p_a - p_b) - p_b F'(p_a - p_b) = 0, \qquad (4.3b)$$

where $F'(v)$ is the derivative of $F(v)$ with respect to v and is simply the density of household mismatch costs at v, $f(v)$. Now one solution to the equations (4.3a) and (4.3b) can be found by setting $p_a = p_b = p^*$ and solving for p^*. As $F(0) = 1 - F(0) = \frac{1}{2}$, this solution is

$$p^* = 1/\{2f(0)\}. \qquad (4.4)$$

Obviously the higher is $f(0)$ the lower are the equilibrium prices. Looking at figure (4.2a) we see that, if p_j^* is the common price level with density f_j, then

$$p_2 > p_1 > p_3.$$

The more consumers have strong preferences for one product rather than the other, the higher the equilibrium prices. At any given p_b, firm a has to choose whether or not to marginally reduce p_a. If $f(p_a - p_b)$ is small in relation to his current market then few customers will be gained, while revenue is lost from existing customers through the lower prices. The same principle applies to firm b, and so the smaller is $f(0)$ the lower is the effective competition and the higher the resulting prices.

It is immediately clear that a number of factors may increase equilibrium prices. If products were more different then the relative density in the middle of the v-distribution might be expected to be lower. Similarly, if consumers perceive products as being more different, the same effect may be expected. Thus the importance of advertising both to change or reinforce consumers' perceptions of product differences and to engender brand loyalty is established, as well as the process of product selection itself.

2.4 Product Design: the Hotelling Debate

In our analogy of characteristics space as a road, we placed our shops at either end, thus maximizing the extent of product differentiation. Now suppose that we moved each shop by the same amount part of the way towards the centre. The new distribution of v would have the rather odd kind of form represented in Figure 4.4, for the uniform household location case, g^1. Consumers in each end segment, to the left of a or to the right of b, have common values of v, denoted v^+ and v^- ($= -v^+$). Thus

Figure 4.4   End segments and 'spikes' of density

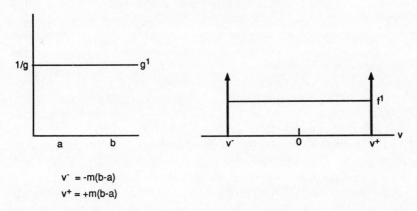

$$v^- = -m(b-a)$$
$$v^+ = +m(b-a)$$

there are 'spikes' or 'mass-points' in the distribution of v and these have a number of implications for the existence and nature of an equilibrium in a two-stage game of, first, product selection – selecting an address for the product – and, second, price setting.

First note that the density $f^1(0)$ is unaffected by moving from Figure 4.2a to figure 4.4. This prompts the possibility that the same prices would then hold in equilibrium. In one of the founding papers in the literature on product differentiation, Hotelling (1929) asks what equilibrium would occur in the two-stage game given that the same levels of prices and profits would arise in a price-setting stage with symmetric addresses such as in Figure 4.4. Arguing that any asymmetric addresses would favour the product nearer the centre (since this would produce an asymmetric distribution of v) the only perfect equilibrium was where each duopolist's product was sited 'back-to-back' in the middle of the length of road. Each firm would wish to move towards the centre in order to achieve a more attractive position for its product with respect to those consumers in addresses between the two products. Thus in equilibrium the products would have minimum product differentiation and there would be 'excessive sameness' (Hotelling, 1929).

The problem with this conclusion was pointed out by d'Aspremont *et al.* (1979) and rests in the spikes of the v distribution which become more prominent as we consider symmetric addresses with v^+ (and v^-) nearer to zero owing to more closely related products. These spikes introduce a fundamental non-concavity into firms' profit functions: if firm b cut its price to (just below) $p_a - v^+$, then it would expect, given its Nash conjecture, to sell to the entire market. As v^+ becomes smaller – and the spike larger – so this prospect of 'mill price undercutting' becomes more profitable. Firm *a* would of course retaliate (a possibility not encompassed by firm *b*'s Nash conjecture) and prices would be bid down. To avoid this, firms will not wish to locate too near each other in the first (product selection) stage of the game. However whether or not an equilibrium exists in the price-setting game is a real problem. D'Aspremont *et al.* show that, if the products are situated in the middle half of the line, then the spikes are sufficiently attractive to lead to price cutting by either firm to obtain the whole market. Obviously no such asymmetric result can constitute an equilibrium, since the no-sales firm can reduce its price to maintain some sales. After a price war stage, firms may reject such predatory pricing in favour of higher prices. This would then prompt a repeat of the price cycle (which is similar to cyclical price behaviour considered by Edgeworth, 1925), and at no prices would the firms be in equilibrium.

A solution to the Hotelling problem has been advanced by Osborne and Pitchik (1987). A mixed strategy equilibrium is proposed for the price game when no pure strategy solution exists. In effect this is a random mix of some prices which ignore the spikes, together with some lower prices (for example, in snap sales). The latter often lead to low aggregate profit, and are more likely (have higher probabilities) when products are nearer. Osborne and Pitchik find that a perfect equilibrium exists with products just within the middle half of the line; firms wish to locate to better strategic advantage but are soon limited by the profit effects of the possibility of price-undercutting competition.

It might be argued that the importance of this debate is limited by two factors. First, it may be unlikely that firms are so naive as to expect to capture all their rival's market without any price response. Eaton (1976) and others have proposed a 'modified zero conjectural variation' which rules out such extreme Nash behaviour. Secondly, the problem is likely to be less if the characteristic space is more general in form, and we will consider such a model in the next section, if mismatch costs are increasing in distance, or if consumers are sufficiently heterogeneous in factors other than their locations (see De Palma *et al.*, 1985). However the Hotelling debate does point to the need for careful design of models portraying oligopoly supply processes.

3 HORIZONTAL PRODUCT DIFFERENTIATION

3.1 Location on a Circle

One of the ways in which the linear representation of product space is unsatisfactory lies in the special role of end-points. One firm can supply consumers between its address and the end of the line – assuming that no other firm locates its product in between – with an obvious natural advantage. This complicates an analysis of a finite market supplied with many product varieties rather than just two, since it prevents the consideration of a completely symmetric model with the simplification of being able to look at a typical firm. The easiest way of avoiding end-points is to think of a product space as the unit length circumference of a circle. Following Salop (1979) and many other contributions, we will adopt this model and also assume that consumers are uniformly distributed with unit density around the circle in terms of their ideal products. Salop's model has some other interesting features; in particular, an 'outside product' is available so that, if prices are too high, consumers will elect to spend their money outside the market. We will assume for the moment that this is not the case (equilibrium prices are not so high) but we will return to such questions in Section 3.3. Finally the mismatch cost for all consumers is again assumed to be m per unit distance.

Consider a segment of the circle's circumference, with three products located at a, b and c, as in Figure 4.5. Assume that the prices of products a and c are p_a and p_c respectively and consider the profit-maximizing price of product b given Nash price conjectures. If b is priced at p_b then sales would be to consumers from $\underline{b}$ to $\overline{b}$ where $\underline{b}$ is such that a consumer at that address has equal total cost (price plus mismatch cost) from buying a or b. Thus $\underline{b}$ satisfies

$$p_a + m(\underline{b} - a) = p_b + m(b - \underline{b}). \tag{4.5a}$$

By the same argument $\overline{b}$ is such that

$$p_c + m(c - \overline{b}) = p_b + m(\overline{b} - b). \tag{4.5b}$$

Solving for $\underline{b}$ from (4.5a) and for $\overline{b}$ from (4.5b) yields

$$\begin{aligned} \overline{b} - \underline{b} &= \{p_c - p_b + m(c+b)\}/2m - \{p_b - p_a + m(a+b)\}/2m \\ &= (\overline{p} - p_b)/m + (c-a)/2, \end{aligned} \tag{4.6}$$

where $\overline{p} = (p_a + p_c)/2$.

Suppose that there are no variable costs, only fixed costs of K. Then profit earned by product b is just

$$\pi_b = p_b(\overline{b} - \underline{b}) - K \tag{4.7}$$

which, using equation (4.6), is maximized by

Figure 4.5 Locations around the arc of a circle

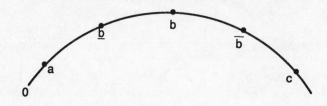

$$p_b{}^* = m(c-a)/4 + \bar{p}/2 \qquad (4.8)$$

and maximum profit is then

$$\pi_b{}^* = (p_b{}^*)^2/m - K. \qquad (4.9)$$

Note that both the optimum price and the associated profit level are independent of the exact location of product b between a and c. The advantage of locating nearer to one neighbouring product is exactly negated by the disadvantage of being further from the other. This suggests the possibility of a symmetric perfect equilibrium in a two-stage game of location and price choice. Suppose there are n firms, each with a single product equidistant from its neighbours. In the price game, a common equilibrium price p is found by setting $p_b{}^* = \bar{p}$ in (4.8) and using $c - a = 2/n$ to yield

$$p = m/n. \qquad (4.10)$$

(This is just an application of the analysis in Section 2.3; $2/n$ consumers buy two adjacent products and the relative density $f(0)$ is $(1/m)/(2/n)$. Thus $1/2f(0)$ in equation (4.4) is simply m/n.) Given their locations, no firm wishes to change its price. Also there is no reason for any firm to move away from a symmetric location. Small changes do not increase profit, and large changes imply close proximity to another product's location, with the accompanying threats of mutually-damaging price wars. Thus symmetric location and equation (4.10) define a perfect equilibrium.

Of course the above argument does not prove uniqueness; there may well be non-symmetric equilibria. However competition from outside goods will tend to strengthen the symmetric case, since asymmetric location will make outside alternatives more attractive to those consumers in the largest vacant arcs. Also there may be special reasons for selecting symmetric equilibria. These reasons relate to entry and entry deterrence issues.

3.2 Entry, Welfare and Variety

From equations (4.9) and (4.10), each firm in a symmetric perfect equilibrium obtains profit equal to

$$\pi = m/n^2 - K. \tag{4.11}$$

If products could freely enter the market then the maximum number of firms that could be accommodated before profits became negative would be the ·highest integer such that equation (4.11) is non-negative. For simplicity let us disregard the integer requirement so that the free-entry number of firms is n_f, where

$$n_f = (m/K)^{\frac{1}{2}} \tag{4.12}$$

Substituting n_f from equation (4.12) into (4.9) implies the free-entry price for all products of p_f:

$$p_f = (Km)^{\frac{1}{2}} \tag{4.13}$$

and equations (4.12) and (4.13) fully describe the free-entry, zero profit, or Chamberlinian symmetric equilibrium (see Chamberlin, 1962). The price is increasing in fixed costs (owing to the effect on entry) and in the level of mismatch costs. The entry process here involves potential entrants foreseeing that incumbents cannot commit themselves to particular locations. When n_f firms have entered, a symmetric location equilibrium results, *providing each firm adjusts its location so as to be in the middle of its market segment*. The role of outside products to promote central location has already been mentioned, and is discussed further in the next section.

This model of a symmetric perfect equilibrium can be contrasted with one where the entry cost K implies a commitment to a particular location as well as to entry itself. We can view firms, in turn, deciding whether or not to enter the market and simultaneously deciding on a product location which is then fixed. A perfect equilibrium in this model would involve each firm forecasting the entry decisions of further firms. The first firm to enter locates anywhere on the circle's circumference; the exact place has no strategic importance. The second firm realizes that it can enforce a profitable market if it locates as far from the first firm's location as possible, but not so far that it is profitable for another firm to locate between them. This maximum distance is (just less than) $2/n_f$ or $(4K/m)^{\frac{1}{2}}$. At this distance any firm entering between the incumbents would have a market of size just less than $1/n_f$: just less than that sufficient to cover the fixed costs of entry.

Other firms can similarly distance themselves in this entry-deterring way. Disregarding the integer requirement for n again, the number of firms that can enter, $2/n_f$ apart, is simply $n_f/2$. Thus, if product design entails a commitment, it can be used strategically in order to limit the number of products supplied to the market and still achieve positive profits in long-run equilibrium. See, for example, Eaton and Lipsey (1978).

An associated question concerns whether there are too many or too few product varieties according to some measure of social welfare. Provided that any profit is distributed back to consumers (rather than being remitted to foreign entrepreneurs, for example), a simple measure of welfare consisting of the average of consumers' utilities reduces to

$W = u -$ average mismatch cost $-$ total fixed cost per consumer,

where u is average gross utility across all consumers. Now average mismatch cost is m times the average distance between ideal and consumed products. This distance varies uniformly between zero and half the distance between products, and is a quarter the distance between products, on average. Total fixed cost per consumer is just nK, (there is one 'unit' of consumers). Thus

$$W = u - m/4n - nK. \tag{4.14}$$

The socially-optimal number of products in a symmetric equilibrium is given by the value of n (again neglecting the integer nature of n) which maximizes (4.14):

$$n_s = (K/4m)^{\frac{1}{2}} = n_f/2. \tag{4.15}$$

It is immediately clear that n_s is half the number of products in a free-entry, zero-profit, Chamberlinian equilibrium, and is in fact equal to the number of products in our alternative equilibrium where there is commitment to locations, some measure of strategic entry deterrence, and positive profits. The reason why the free-entry equilibrium yields too many products is straightforward. The mismatch cost reduction from an additional product has less social value to the community than private value to the supplying firm since the latter does not take account of the reduced economies of scale (economies of fixed cost) of other firms caused by new entry.

The analysis here suggests that strategic product location to obtain long-run positive profits reduces the number of products and increases economies of scale and that this reduced 'product proliferation' is welfare-improving. Note however that going from n_f to $n_f/2$ products will not generally be a Pareto improvement: some consumers will lose their ideal available product and their share of allocated profits is unlikely to be a sufficient compensation. Also any such welfare results are only indicative of the kinds of processes that may happen. The special nature of the model prevents any claim to generality.

3.3 Adding Outside Products

If the price level is sufficiently high, the equilibria discussed above may fail as some consumers choose to eschew the market and buy outside goods instead. Suppose that a consumer located at h between products a and b has net utility of

$u - p_a - m(h-a)$ if he buys product a;
$u - p_b - m(b-h)$ if he buys product b;
0 if he buys the outside product.

Now sales of product a are limited by both the alternatives of buying product b and the outside product. Sales are $h^* - a$ where

$$h^* - a = \min \{(u-p_a)/m, (p_b-p_a)/2m + 1/2n\}. \tag{4.16}$$

The first expression in $\min \{.,.\}$ in equation (4.16) is the furthermost customer reached who does not prefer the outside product, while the second expression is that reached who does not prefer product b. If we take the free entry assumption, where all prices are equal to p_f, then, if

$(u - p_f)/m > 1/2n,$

the outside product is immaterial and the analysis of the last subsection is appropriate. Using the solution for p_f found in equation (4.13) this condition is just that $u > 1.5m/n$. Salop (1979) terms this case the 'competitive' case. On the other hand, the price that maximizes profit when demand is effectively constrained only by the outside product is simply $u/2$ ($pu/2$ maximizes $p(u-p)/m$). If all products in the market adopted this and found that they were not actively competing with each other then $1/2n > u/2m$ (from equation 4.16)) or $u < m/n$. Thus, if the outside product is a poor substitute (u high), it can be ignored; if it is a sufficiently good substitute, inter-variety competition can be ignored – indicating that the definition of the market may have been ill-judged. There is also a set of conditions such that $m/n < u < 1.5m/n$ where both constraints hold simultaneously. Here firms reduce prices to expand demand while they only compete with the outside product, but cease when faced with much less elastic demand when they have to compete with neighbouring products as well. Thus, in this 'kinked equilibrium' case (Salop, 1979), there is no active competition between products supplied to the market, despite the fact that all consumers are supplied. To sell more means attracting customers for whom the seller's variety is essentially third-best; both the outside product and the neighbouring product are preferred by potential customers.

An interesting feature of the kinked equilibrium is some rather perverse comparative statics. The equilibrium price at the 'kink' is found by equating the two expressions in min $\{, . ,\}$ in equation (4.16) for when $p_a = p_b$. Thus $p = u - m/2n$. Note that p increases if the number of supplying firms increases, and decreases if the cost of mismatch increases! The reason is that, for small changes in parameters, the equilibrium remains at the kink; the extra fixed cost of more products is passed on to consumers, while higher mismatch costs persuade firms to reduce prices until they are just at the kink again. This can be contrasted with the competitive case, where prices defined by equation (4.10) decrease with the number of firms and decrease with mismatch costs.

4   VERTICAL PRODUCT DIFFERENTIATION

4.1   The Demand for Different Qualities

If individual consumers value additional quality by differing amounts then the possibility arises of different quality products being priced at levels which achieve positive sales in a market equilibrium. Of course, if consumers differ only moderately, then products might be expected to differ little in quality. Since price competition is usually more intensive the less heterogeneous the products, the number of products existing in an equilibrium may be very restricted and may more reflect the range of differences in consumers, and thus the demand for this kind of variety, than the number of consumers.

Our analysis will entail a simplified model of vertical product differentiation of the kind used in Jaskold Gabszewicz and Thisse (1979, 1980) and Shaked and Sutton (1982, 1983). Two questions are of interest. First, whether the number of firms which can be supported by the market always grows with market size. The answer to this will be no; a market with an infinite number of consumers can be in equilibrium with a finite number of firms. Secondly, if there are just a few products supplied, how different will be their qualities and their profitability?

Figure 4.6 Quality differentiation as product locations

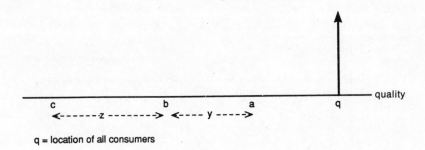

q = location of all consumers

Figure (4.6) reproduces Figure 4.3 with some additional notation. The distances between products and the location of the ideal or reference product (of all consumers) are shown, and the mismatch cost parameter m varies among the consumers located at q according to an assumed uniform density $h(m)$ such that:

$$h(m) = h \qquad \underline{m} < m < \bar{m}$$
$$\quad\quad\quad = 0 \qquad \text{otherwise.}$$

Variable production costs of any quality product continue to be assumed zero. Fixed costs of entry are assumed to be positive but arbitrarily near zero. In this framework, providing that positive sales of a product can be made at a positive price, that product is viable. If either sales are zero or price is zero then that product is not viable, since the fixed cost would not be covered.

From Figure 4.6 and the density of m we can state that consumers with mismatch parameter m will prefer product a to product b if

$$p_a < p_b + my \tag{4.17}$$

and will prefer product b to product c if

$$p_b < p_c + mz. \tag{4.18}$$

Consumer choices for arbitrary prices are indicated in Figure 4.7. Obviously, if p_b is virtually zero and $\underline{m} > 0$, no sales of product c will take place, even when p_c is zero. Is there any situation where no sales of b will occur either? If $p_b \approx 0$ then a's profit-maximizing price is that which maximizes its price times sales:

$$\pi_a = p_a h \{ \bar{m} - \max(\underline{m}, p_a / y) \}. \tag{4.19}$$

Figure 4.7   Product choices for consumers

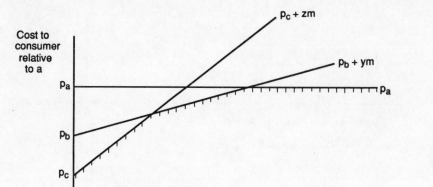

Product a will sell to all consumers apart from those (if any) who have m values between $\underline{m}$ and p_a/y and who therefore prefer product b at a zero price – see equation (4.17). The optimal p_a can reflect either of two cases. Case (1) is where some sales are made of product b, and is depicted in Figure 4.8a. Assuming that p_a will be chosen such that max $(\underline{m}, p_a/y) = p_a/y$, the optimal p_a is that which maximizes $p_a h(\bar{m} - p_a/y)$, and this is $p_a = y\bar{m}/2$. Provided then that $p_a/y > \underline{m}$, that is $\bar{m}/2 > \underline{m}$, this is consistent. Case (2) is depicted in Figure 4.8b. Here firm a increases price until the point where any further increase would lose sales to product b, that is where $p_a = y\underline{m}$, but does not find it profitable to increase price more. For this case to be consistent, $\bar{m} < 2\underline{m}$. Thus the two cases are:

Case (1) $p_a = \bar{m}y/2$ if $\bar{m}/2 > \underline{m}$;
Case (2) $p_a = \bar{m}y$ if $\bar{m}/2 < \underline{m}$.

Sales are the minimum of $h(\bar{m} - \underline{m})$ and $h\bar{m}/2$. If the whole market is supplied by product a then b achieves no sales at a virtually zero price, and is thus not a viable product. Thus no second (inferior) product is viable if $\bar{m} < 2\underline{m}$, when there is no room for other than the highest-quality product. The market is a natural monopoly. Note that neither the density of consumers, h, nor the quality difference, y, affects this condition.

4.2   A Natural Duopoly

Now consider that the market is not a natural monopoly and that products a and b can exist with positive sales and prices. Thus we know that

Figure 4.8   A natural monopoly or not?

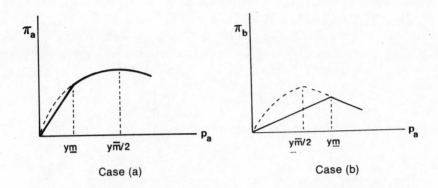

Case (a)   Case (b)

$\bar{m} > 2\underline{m}$. Can a product c of lower quality than either a or b also achieve positive sales with a positive price? For this to happen, p_b must be sufficiently high. Firm b's profit is its price times its sales and, when p_c is virtually zero, this is given by:

$$\pi_b = p_b h\{(p_a - p_b)/y - \max(\underline{m}, \ p_b/z)\}. \tag{4.20}$$

Product b will sell to consumers with m parameters between $(p_a - p_b)/y$ (from equation (4.17)) and p_b/z (from equation (4.18) when $p_c = 0$). However, if $p_b/z < \underline{m}$, there is zero density between p_b/z and $\underline{m}$, and no sales are possible in this range. The optimal p_b is defined according to three possible cases. In Figure 4.9, π_b is sketched for both functional forms: for $\underline{m} < p_b/z$ and for $\underline{m} > p_b/z$. The true function switches from one to the other at $p_b = z\underline{m}$. In case (1), $\underline{m}$ is sufficiently high for no sales to be lost to product c, and this is shown in Figure 4.9(a). Case (2) in Figure 4.9(b) is where a higher price yields higher π_b while $p_b < z\underline{m}$, but increasing price beyond $z\underline{m}$ decreases π_b owing to additional sales losses to product c. At $p_b = z\underline{m}$ product c obtains no positive sales. In case (3) in Figure 4.9(c), firm b's optimal price allows c some positive sales at a zero price, and thus product c can earn some positive revenue at some positive price. The three cases can be summarized as:

Case (1) $p_b = (p_a - \underline{m}y)/2$ if $\underline{m} > (p_a - y\underline{m})/2z$;
Case (2) $p_b = z\underline{m}$ if $p_a/(2z + 2y) < \underline{m} < (p_a - y\underline{m})/2z$;
Case (3) $p_b = p_a z/(2z + 2y)$ if $\underline{m} < p_a/(2z + 2y)$.

The price p_a is of course endogenous, and is that price which maximizes

Figure 4.9   A natural duopoly or not?

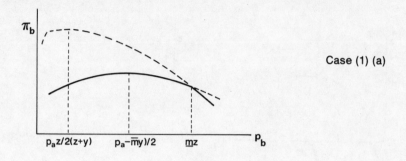

Case (1) (a)

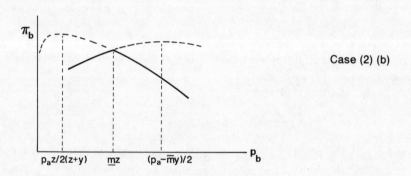

Case (2) (b)

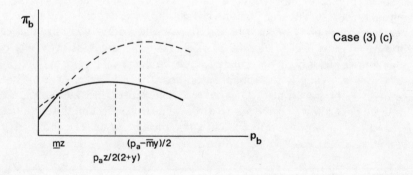

Case (3) (c)

$$\pi_a = p_a h\{\bar{m} - (p_a - p_b)/y\} \tag{4.21}$$

so that

$$p_a = (\bar{m}y + p_b)/2. \tag{4.22}$$

Using p_a from equation (4.22) yields

Case (1) $p_b = y(\bar{m} - 2\underline{m})/3$
$p_a = y(2\bar{m} - \underline{m})/3$
$\quad\quad$ if $y(\bar{m} - 2\underline{m})/3 < \underline{m}z$ so that $\bar{m} < \underline{m}(2 + 3z/y)$;

Case (2) $p_b = z\underline{m}$
$p_a = (\bar{m}y + \underline{m}z)/2$ $\quad\quad$ if $\underline{m}(4 + 3z/y) > \bar{m} > \underline{m}(2 + 3z/y)$;

Case (3) $p_b = zy\bar{m}/(4y + 3z)$
$p_a = 2(z + y)y\bar{m}/(4y + 3z)$
$\quad\quad$ if $y\bar{m}/(4y + 3z) > \underline{m}$ so that $\bar{m} > \underline{m}(4 + 3z/y)$.

Thus there is no room for product c to sell at a positive price if products a and b cover all the market, and this occurs when

$$\bar{m} < 4\underline{m} + 3\underline{m}z/y. \tag{4.23}$$

As z can be any non-negative value, a sufficient condition for this to hold is that $\bar{m} < 4\underline{m}$. Thus if $2\underline{m} < \bar{m} < 4\underline{m}$, exactly two products can exist with positive sales. If $\bar{m} > 4\underline{m}$ then, for a sufficiently small z, case (3) would be operative and at least three products could exist with positive sales. As the ratio of $\bar{m}/\underline{m}$ increases, so more products could be accommodated within the market.

The intuition behind these results is very simple. The demand for quality variety is determined by differences among consumers, not by the number of consumers. For any given range of consumers, price competition among the top-quality brands leads to all consumers being prepared to buy one of these brands rather than a lower-quality product at even a zero price. The results in this and the last section have merely determined the ranges of consumer heterogeneity which lead to a maximum of one or of two products with positive sales.

4.3 Product Selection

The duopoly case implied by the restriction $4\underline{m} > \bar{m} > 2\underline{m}$ permits a simple analysis of product selection: that is, the choice of quality locations a and b. Suppose that firms enter the market (by paying the fixed cost). Then they each choose their product quality in a Nash game with the outcome of the subsequent price game as their payoffs. Let a be the highest possible quality level, given current technology.

If more than two firms entered the market then only the two firms with the highest-quality products would make positive sales. Each firm would increase its quality to beat its competitors and the only equilibrium would be for all firms to locate at a. This implies a zero price for all firms (as $z = y = 0$) and thus zero revenue. Fixed costs are not covered and the entry decisions of the third and subsequent firms are seen to be irrational. A perfect equilibrium therefore involves just two firms entering the market. We will, however, assume there is an additional product available at a very low-quality level (at c) and which is sustained by demand from another market. It is thus an 'outside product'. We can then show that the duopoly equilibrium will involve a price game where the solution is not of the case (1) form.

Substituting the equilibrium prices for case (1) into equations (4.20) and (4.21) leads to profits of the form

$$\pi_a = hy(2\bar{m} - \underline{m})^2/9 \tag{4.24}$$

$$\pi_b = hy(\bar{m} - 2\underline{m})^2/9. \tag{4.25}$$

As y is the difference in quality between a and b, both firms will wish to increase y by either increasing a's quality or decreasing b's quality. Thus product a will be located at the maximum quality possible and b at the lowest. However the latter is bounded since, as b decreases, it becomes nearer to product c; z/y decreases and case (1) converts to case (2). Then an interior maximum for firm b involves a location for product b some distance from both a and c. The conclusion is that, subject to the constraint imposed by the outside product, maximum product differentiation in quality is seen in a perfect equilibrium.

5   FURTHER REMARKS AND CONCLUSIONS

5.1   Changing the Assumptions

The very special functional forms that we have adopted have served to illustrate the role of product differentiation in the market supply process. However the assumptions on consumers and firms are a matter of more general concern, and it is important to see how far the approach we have adopted can be extended to include variations in these assumptions.

One central question concerns the level of information of consumers. We have been concerned mostly with situations of perfect information, but an interesting variant would involve there being less perfect information the more product varieties exist. Then advertising may be used to persuade, and possibly misinform, consumers as to the quality levels of available products (see, for example, Schmalensee, 1978). Grossman and Shapiro (1984) use a Salop-type model to show that there will be excessive advertising in equilibrium: each firm will want to inform consumers about its product's location, and its perceived private gain from marginal advertising expenditure is greater than the social gain.

Our assumption that each firm supplies only one product can be relaxed. However the clearest picture of multi-product firms can be seen in terms of each firm's products being grouped together so that competition with other firms' products is minimized. Thus, in our notion of horizontal product differentiation, a particular firm would wish to locate its products next to each other and charge monopoly prices to consumers who would bear high mismatch costs if they bought from another firm (see, for example, Prescott and Visscher, 1977; Brander and Eaton, 1984). The entry deterrence aspects of multi-product firms are also related to this. An alternative view is contained in Judd (1985). He argues that, if a firm supplies a number of neighbouring products, it will be less able to threaten to reduce prices of its peripheral products to counter price competition from other firms, since this would have knock-on effects for profits of its interior products.

The location model of horizontal product differentiation has also been applied to monopolies (see, for example, Bental and Spiegel, 1984), to multinational corporations (Lyons, 1984) and to the organization of retailing (Mathewson and Winter, 1984).

The same comments concerning multi-product firms and product selection usually apply to product selection in models of vertical product selection. If a firm can achieve a monopoly within its own market segment, then monopoly profits can be extracted. Then the finite nature of the number of products which can be supported in an equilibrium is replaced by a finite number of firms, each supplying a range of similar-quality products. Vertical market segmentation by a pure monopolist is analysed by Mussa and Rosen (1978). The form of analysis is similar to that of the question of non-linear prices; see, for example, Spence (1977a).

Our analysis of address models has treated horizontal and vertical product differentiation as separate phenomena, and has not attempted to combine the two forms in a single model. Such a combination is difficult to achieve, particularly in terms of researching the kind of products which would be selected by firms. A simple approach in Ireland (1987, Chapter 7) argues that horizontal differentiation would be maximized, and that this would lead to each firm choosing the same quality of product. No firm would choose a lower quality without cost savings, since a Bertrand price competition would be limited by the presence of horizontal product differentiation. More general questions concerning industry structure and product differentiation are considered in Shaked and Sutton (1987). They discuss the interplay between the cost of quality improvements and whether firms' individual market shares become arbitrarily small as the market becomes large.

All the above extensions essentially maintain the address model approach. Thus which consumers buy which products is part of the solution to the models. An alternative approach to product differentiation would be to postulate an arbitrary demand function, which stated how aggregate demands for the various product varieties were related, but was not derived specifically from differences among individual consumer tastes or incomes. Such an approach is necessary when the number of products in direct competition with each other is more than a few. Lack of space prevents discussion here, but the interested reader should look at Yarrow (1985) or Ireland (1987, Chapter 9) for an introduction.

5.2   Conclusions

The functional-form-specific nature of our analysis prevents results from having the status of theorems. Rather the models we have looked at should be considered as illustrations of how product differentiation has strategic value in setting the economic environment for firms engaged in price competition. Product design is the linking middle stage in the process of market supply. On the one hand there are strategic advantages which allow higher equilibrium prices; on the other there are entry-limiting factors. Thus the kind of product adopted will have a niche in the market: it will sell to a particular selected segment of the market. This segment may relate to specific individual taste or to the consumers' view of the value of marginal quality, or to a combination of both horizontal and vertical factors.

The product selection decision will also be influenced by the desire to deter entry of competing products. Thus if the market segment is too profitable it may attract the entry of competitors. Judicious location and the possibility of supplying multiple varieties may permit above-normal profit to be earned in the long run. If product selection and the resulting equilibrium prices can be predicted at the entry stage, then a perfect equilibrium in the supply process can be deduced. The structure of the industry in equilibrium, and particularly the number of firms and product varieties that are viable, depends on the kind of product differentiation that can be supported by current technology and tastes.

5. Price Discrimination

George Norman

---

1 INTRODUCTION

Price discrimination is a remarkably widespread business practice that has survived despite considerable attempts by policy makers to limit its application. Equally it is a practice that has received surprisingly little attention in standard microeconomic analysis. If price discrimination is to be found anywhere in the textbooks, it is usually as a *curiosum* in the chapter on monopoly. Even then, the range and extent of price discrimination is sadly understated. Only with developments in 'the new industrial economics' have we begun to put analytic meat on observed business practices. There is no doubt that, in this area, as with so many others considered in this book, microeconomic analysis has much to gain from its integration with the theory of industrial organization.

1.1 Some Definitions

We begin with a definition of what is meant by price discrimination. There are many possible candidates – for an extensive discussion of these, see the excellent analysis by Phlips (1983). The definition we prefer is that suggested by Phlips:

> price discrimination should be defined as implying that two varieties of a commodity are sold (by the same seller) to two buyers at different *net* prices, the net price being the price (paid by the buyer) corrected for the cost associated with the product differentiation. (Phlips, 1983, p. 6)

An important element of this definition is that it explicitly allows for product differentiation. Such differentiation can take many forms: goods can be differentiated in terms of characteristics such as their location, colour, taste and so on, or the time at which they are made available, or in terms of their quality. Typically such product differentiation is costly; for example, the goods have to be transported or stored, and improved

107

quality typically implies changes in product design and content. Price discrimination exists, on this definition, when the difference in the prices of two differentiated goods does not equal the costs of differentiation.

A special case of the definition arises where two *identical* goods are sold at different prices to two different buyers. Since there is no cost associated with product differentiation, the net prices of the two identical goods must be different.

The ability of a seller to employ discriminatory prices necessitates that the seller has at least some degree of monopoly power. Note that we refer to 'some degree' of monopoly power. Price discrimination is a natural feature of monopoly but we shall see that it is at least as equally a feature of oligopoly and an industrial organization world of imperfectly competitive markets. In this type of world, sellers confront buyers differentiated by locations, tastes or incomes. As a consequence, buyers' demands are not the perfectly elastic functions of product prices that characterize perfect competition.

There are, of course, constraints on the extent to which a seller can price discriminate between buyers. First, the seller must be able to separate his consumers into distinct groups with different demands. Some natural exogenous divisions such as age and location immediately suggest themselves and others, such as income, may be feasible in particular situations. Endogenous divisions are also possible, based upon criteria that cannot be directly observed by the seller in advance. The seller may, nevertheless, be able to encourage buyers to self-select into different categories with respect to features such as time of purchase or the quality of good demanded that are not under the explicit control of the seller.

Secondly, the seller must be able to prevent arbitrage by buyers. Two types of arbitrage can be considered related, roughly, to the exogenous/ endogenous division of buyers noted above. Consider, first, price discrimination related to exogenous consumer characteristics. Assume that the net prices charged to two different types of consumer differ by more than the transactions costs incurred by these consumers in transferring the goods between themselves. Then the low-price buyers have an incentive to buy the product and sell it to the high-price buyers. As an example, there is obvious potential for arbitrage available to students with discount cards acceptable in major department stores. Of course this type of arbitrage is not always possible, for example where transactions costs between consumers are high. Age discounts for entry to amusement parks, for bus, rail and air travel are usually supported by heavy fines imposed on buyers who deliberately misrepresent their ages. Similarly many products are difficult to transfer: medical treatment and other similar services are obvious examples.

Where the division of consumers is endogenous, arbitrage arises when the consumer chooses not to consume the product that has been designed for him. This is most easily illustrated where goods are differentiated by quality, buyers are distributed according to their incomes, but the seller knows only the aggregate distribution of consumer incomes. Typically a seller would want to encourage high-income consumers to purchase high-quality goods at high prices. The seller's ability to price discriminate across product quality in this way is limited by an 'incentive compatibility' constraint. Consumers will only sort themselves in the desired manner if the difference in price is at least justified by the difference in quality.

The desire on the part of a monopolist to price discriminate should be obvious. Such a pricing policy will typically be more profitable than a non-discriminatory scheme. After all, the monopolist always has the option of not discriminating. We shall see that matters are much less clear-cut with oligopoly. Price discrimination may be less profitable than the situation in which all firms do not discriminate but the no-discrimination case may not be a Nash equilibrium of the non-cooperative game played between the firms.

In developing the discussion further, it is convenient to follow Pigou (1932, Part 2, Chapter 17) and distinguish three types of price discrimination. *First-degree* discrimination

> would involve the charge of a different price against all the different units of commodity, in such wise that the price exacted for each was equal to the demand price for it, and no consumers' surplus was left to the buyers. (p. 279)

Such perfect price discrimination is not always attainable in practice, either because of potential arbitrage between consumers or because the seller has insufficient information about buyers. *Second-degree* price discrimination may be possible in such cases. Assume that buyers can be separated into *n* groups on the basis of some criterion that cannot be observed directly by the seller. The seller can still extract some consumer surplus by choosing a set of prices that encourage the consumers to self-select into the various groups. *Third-degree* discrimination

> would obtain if the monopolist were able to distinguish among his customers *n* different groups, separated from one another more or less by some practicable mark, and could charge a separate monopoly price to the members of each group . . . . This degree, it will be noticed, differs fundamentally from either of the preceding degrees, in that it may involve the refusal to satisfy, in one market, demands represented by demand prices in excess of some of those which, in another market, are satisfied. (p. 279)

The distinction between second- and third-degree price discrimination is that the buyer grouping in the latter case is based on an observable (exogenous) signal. Such a signal confers on the seller the power to choose whether or not to supply particular buyer groups.

1.2 Additional Reading

It is impossible in a single chapter to do justice to the full range of literature now available on price discrimination. The examples discussed in the sections below cover, first, some of those that are commonly considered to be particularly important and, secondly, those that reflect the author's own particular interests (or prejudices). A wealth of additional reading can be recommended. Reference has already been made to Phlips' (1983) extended discussion. There are, in addition, two excellent survey articles: Varian (1989) and Phlips (1988). For an extensive discussion of price discrimination by monopolists, see Tirole (1988, Chapter 3), while some of the introductory aspects of price discrimination in oligopolistic markets can be found in Greenhut, Norman and Hung (1987). If this is not sufficient then the bibliographies offered by these authors will more than complete the set.

2   PRICE DISCRIMINATION IN PRACTICE[1]

The examples presented below are by no means exhaustive. They are intended merely to give a flavour of typical business practices. It is tempting to suggest, in fact, that cases of price discrimination can be found in almost every 'real-life' market.

Example 1 : two-part tariffs
For many goods and services, the pricing schedule consists of a fixed initial fee plus a charge related to subsequent usage. Taxi charges and the charge for utilities such as gas, electricity and water are obvious examples, as are entry charges for theme parks such as Disneyland. The initial fee and usage charge are often differentiated according to an observable criterion: age, business or personal use and time of day are typical criteria.

Example 2: quantity discounts
In many cases sellers will offer quantity discounts to buyers, in the sense that the price of, say, four units of a good is less than four times the price of one unit. To effect this type of price discrimination, the higher-quantity/lower-unit-price offer typically takes the form of a bundled commodity; a six-pack, for example, that the consumer cannot unbundle before purchase, or a season of opera tickets that must be reserved, and paid for, in advance.

Table 5.1   Membership charges for American Economic Review

Income ($)	Annual fee ($)
less than 30 000	60.00
above 30 000 but less than 40, 000	68.80
above 40 000	77.60
Junior members (registered students)	38.00

Table 5.2   Academic journal prices

| Journal | Price | |
	Institution	Personal
Economic Journal	£68.00	£28.00
Economica	£22.50	£12.50
Review of Economic Studies		
1 year	£50.00	£18.00
3 years	—	£45.00
American Economic Review	$200.00	(See Table 5.1)

Example 3: price discrimination by income
It is always encouraging to find economists practising what they preach. Table 5.1 gives the current membership charges for the *American Economic Review*.

An interesting feature of this example of price discrimination is that there appears to be little attempt to check upon the accuracy of the declared income. Presumably academic economists are assumed either to be honest or to be boastful.

Example 4: price discrimination by buyer type
Reference has already been made to two-part tariffs for services differentiated according to whether consumption is for business or for personal use. Table 5.2 presents another example: the differential in price charged for economic journals to institutions (typically libraries) and individuals. The good being offered is, in this case, identical but usage may, of course, not be: see Liebovitz (1986) and Erkkila (1986) for a discussion of this example.

Example 5: price discrimination by type or quality
Anyone who buys economics books knows that there is usually a

Table 5.3   Hardback and paperback book prices

Title	No of pages	Price	
		Hardback	Paperback
Macroeconomic Theory	256	£30.00	£10.95
Economics of Business Enterprise	320	£40.00	£9.95
Economics of Bargaining	272	£35.00	£12.95
Advanced Econometrics	516	£50.00	£17.50
Handboook of International Economics; vol. 1	624	$69.50	$34.95

significant difference between the hardback and paperback price, a difference that would appear to be unrelated to differences in the costs of production of the two types of book. After all, the actual content of the two types of book is identical. Table 5.3 gives some recent examples.

3   MONOPOLY

3.1   Perfect Price Discrimination

Suppose the simplest possible demand conditions, in which each buyer i has a known reservation price v_i for a good and has unit demand for the good at any price less than or equal to the reservation price. The monopoly seller can then extract the entire consumer surplus by charging consumer i a price $p_i = v_i$ provided, of course, that arbitrage can be prevented.

The more interesting case arises when consumers are identical but consumer demand is a decreasing function of price. Now it makes little sense to talk of the individual consumer's reservation price, nor is it possible to sell individual units of the product to each consumer at different prices. Nevertheless it is still possible for the seller to extract consumer surplus by adopting a non-linear pricing strategy. For a detailed discussion of this case applied to pricing of theme parks such as Disneyland, see Oi (1971). See also Schmalensee (1982).

To fix our ideas for later discussion, assume that consumer preferences are given by the utility function (see Tirole, 1988, Chapter 3):

$$U = \begin{cases} \theta V(q) - T & \text{if they pay } T \text{ and consume } q \text{ units of the good;} \\ 0 & \text{if they do not buy;} \end{cases} \quad (5.1)$$

where $V(0) = 0$, $V'(q) > 0$, $V''(q) < 0$ and θ is a taste parameter. This preference function is illustrated in (q, T) space in Figure 5.1(a). Note that the indifference curves are vertical translates of each other: they have the same slope at any given quantity. The curve $R(q)$ is the consumer's reservation tariff. $R(q)$ is the maximum amount the consumer is willing to pay for q units of the commodity: hence $U(q, R(q)) = 0$. Consumer surplus increases the *lower* the indifference curve the consumer attains.

These preferences generate the consumer demand function of Figure 5.1(b):

$$p = \theta V'(q) \tag{5.2}$$

which, from the quasi-linear preference structure of equation (5.1), has no income effects.

As a specific example, we may assume that:

$$V(q) = \frac{1 - (1 - q)^2}{2}. \tag{5.3}$$

Then $V'(q) = 1 - q$ and the demand function is $q = 1 - p/\theta$.

Assume further that the monopolist's cost function is

$$c = c(q), \tag{5.4}$$

where $c(0) = 0$; $c'(q) > 0$; $c''(q) \geq 0$.

The monopolist's profit is then

$$\pi(q) = T - c(q) \tag{5.5}$$

and is illustrated in Figure 5.1(a) by the monopolist's isoprofit curves. Profit on each curve is measured by the vertical intercept of that curve. The marginal cost curve is illustrated in Figure 5.1(b).

Now assume that the monopolist charges a linear price schedule $T = pq$. Consumers will maximize utility at point C in Figure 5.1(a) by consuming q_p with profit to the monopolist of π_p. The monopolist can increase his profit immediately by introducing a fixed fee CD ($= OA$), equal to the consumer surplus at C, taking consumers to point D.

Since the isoprofit curve at D cuts the reservation outlay schedule, D is not optimal for the monopolist. Profit is maximized at point E, with demand q^*, where an isoprofit curve is tangent to the reservation outlay schedule. Point E is achieved by the monopolist charging the affine pricing schedule:

$$T(q) = A^* + p^*q, \tag{5.6}$$

where:

1. the price per unit p^* is equal to marginal cost $c'(q^*)$. Such a linear

Figure 5.1   Quasi-linear preferences and demand

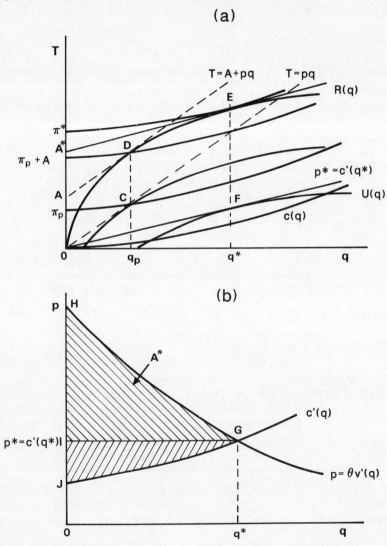

pricing schedule would lead to consumption at point F and consumer surplus FE. Hence:

2. the fixed fee A^* is equal to consumer surplus FE at the price per unit p^*. This pricing policy can also be illustrated in Figure 5.1(b). Setting a unit price $p^* = c'(q^*)$ and a fixed fee equal to consumer surplus (area HIG) realizes profit given by the shaded area JGH. No other pricing policy can improve on this.

It might be argued, of course, that the pricing schedule (5.6) is not discriminatory according to our definition. In response, it should be noted that, since average price is a declining function of output, (5.6) is indeed discriminatory in that different units are being sold, effectively, for different prices. The more convincing response is to extend the analysis by assuming that consumers are not all identical. Rather we might assume that consumers fall into distinct groups on the basis of some exogenous, observable criterion (age, location and so on), such that utility for consumers in group i is

$$U_i = \begin{cases} \theta_i V(q) - T & \text{for } q > 0 \\ 0 & \text{for } q = 0, \end{cases} \tag{5.7}$$

where $\theta_i < \theta_{i+1}$.

Figure 5.2 illustrates this case for two groups of consumers: to keep matters simple we assume constant marginal costs and so no feedback into marginal costs from the output levels supplied to each group. The perfectly discriminating, profit-maximizing policy is to offer each consumer in group i the affine pricing schedule:

$$T^*_i(q) = A^*_i + p^*_i q, \tag{5.8}$$

where p^*_i equals marginal cost[2] and A^*_i is consumer surplus for each consumer in group i at price p^*_i: DC for group 1 consumers and FE for group 2 consumers in Figure 5.2. Pricing policy (5.8) is obviously discriminatory. The application of this result to age discounts, for example, should be obvious.

3.2 Second-degree Price Discrimination

Pricing policy (5.8) assumes that the monopolist can distinguish between buyers according to some direct, observable criterion. Suppose, however, that, while the monopolist knows that buyers are heterogeneous, the defining criterion is unobservable (endogenous). Then pricing policy (5.8) will not have the desired effect since it does not satisfy the incentive compatibility constraint. In the two group case of Figure 5.2, group 2 buyers will represent themselves as group 1 buyers, consuming at C and enjoying a positive surplus.

What the monopolist must now find is a pricing policy that encourages the consumers to sort themselves into the 'correct' groups.

A two-part tariff

Assume that the monopolist offers all consumers a two-part tariff $T = A + pq$ as in Section 3.1. The monopolist wishes to choose A and p to maximize aggregate profit. From Figure 5.3 it is apparent that this is unlikely to be the pricing schedule $T = A^*_2 + p^*_2 q$ of equation (5.8) since group 1 consumers will leave the market.[3] Consider, therefore, the pricing schedule $T = A^*_1 + p^*_1 q$ such that $p^*_1 = c$.

Assume that there are N_1 consumers in group 1 and N_2 consumers in group 2. Then profit to the monopolist is $\pi = (N_1 + N_2)A^*_1$: the sum of the fixed charges. Group 1 consumers maximize utility at B and group 2 consumers at D. Consumers in both groups continue to buy q^*_i: see Figure 5.3. Now assume that price is increased by the amount Δp. In order to ensure that group 1 consumers continue to buy the good, the fixed charge has to be reduced by ΔA. Since the seller is extracting the entire surplus from group 1 consumers, if the change in price is 'small' the overall impact

Figure 5.2   First-degree discrimination

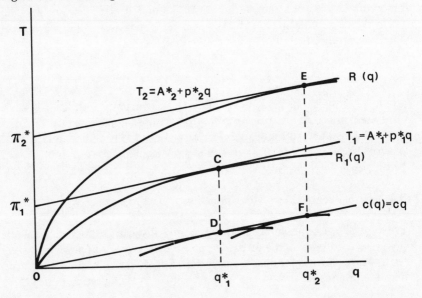

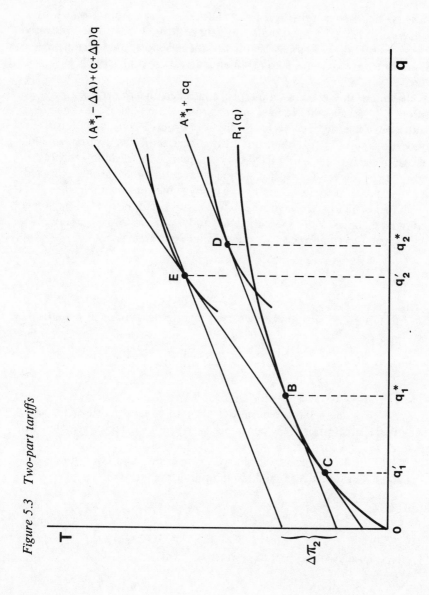

Figure 5.3   Two-part tariffs

of these changes in price and fixed charge on profit from group 1 consumers is of second order: the isoprofit curve through C is not significantly lower than that through B. This is not the case for group 2 consumers. Equilibrium moves from D to E, with an increase in profit per consumer of $\Delta\pi_2$.

Of course this process cannot be continued indefinitely. As price is further increased the reduction in profit from group 1 consumers increases, while the increase in profit from group 2 consumers falls. The important point is that the optimal two-part tariff has a price per unit above marginal cost and a fixed charge equal to the resulting surplus of group 1 consumers. Group 1 consumers have the whole surplus extracted while group 2 consumers continue to enjoy some consumer surplus.

To make this discussion more explicit, assume that the utility function is given by equation (5.3). Individual demand is $q_i = D_i(p) = 1 - p/\theta_i$. Net consumer surplus at price p for each group i consumer is:

$$S_i(p) = \frac{(\theta_i - p)^2}{2\theta_i}. \tag{5.9}$$

If both groups of consumers are served, aggregate demand at price p is:

$$D(p) = N_1 D_1(p) + N_2 D_2(p) = N\left(1 - \frac{p}{\theta}\right), \tag{5.10}$$

where $1/\theta = \lambda/\theta_1 + (1 - \lambda)/\theta_2$ and $\lambda = N_1/(N_1 + N_2)$ = proportion of group 1 consumers; θ is the harmonic mean of θ_1 and θ_2 with λ as weight. At any marginal price p, the consumer surplus for each group 2 consumer exceeds that for each group 1 consumer. A fixed charge A that just extracts all the group 1 consumers' surplus will also ensure that both groups buy the good. Thus $A = S_1(p)$ and the monopolist maximizes

$$(N_1 + N_2) S_1(p) + (p - c) D(p) = N\frac{(\theta_1 - p)^2}{2\theta_1} + N(p - c)\left(1 - \frac{p}{\theta}\right).$$

Differentiating with respect to p gives:

$$\begin{aligned} p^* &= c/(2 - \theta/\theta_1) \\ A^* &= S_1(p^*). \end{aligned} \tag{5.11}$$

Non-linear prices

A two-part tariff is not the second-degree price discrimination tariff that maximizes the monopolist's profit. Consider Figure 5.4, in which we illustrate the optimal two-part tariff, $A^* + p^*q$. Group 1 consumers maximize utility at C, and group 2 consumers at D. The same outcome could be achieved by the monopolist offering the discrete, non-linear, outlay schedules (q_1, T_1) and (q_2, T_2); that is, offering to sell two 'bundles': q_1 at total price T_1 and q_2 at total price T_2. But then the monopolist can further increase profit by increasing the tariff T_2 to the level T'_2 where group 2 consumers just prefer the bundle (q_2, T'_2) to the bundle (q_1, T_1). This is the point E in Figure 5.4, which lies on the group 2 indifference curve $S'_2(q)$ through C. Even point E is not profit-maximizing, since at E the monopolist's isoprofit curve cuts the indifference curve. *Given* the bundle (q_1, T_1), the monopolist should offer a second bundle (q'_2, T''_2) which maximizes profit from group 2 consumers while being incentive-compatible; that is, satisfying the arbitrage constraint: point F in Figure 5.4. In general, therefore, the optimal non-linear tariff is such that

1. the lower-demand buyers enjoy no net surplus;
2. the higher-demand buyers enjoy positive net surplus;
3. the highest-demand buyers purchase the socially optimal quantity;
4. incentive compatibility constraints are satisfied so that each buyer group purchases the (q_i, T_i) bundle designed for it.

The example analysed in the preceding sub-section allows us to be more

Figure 5.4   Non-linear prices

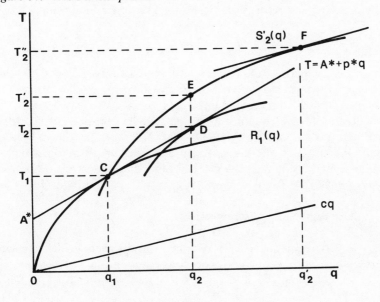

specific. Consider Figure 5.5. We know from (3) above that, no matter the (q_1, T_1) bundle offered to group 1 buyers, group 2 buyers will purchase the socially optimal quantity $q_2(c)$. The tariff T_2 charged for this quantity is, however, dependent upon (q_1, T_1). To satisfy the incentive compatibility constraint, the bundle $(q_2(c), T_2)$ must generate at least as much surplus for group 2 consumers as the bundle (q_1, T_1). This surplus is $R_2(q_1) - R_1(q_1)$: AB in Figure 5.5, equal, by construction, to CD. Hence the tariff T_2 must satisfy:

$$R_2(q_2(c)) - T_2 \geq R_2(q_1) - R_1(q_1).$$

Since this will be satisfied as an equality, we have:

$$T_2 = R_2(q_2(c)) - (R_2(q_1) - R_1(q_1)).$$

We also know from (1) that $T_1 = R_1(q_1)$. The monopolist's profit function is, therefore:

$$\begin{aligned} \pi &= N_2(T_2 - cq_2(c)) + N_1(T_1 - cq_1) \\ &= N_2(R_2(q_2(c)) - cq_2(c)) + N_1(R_1(q_1) - cq_1) - \\ &\quad N_2(R_2(q_1) - R_1(q_1)). \end{aligned}$$

The first term is fixed, since $q_2(c)$ is defined. Hence to maximize profit the monopolist chooses q_1 to maximize $(N_1 + N_2)R_1(q_1) - N_2 R_2(q_1) - N_1 cq_1$. Differentiating and reorganizing gives the first-order condition

$$R'_1(q^*_1) = \lambda c + (1 - \lambda) R'_2(q^*_1). \tag{5.12}$$

Group 1 consumers are offered a sub-optimal quantity, $R'_1(q^*_1) > c$, since by reducing the quantity offered to group 1 buyers the seller can increase the profit earned from group 2 buyers.

Generalizations of this result can be found in Spence (1977a, 1980), Goldman, Leland and Sibley (1984), Katz (1983). In practice it typically results in the seller offering quantity discounts or, in markets such as insurance markets, in the seller designing individual contracts for different types of buyer: see Rothschild and Stiglitz (1976) and Stiglitz (1977).

3.3 Third-degree price discrimination

Suppose that a monopolist seller of a single product can divide buyers into n groups on the basis of some exogenous criterion, such as location, age, sex or occupation. Each group has a downward-sloping aggregate demand curve $q_i = D_i(p_i)$ for the product. This demand curve is known to the monopolist and demand curves vary between groups. Suppose also that the monopolist is able to price discriminate between groups but cannot discriminate (either first or second degree) within a group. Thus a linear tariff $T_i = p_i q_i$ must be charged to each group. Let the monopolist's cost function be $c(q)$ where $q = \sum_{i=1}^{n} q_i$. Then aggregate profit is

$$\pi_i = \sum_{i=1}^{n} p_i D_i(p_i) - c\left(\sum_{i=1}^{n} D_i(p_i)\right)$$

and is maximized by the familiar inverse-elasticity rule:

$$p_i\left(1 - \frac{1}{\varepsilon_i}\right) = c'(q), \tag{5.13}$$

where $\varepsilon_i = -D'_i(p_i)\, p_i/D_i(p_i)$ is the elasticity of demand in market i. The left-hand side of (5.13) is marginal revenue and the right-hand side is marginal cost. From (5.13):

Figure 5.5   Optimal non-linear prices

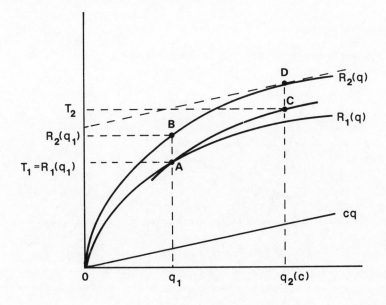

$$\frac{p_i}{p_j} = \frac{\varepsilon_i}{(\varepsilon_i - 1)} \bigg/ \frac{\varepsilon_j}{(\varepsilon_j - 1)} > 1 \text{ if } \varepsilon_i < \varepsilon_j.$$

(5.14)

The monopolist should charge more in markets with inelastic demands: see Figure 5.6. We can see, therefore, why business travellers are charged more than students, why hardback books are sold at a premium and why prices may vary between countries and between cities.

As an example, assume that a centrally-located seller supplies consumers in a number of different cities: see Greenhut, Norman and Hung (1987) for a more detailed discussion. Transport costs per unit sold to city i are t_i and aggregate demand in city i is $q_i = D(p_i)$: the demand *function* is assumed identical across cities. For simplicity, marginal production costs are assumed constant at c per unit, as a result of which aggregate profit is maximized by maximizing profit in each city individually. The price charged to consumers in city i is given from (5.13) by:

$$p_i \left(1 - \frac{1}{\varepsilon_i} \right) = c + t_i.$$

(5.15)

Figure 5.6   Third-degree discrimination

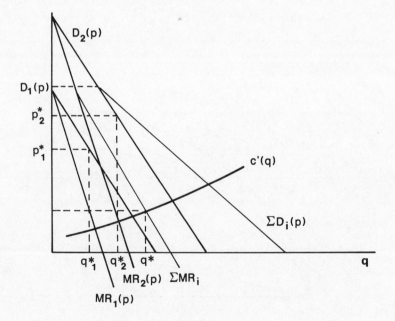

Suppose that demand in each city is given by

$$D(p) \quad \begin{aligned} &= \left(\frac{x}{b}(a - p)\right)^{1/x} \quad (x > -1; x \neq 0) \\ &= a\,e^{-bp} \quad\quad\quad x = 0 \end{aligned} \quad\quad (a, b > 0). \quad\quad (5.16)$$

If $x = 1$, this is simply a linear demand function, if $x < 1$ it is convex and if $x > 1$ it is concave. If $x < 0$ demand is more convex than the exponential demand function $D(p) = ae^{-bp}$. Elasticity of demand is

$$\varepsilon \quad \begin{aligned} &= p/x\,(a - p) \quad \text{if } x \neq 0 \\ &= bp \quad\quad\quad\quad \text{if } x = 0. \end{aligned}$$

Substitute in (5.15) and solve for p:

$$\begin{aligned} p_i &= \frac{ax + c}{1 + x} + \frac{t_i}{1 + x} \quad \text{if } x \neq 0 \\ p_i &= \frac{1}{b} + c + t_i \quad\quad\quad \text{if } x = 0. \end{aligned} \quad\quad (5.17)$$

The net price charged by the seller is the price adjusted for the costs of product differentiation. In this example, products are differentiated by being transported to different cities at unit cost t_i. The net price (which might also be called the *mill* price) charged to consumers in city i is $m_i = p_i - t_i$:

$$m_i = \quad \begin{aligned} &\frac{ax + c}{1 + x} - \frac{t_i\,x}{1 + x} \quad \text{if } x \neq 0 \\ &\frac{1}{b} + c \quad\quad\quad\quad \text{if } x = 0. \end{aligned} \quad\quad (5.18)$$

Only in the case of exponential demand is net price invariant between cities; that is, only then does the seller adopt f.o.b. pricing. For less convex demands ($x > 0$) net price falls the more distant the city and for more convex demands ($x < 0$) net price rises with distance. In the special case of linear demand, only 50 per cent of the freight costs are actually charged. The direction of price discrimination, in other words, is affected by the precise form of the demand function. Examples of this type of price discrimination can be found in Phlips (1983).

4   OLIGOPOLY

The strategic instruments used by competing firms 'matter' in the great
majority of models of oligopolistic competition in that they have a marked
influence on the resulting equilibrium. We shall concentrate upon two
possible strategic instruments, quantity and price. In contrast to the
discussion of price discrimination in monopoly, we shall concentrate in
the oligopolistic case upon third-degree price discrimination.[4]

4.1   Third-degree Price Discrimination : Cournot–Nash

The most highly developed models of price discrimination in oligopoly are
models of spatial discrimination. This should not, however, be taken to be
a major limitation. 'Space' can be treated as an analogy for a wide variety
of economic phenomena that underpin differences in consumer tastes and
lead to a division between consumers and producers: see Greenhut, Norman and Hung (1987) and Phlips (1983) for particular examples.

Consider, then, a spatial market populated by a group of n competing
sellers producing a homogeneous good that can be sold in a series of
separated markets. The strategic instrument being chosen by each seller is
the quantity of the product it will offer to sell in each market and we seek
to identify the resulting non-cooperative, Cournot–Nash equilibrium.

In this setting it is highly likely that sellers will invade each other's
'local' markets. Since the equilibrium price in each market is determined
by the aggregate quantity supplied to that market, price discrimination is
likely to characterize the resulting equilibrium. Indeed it is highly likely
that we shall see at least as great a degree of price discrimination being
applied by the oligopolistic firm as would be applied by a monopolist.

Consider a market k in which the aggregate inverse demand curve is:

$$p_k = \alpha_k - \beta_k Q_k,$$

where $\alpha_k, \beta_k > 0$ and Q_k is aggregate supply to market k. Assume, further,
that this market is supplied by a sub-group K of sellers, each of which
supplies the quantity q_{ik} ($i \in K$). So that $Q_k = \sum_{i \in K} q_{ik}$. Let firm i's marginal
production costs be constant at c_i and its transport costs to market k be
linear at t_{ik} per unit transported. The profit to firm i in supplying market k
is then

$$\pi_{ik} = q_{ik} (\alpha_k - \beta_k Q_k) - c_i q_{ik} - t_{ik} q_{ik}.$$

Assume that K contains n_k sellers. Then the Cournot–Nash equilibrium is the solution of the system of n_k first-order conditions – reaction functions – generated by these profit equations:

$$p_k - \beta_k q_{ik} - c_i - t_i = 0. \qquad (i \in K)$$

Summing over the n_k firms gives, after dividing by n_k:

$$p_k - \beta_k \frac{Q_k}{n_k} = \bar{c}_k + \bar{t}_k,$$

where

$$\bar{c}_k = \sum_{i \in K} c_i / n_k; \quad \bar{t}_k = \sum_{i \in K} t_{ik} / n_k.$$

In other words, $\bar{c}_k + \bar{t}_k$ is the mean of the marginal production and transport costs of all sellers supplying market k. Reorganizing gives the equilibrium price:

$$p^*_k = \frac{1}{n_k + 1} (\alpha_k + n_k \bar{c}_k + n_k \bar{t}_k). \tag{5.19}$$

As might be expected, this is independent of β_k.

To see how this equation gives rise to price discrimination we can consider a range of possible cases, based upon the simple example illustrated in Figure 5.7, in which there are three markets located at 0, 1 and 2 ($k = 0, 1, 2$).

Case 1
Assume that each market contains a single local seller who is able to sell in every market, so that $n_k = 3$ for $k = 0, 1, 2$. Assume that $c_i = 0$ for each seller and that transport costs are $t_{ij} = t|i - j|$. Hence $\bar{c}_k = 0$, $\bar{t}_0 = t$, $\bar{t}_1 = 2t/3$, $\bar{t}_2 = t$ and

$$\begin{cases} p^*_0 = (\alpha_0 + 3t)/4 \\ p^*_1 = (\alpha_1 + 2t)/4 \\ p^*_2 = (\alpha_2 + 3t)/4. \end{cases}$$

Figure 5.7   A simple spatial market

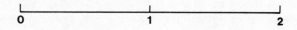

If all consumers are identical so that $\alpha_k = \alpha$ $(k = 0, 1, 2)$ then the Cournot–Nash equilibrium prices in markets 0 and 2 are equal and are *higher* than the equilibrium price in market 1. The sellers located at 0 and 2 absorb more than 100 per cent of freight costs in order to be able to compete in market 1.

Case 2
Again assume that $\alpha_k = \alpha$ $(k = 0, 1, 2)$ and that $c_k = \bar{c}_k = 0$, but now assume that there are n sellers, all located at 0 and all selling in every market. Then $\bar{t}_0 = 0, \bar{t}_1 = t, \bar{t}_2 = 2t$ and

$$p^*_0 = \alpha/(n + 1)$$
$$p^*_1 = (\alpha + nt)/(n + 1)$$
$$p^*_2 = (\alpha + 2nt)/(n + 1).$$

Price increases with distance at the rate $n/(n + 1)$. There is freight absorption which is at a lower rate than for a monopolist. In the limit, as n becomes 'large', prices tend to f.o.b. prices, that is, to non-discriminatory prices.

Case 3
As in Case 2, but now assume that there are s_0 sellers located in market 0 and s_2 sellers located in market 2, with no sellers located in market 1. Hence $n_k = s_0 + s_2, \bar{t}_0 = 2 s_2 t/(s_0 + s_2), \bar{t}_1 = t, \bar{t}_2 = 2 s_0 t/(s_0 + s_2)$ and

$$p^*_0 = (\alpha_0 + 2 s_2 t)/(s_0 + s_2)$$
$$p^*_1 = (\alpha + (s_0 + s_2)t)/(s_0 + s_2)$$
$$p^*_2 = (\alpha + 2 s_0 t)/(s_0 + s_2).$$

Note that

$$p^*_1 - p^*_0 = p^*_2 - p^*_1 = (s_0 - s_2)t/(s_0 + s_2).$$

Thus, if $s_0 = s_2$, delivered prices are uniform in every market: there is 100 per cent freight absorption by all sellers. If $s_0 > s_2$, prices are lower in market 0 than in market 1 or 2. Now sellers located in market 2 have to absorb more than 100 per cent of freight costs in order to be able to compete in markets 0 and 1 with the greater number of sellers located in market 0 (and vice versa if $s_2 > s_0$).

Case 4
As in Case 1, but now assume $\alpha_0 > \alpha_1 > \alpha_2$. Thus demand is more elastic at any price in market j than market k for $j > k$. Then

$$p^*_0 > p^*_1; \ p^*_0 > p^*_2 \text{ but } p^*_1 \gtreqless p^*_2.$$

Comparing markets 0 and 2, price is higher in the market with the less elastic demand, as in the monopoly case. But this need not be the case, as can be seen by comparing prices in markets 1 and 2. Because market 1 is, on average, nearer to the competing sellers than the other markets, competition in market 1 is stronger and may offset the effect of a lower demand elasticity as compared with market 2.

Case 5

As in Case 1, but now assume that each seller can sell only in the local market and the immediately adjacent market. Thus

$$n_0 = n_2 = 2, n_1 = 3, \bar{t}_0 = t/2, \bar{t}_1 = 2t/3, \bar{t}_2 = t/2 \text{ and}$$

$$p^*_0 = (\alpha_0 + t)/3$$
$$p^*_1 = (\alpha_1 + 2t)/4$$
$$p^*_2 = (\alpha_2 + t)/3.$$

If $\alpha_k = \alpha \ (k = 0, 1, 2)$ then $p^*_1 < p^*_0 = p^*_2$ if $t < \alpha$ (as might be expected).[5]

Many other cases can be considered: see Greenhut and Greenhut (1975) and Neven and Phlips (1985). The essential point that emerges is that the pattern of delivered price emerging from this type of competition is likely to be heterogeneous and to evidence extensive price discrimination, even in the absence of differences in demand conditions. Variations in competitive pressures in the various markets supplied by a particular seller are alone sufficient to generate discriminatory pricing.

4.2   Third-degree Price Discrimination : Bertrand–Nash

One of the first spatial analysts to consider price as a strategic instrument was Hoover (1937, 1945). His work has recently been developed and sophisticated, first by Gee (1976) and more recently by Lederer and Hurter (1986) and MacLeod, Norman and Thisse (1988).[6]

Consider a model similar to that discussed in Section 4.1, but now assume that buyers are evenly distributed at unit density over the entire line market from 0 to 2. Further assume that the set K of sellers consists of one seller at each of three separate locations 0, 1 and 2. We might consider this market to be a High Street containing three retail outlets. Assume that all buyers are identical, with inverse demand functions:

$$p(r) = \alpha - \beta q(r)$$

where $p(r)$ is price and $q(r)$ quantity for the buyer distance r from the left-hand edge of the market. Transport costs are assumed, as above, to be linear in distance and quantity with t the unit transport rate. Marginal production costs for each seller are assumed constant at c_i. Consider seller i ($i = 0, 1, 2$). In the absence of competition from any other seller, we know from section 3 that the optimal, monopoly third-degree price-discriminatory scheme involves 50 per cent freight absorption, giving the delivered price schedule

$$p_i^M (r) = \frac{1}{2}(\alpha + c_i) + \frac{1}{2} t|i - r| \qquad (i = 0, 1, 2)$$

as illustrated in Figure 5.8.

If sellers are in competition for particular buyers, $p_i^M (r)$ is not an equilibrium. The Bertrand–Nash equilibrium price schedule can be identified by treating the competitive interaction between sellers as being Bertrand-at-every-point, in which case each buyer will be supplied by the lowest-cost seller at a price equal to (ε below) the marginal production and transport costs of the second-lowest-cost seller. The resulting equilibrium price schedule for seller i in K is:

$$p_i^*(r) = \begin{cases} p_i^M(r) \text{ if } p_i^M(r) \le c_j + t|j - r| \text{ for all } j \in K, j \ne i \\ c_j + t|j - r| \text{ if } p_i^M(r) > c_j + t|j - r| \text{ and} \\ \qquad c_j + t|j - r| \le c_l + t|l - r| \text{ for all } j, l \in K; j, l \ne i. \\ c_i + t|i - r| \text{ otherwise.} \end{cases} \qquad (5.20)$$

(For a detailed discussion see Thisse and Vives, 1988.)

The first two components of this price schedule are illustrated by the heavy lines in Figure 5.8. Seller i exploits its monopoly power if possible (note that, in our illustration, there is no set of buyers for which seller 1 has monopoly power) or undercuts its competitors if possible and otherwise offers to sell at marginal cost (but sells nothing since it is undercut by its rivals).

The resulting price discrimination is extreme: price falls with distance from the seller in any region in which there is competition for buyers: a pattern that is characteristic, for example, of basing-point pricing – see Thisse and Vives (1988); Benson *et al.* (1990); Machlup (1949) – in which price is typically quoted as mill price plus transport costs from a dominant centre (the basing point) no matter the location of the seller.

By contrast to the model of section 4.1, the model outlined above does not allow for interpenetration of buyer markets by several sellers. This is, of course, a consequence of assuming that the product is homogeneous.

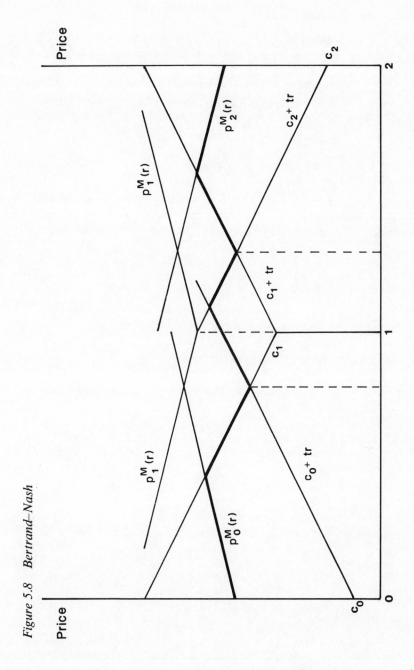

Figure 5.8 Bertrand–Nash

129

Assume, then, that the various sellers do not produce perfect substitutes. Such a case has been developed by Norman (1983): see also Mertens (1990).

Assume that there are two sellers supplying a differentiated product to buyers distributed over a line market. Demand by buyers at location r for each product is:

$$q^1(r) = \alpha_1 - \beta_{11} p_1(r) + \beta_{12} p_2(r)$$
$$q^2(r) = \alpha_2 + \beta_{21} p_1(r) - \beta_{22} p_2(r),$$

where $\alpha_i, \beta_{ij} > 0$, $i, j = 1, 2$. Transport costs are assumed linear in distance and quantity at unit rate t and marginal production costs are normalized to zero. Profit to each firm from buyers at r is then:

$$\pi^1(r) = (p_1(r) - t_1(r)) q^1(r)$$
$$\pi^2(r) = (p_2(r) - t_2(r)) q^2(r),$$

where $t_i(r)$ is the transport cost incurred by firm i in supplying r. The reaction functions (with price as the strategic variable) are:

$$2\beta_{11} p_1(r) - \beta_{12} p_2(r) = \alpha_1 + \beta_{11} t_1(r)$$
$$-\beta_{12} p_1(r) + 2\beta_{22} p_2(r) = \alpha_2 + \beta_{22} t_2(r)$$

Solving gives the delivered price schedules:

$$p^*_1(r) = [(2\beta_{22} \alpha_1 + \beta_{12} \alpha_2) + 2\beta_{11} \beta_{22} t_1(r) + \beta_{12} \beta_{22} t_2(r)]/\Delta$$
$$p^*_2(r) = [(2\beta_{11} \alpha_2 + \beta_{21} \alpha_1) + \beta_{21} \beta_{11} t_1(r) + 2\beta_{22} \beta_{11} t_2(r)]/\Delta, \quad (5.21)$$

where $\Delta = 4\beta_{11} \beta_{22} - \beta_{12} \beta_{21}$.

Case 1: sellers sharing locations
Assume that both sellers are located at the left-hand side of the line market. Then $t_i(r) = tr$ $(i = 1, 2)$ and the slopes of the delivered price schedules are:

$$S_i = \frac{\partial p^*_1(r)}{\partial(r)} = \frac{2\beta_{ii} \beta_{ij} + \beta_{ij} \beta_{jj}}{4\beta_{ii} \beta_{jj} - \beta_{ij} \beta_{ji}} \geq \frac{1}{2} \quad (i, j = 1, 2).$$

The degree of spatial price discrimination is $1 - S_i$ and will, in general, be less than that adopted by a single product monopolist. Seller 1 will apply a greater degree of price discrimination than seller 2 if $\beta_{12} \beta_{22} \leq \beta_{11} \beta_{21}$; that is, if $\beta_{12}/\beta_{11} < \beta_{21}/\beta_{22}$. This can be rewritten:

$$\frac{\beta_{ij}}{\beta_{ii}} = \frac{\varepsilon_{ij}\, p_i\, (r)}{|\varepsilon_{ii}|\, p_j\, (r)} \qquad (i, j = 1, 2; \ i \neq j),$$

where ε_{ij} is the cross-price and ε_{ii} the own-price elasticity of demand. For given $p_i\, (r)$, $p_j\, (r)$ the ratio β_{ij}/β_{ii} will be smaller the lower is the ratio of the cross-price elasticity of demand relative to the own-price elasticity of demand. This ratio can be interpreted as an index of buyers' perceptions of the degree of product differentiation : the lower the ratio the greater the extent to which product i is seen as being differentiated from product j. Thus seller i will adopt more discriminatory prices than seller j if product i is perceived as being more differentiated from j than is j from i.

Case 2: sellers not sharing locations
Assume the line market is of length L and that the sellers are located at opposite ends of the market. Then $t_1\, (r) = tr$ and $t_2\, (r) = t\, (L - r)$. The slopes of the delivered price schedules are

$$S_i = \frac{2\, \beta_{ii}\, \beta_{jj} + \beta_{ij}\, \beta_{jj}}{4\, \beta_{ii}\, \beta_{jj} - \beta_{ij}\, \beta_{ji}} \qquad (i, j = 1, 2; i \neq j),$$

where S_2 is measured from L. For price to fall with distance as in the homogeneous product case it is necessary that $2\, \beta_{ii} - \beta_{ij} < 0$; that is, that the cross-price elasticity of demand considerably exceeds the own-price elasticity, implying that the products are very close substitutes. If $2\, \beta_{ii} - \beta_{ij} > 0$ and $\beta_{ij} > 0$ then $S_i < \frac{1}{2}$ and prices are more discriminatory than under monopoly. But now the relative degree of price discrimination is the reverse of the 'sharing location' case.

While we have assumed that buyers are evenly distributed over the entire market space, it should be obvious that exactly the same analysis can be applied to the case in which buyers are localized in 'towns' or 'countries'. If this is done, we now have a model that is capable of explaining, for example, why motor car prices are typically higher in the United Kingdom than in the rest of Europe.

5. SOME WELFARE CONSIDERATIONS

This section will be kept brief: for a more extensive discussion see Phlips (1988) and Tirole (1988).

When we consider price discrimination with monopoly a number of interesting points emerge. In particular, first-degree price discrimination generates the socially optimal level of consumption, at which price equals marginal cost. Of course it is also a pricing system in which the entire surplus is taken by the seller, leading to some problematic distributional issues. With second-degree price discrimination, non-linear pricing also leads to one group of consumers being offered the socially optimal price/quantity bundle.

The comparison of non-discriminatory (uniform) prices with non-linear prices leads to a number of other interesting results. It is a simple matter to show, for example, that a non-linear, two-part tariff can generate more aggregate welfare than a linear tariff: see Littlechild (1975), Phlips (1988). This is illustrated in Figure 5.9.

Given any linear tariff pq – illustrated by a straight line through the origin with slope p – it is always possible to find a two-part tariff with fixed fee A and unit price $\hat{p} < p$ such that the gains of consumers who buy more than $\hat{q}$ units, where $\hat{q}$ is the intersection of the two outlay schedules, are greater than the losses of consumers who buy less than $\hat{q}$ units. The gains and losses in Figure 5.9 are measured by the shaded areas between the two pricing schedules. It is always possible by appropriate choice of A and $\hat{p}$ to make the area to the right of $\hat{q}$ greater than the area to the left. Since gains exceed losses, there is scope for overall welfare improvement through a compensation scheme.

Figure 5.9   Linear v. non-linear outlay schedule

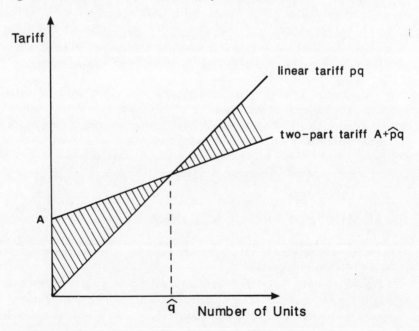

This result has been extended by Willig (1978) to obviate the need for a compensation scheme. We might, instead, offer buyers the choice of a uniform price or a two-part tariff. What Willig shows is that such a scheme will improve buyers' individual (and aggregate) welfare *and* seller's profit – a very powerful result.

Consider Figure 5.10 and assume that the uniform price is p. Now offer consumers the option of paying a fixed charge $A_1 = \gamma t$ for the right to buy at price $(p - t)$. Those with demands $q > \gamma$ will choose the two-part tariff and those with demands less than γ the linear tariff. Clearly no consumer loses and some gain: a Pareto-improvement for consumers.

What Willig also shows is that, by appropriate choice of γ and t, it is possible to increase the seller's profit: intuitively, the change in pricing policy to a two-part tariff for high-demand consumers increases their consumption. If γ and t are chosen optimally, the additional revenue from the increased consumption can be made to more than offset the loss in revenue of the lower price charged on the original consumption bundle.

Turning to third-degree price discrimination, distributional issues arise once again. Compared to non-discriminatory pricing schemes, buyers in high-elasticity markets gain and those in low-elasticity markets lose. For

Figure 5.10   Option between a uniform price and a two-part tariff

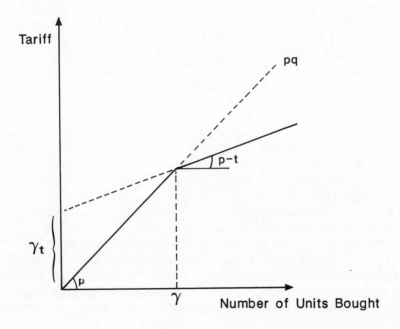

example, in spatial markets with less convex demand, more distant buyers benefit at the expense of more proximate buyers.

Other welfare issues arise, and have been analysed by Beckmann (1976), Robinson (1933), Schmalensee (1981): see also Greenhut, Norman and Hung (1987). It is simplest to present these results in a spatial framework.

If attention is confined to linear demand curves *and* it is assumed that the firm supplies the *same* market radius (denoted R) under a discriminatory and non-discriminatory (f.o.b.) pricing system, then the following results apply (subscript f denotes f.o.b. pricing and d discriminatory pricing):

Delivered prices:
$$p_f(r) < p_d(r) \quad \text{for } r < R/2$$
$$p_f(r) > p_d(r) \quad \text{for } r > R/2$$

Aggregate output: $Q_f = Q_d$

Profit: $\pi_d > \pi_f$

Consumer surplus: $CS_f > CS_d$

Total surplus: $TS_f > TS_d$.

Discriminatory pricing increases profit (as is to be expected), leaves output unaffected and reduces consumer and total surplus.

These results are critically affected by two assumptions: linear demand and the constraint that market area is unaffected by pricing policy. Dropping either or both will change the results. For example, discriminatory pricing will allow the monopolist to serve markets that might otherwise not be served. It is obvious that this change in market area can lead to a reversal of the output and surplus comparisons presented above. Similarly, if demand is convex, price discrimination approximates more closely to f.o.b. pricing, narrowing the welfare differences between the two pricing policies. By contrast, if demand is concave, prices become more discriminatory. Within a *given* market area this will worsen the welfare effects of discriminatory prices, but within an endogenously determined market area increases the likelihood of price discrimination increasing consumer and total surplus.

The potential for price discrimination to enhance buyers' welfare also arises in oligopolistic markets. Under monopoly, price discrimination is typically a device employed by the seller to appropriate buyer surplus. In oligopolistic markets, by contrast, price discrimination has the potential for strengthening competitive forces. This can be seen in the context of the Cournot model of Section 4.1. Price discrimination facilitates market interpenetration by sellers with competition being Cournot-at-every-point. If we were to impose the constraint that firms do not price discriminate, in other words that all firms sell f.o.b., then with homogeneous products markets would effectively be separated. Competition would arise solely at the boundaries of contiguous market areas or between (a small number of) coincidentally located sellers. Price would typically be higher and buyer surplus lower in the absence of price discrimination.

Similar comments apply when the oligopolists compete in prices (Bertrand competition) as in Section 4.2. Now there is a further complication in that, if firms do *not* price discriminate, non-existence of a price equilibrium can result (see MacLeod *et al.*, 1988), if the competing firms are 'close' to each other.

Assume, then, a spatial model in which buyers' demands are linear, as in Section 4.2, and the firms' locations are fixed such that the f.o.b. price equilibrium exists. Further assume that production costs are normalized to zero. Then the analysis of Greenhut, Norman and Hung (1987, p. 59) shows that the equilibrium f.o.b. mill price is given by:

$$m = \frac{2 t R (\alpha - m - t R/2)}{(\alpha - m + t R)}.$$

To facilitate comparison, assume two firms located at opposite ends of a market of unit length. Then $R = \frac{1}{2}$ and the mill price is:

$$m = \frac{1}{2} (\alpha + 3 t/2) - \frac{1}{2} \sqrt{(\alpha^2 - \alpha t + 13 t^2/4)}.$$

With price discrimination, the equilibrium price is

$$p(r) \quad \begin{aligned} &= t - tr & \text{for } r \leq \frac{1}{2} \\ &= \frac{t}{2} + t(r - \frac{1}{2}) & \text{for } r \geq \frac{1}{2}. \end{aligned}$$

These two sets of prices give rise to very different distributions of buyer surplus. Further, so long as $\alpha > 3 t/2$, the non-discriminatory f.o.b. prices are, on average, higher than the discriminatory prices.

6   SUMMARY AND CONCLUSIONS

There is little point in repeating the various results that have been presented in this chapter. What should have emerged from the analysis is an indication that price discrimination is extensive and takes a wide variety of forms. Indeed space constraints are such that the full variety of price discrimination has only been hinted at above. Many other applications could have been considered.

A further important point to emerge is that price discrimination need not be harmful to buyers, even in monopoly markets. Such a pricing policy may be necessary to ensure that particular markets are served. It has also been shown that non-linear prices can Pareto-dominate non-discriminatory prices.

In a more general sense, price discrimination can facilitate market entry and market interpenetration by competing sellers, with buyers being offered a greater variety of goods than would otherwise be available.

NOTES

1. Not all of the examples presented in this section will be 'explained' in the subsequent analysis. Where no explanation is offered, the interested reader should refer to the additional readings noted in section 1.2.
2. With non-linear costs, this is marginal cost of aggregate output.
3. An exception to this would be if the proportion of group 2 consumers were 'high' or if θ_2 were 'significantly greater' than θ_1.
4. Some analysis of second-degree price discrimination is now available, but this is technically very complicated: see Gal-Or (1988); Oren, Smith and Wilson (1983).
5. This case would arise if, for example, $p^*_0 - t_{02} = p^*_0 - 2t = (a_0 - 5t)/3 < 0$, in which case the seller located at 0 could not sell at a profit in market 2.
6. Problems of non-existence of equilibria have plagued spatial price models in the *absence* of price discrimination (Gabszewicz and Thisse, 1986). These problems tend to be resolved when price discrimination is allowed.

137-58

G34 L12 L13

6. Towards a Theory of Horizontal Mergers

Gérard Gaudet and Stephen W. Salant

INTRODUCTION

The purpose of this chapter is to explain and illustrate some recent developments in the theory of horizontal mergers. In Section 2, we derive the key property of oligopoly models – analysed in detail in Gaudet and Salant (1991a) – on which our subsequent merger analysis is based. This property has widespread implications, not only for the theory of mergers but also for international trade theory, the relationship of Stackelberg to Cournot equilibrium and other topics. We briefly discuss these implications before focusing on mergers.

To clarify its implications for the theory of mergers, we examine two examples in Section 3. In the first example, we consider the merger of firms engaged in Cournot competition and producing perfect substitutes – such as oil extractors. In the second example, we consider the merger of firms engaged in Bertrand competition and producing complementary inputs – such as different railroads whose tracks adjoin 'end-to-end' and whose services are therefore *jointly* needed to ship a good from one end of the line to the other.

In each case we assume provisionally that the firms merge and focus on two issues: (1) how the merger would affect the *private profitability* of the merging firms and, as a separate matter, (2) how it would affect *social welfare*. Paradoxically – as was first proved in Salant, Switzer and Reynolds (1983) – some exogenous mergers would induce losses for the merging firms.

Section 4 analyses a two-stage game – first formulated by Kamien and Zang (1990) – in which the merger decision is endogenized. We discuss the basic characteristics of the equilibrium and prove that none of the unprofitable mergers previously noted would occur endogenously under *laissez-faire*. Indeed, in the acquisition game we consider, some exogenous mergers which would *increase* the profits of the merging firms do not occur. We briefly explain why and then use the two examples from the previous section to illustrate that socially undesirable mergers may occur in equilibrium and socially desirable mergers may fail to occur. This suggests two types of situations where government intervention might be contemplated. Section 5 discusses extensions and concludes the chapter.

Our goal here is a modest one: to integrate selectively a few recent contributions to the theory of horizontal mergers, to point out fundamental differences between the merger of firms producing substitutes and firms producing complements and to suggest, by means of illustrations, a few results of importance to policy. References have been included to guide readers interested in particular merger models to the relevant technical literature.

2　A COMPARATIVE-STATIC PROPERTY OF OLIGOPOLY MODELS

Merger theory builds on oligopoly theory.[1] Our task in this section is to clarify one aspect of oligopoly models on which our future analysis depends. The remaining sections will apply this property to mergers. In the remainder of this section we discuss a few of its other important applications.

As an opening teaser, consider an industry in which three identical firms produce a homogeneous good at constant marginal cost and engage in Cournot (quantity) competition. For simplicity, assume the demand curve is linear.

1.　If two of the firms are located in the 'home country' while the third firm is located in another country, is the optimal trade policy for the home government an export subsidy? For simplicity, assume the government of the 'other country' (where the other firm is located) is pre-committed to *laissez-faire*; furthermore assume that no home residents consume the good so the entire output is exported.
2.　Assume that a 'Stackelberg leader' gains control of two firms and can pre-commit to outputs at each before the third firm responds. Will the leader strictly increase their outputs relative to the levels under Cournot competition?

One might well answer both questions in the affirmative. It might *seem* that an export subsidy is the optimal trade policy since that result has been shown by Brander and Spencer (1983) to hold where there are *two* firms in total – one in the home country and one in the other country.

It might *seem* that a Stackelberg leader would wish to increase the output at each of the firms, since, in the textbook case where the Stackelberg leader controls only one firm, it is profitable for him to produce more than in Cournot equilibrium. However compelling each of these answers may seem, each is incorrect. The correct answer to each question is 'no!'

Consider an industry composed of n firms with identical cost functions in a symmetric Cournot equilibrium. Suppose the equilibrium is displaced by an exogenously-induced *marginal* contraction of the output of a subset of s of these firms. To resolve each of the foregoing teasers, we must identify the circumstances in which the profits of each firm in the subset would increase as a result of the exogenous output contraction.

First note that, since each of the s firms is optimizing, a marginal contraction in its own output in a neighbourhood of equilibrium would have no effect on its profits were it not for the induced changes in the output of the $n - 1$ other firms. Assuming goods are substitutes in demand, the profit of each contracting firm will increase if and only if the aggregate output of the other $n - 1$ firms decreases.

By assumption, the output of $s - 1$ of these firms decreases since they are in the designated subset. Assuming downward-sloping reaction functions (strategic substitutes), the output of the other $n - s$ firms will increase. To determine which effect dominates and under what circumstances requires some algebra.

Let $P(\cdot)$ denote the inverse demand function, $C(\cdot)$ the identical total cost function of each firm and Q_{-i} the aggregate output of every firm other than i. Denote the output of each of the $n - s$ firms as q and let $\bar{q}$ denote the output of each of the s firms whose output will be contracted exogenously. Since a symmetric equilibrium is being displaced, $q = \bar{q}$ at the initial equilibrium. Nonetheless it is important to distinguish the two variables in the notation since one variable is displaced exogenously while the other adjusts endogenously in response. If firm i is one of the firms whose output is being contracted, then, given these definitions:

$$Q_{-i} = (n - s)q + (s - 1)\bar{q}. \tag{6.1}$$

Let π denote the profit of this firm. It can be expressed as a function of two variables:

$$\pi(\bar{q}, Q_{-i}) = \bar{q}P(\bar{q} + Q_{-i}) - C(\bar{q}). \tag{6.2}$$

Under standard assumptions, if $q = \bar{q}$, a unique, symmetric Nash equilibrium in pure strategies will exist[2]. At the equilibrium,

$$\pi_1(\bar{q}, Q_{-i}) = 0, \tag{6.3}$$

where the subscript on π denotes partial differentiation with respect to the subscripted argument.

To determine the effect on firm i's equilibrium profits of a change in $\bar{q}$, we totally differentiate the expression for its equilibrium profits:

$$\frac{d\pi}{d\bar{q}} = \pi_1 + \pi_2 \frac{dQ_{-i}}{d\bar{q}}. \tag{6.4}$$

$$0 \quad - \quad ?$$

From equation (6.1):

$$\frac{dQ_{-i}}{d\bar{q}} = (n - s)\frac{dq}{d\bar{q}} + (s - 1). \tag{6.5}$$

Clearly, in the special case where $s = n$, $dQ_{-i}/d\bar{q} > 0$ and a marginal contraction in the output of the s firms will cause Q_{-i} to fall and hence the profits of firm i to increase. This explains why it is always profitable for a monopolist who takes over an industry of n independent firms to contract the production of each. If, at the other extreme, $s = 1$, then $dQ_{-i}/d\bar{q} < 0$ and a marginal contraction in the output of this firm will have the effect of increasing the output of the other firms and hence reducing the profit of the contracting firm. This explains why a Stackelberg leader who takes over one firm in a duopoly will *expand* its production.

To understand what happens in intermediate cases, we must evaluate $dq/d\bar{q}$. This is done by differentiating the first-order condition of the typical firm which is not being contracted. After some simplification, we conclude.[3]

$$\frac{d\pi}{d\bar{q}} \mathop{\gtrless}^{\geq}_{<} 0 \Leftrightarrow s - \alpha(n - s) \mathop{\lessgtr}^{\leq}_{>} 1, \tag{6.6}$$

where

$$\alpha = \frac{P' + qP''}{P' - C''}. \tag{6.7}$$

To interpret this condition, consider first the benchmark case of linear demand and constant marginal costs. Then $\alpha = 1$ and the condition says that a marginal contraction raises the profits of the firms in the subset if and only if the number of firms in the subset, s, exceeds the number of other firms, $n - s$, by strictly more than one. In the general case, if $P' + qP'' < 0$, reaction functions will be downward-sloping. If in addition

$P' - C'' < 0$, which is a common stability condition in oligopoly models, α will be positive.[4] It is helpful to regard α as a multiplicative adjustment in the number of outside firms. The adjustment factor differs from unity in predictable ways when non-linearities are introduced.

In the linear cases outlined at the beginning of the section, $s = 2, n = 3$, and $\alpha = 1$. Since $s - \alpha (n - s) = 1$, a marginal change (contraction or expansion) will have no effect on the profits of firms in the subset. This explains each of the cases referred to at the outset. With two firms in the home country and one outside, the optimal trade policy in the home country is free trade rather than a subsidy or tariff. A tariff would be the optimal policy if we dropped the linearity assumption in a way which decreased[5] α or, alternatively, if we maintained the linearity assumption but appropriately increased the number of home firms relative to foreign firms (for example, $s = 3, n = 4$).

A Stackelberg leader would not alter the outputs of the two firms relative to their Cournot level. If he controlled only one firm in a two-firm industry, he would want to *expand* its production to maximize profits. This is the duopoly case which dominates most textbook treatments.[6] But if instead he controlled three of four firms, then in the linear case he would want to *contract* their production relative to their Cournot levels.

So far, we have considered only the case of quantity competition. But similar results hold when firms compete in price, provided reaction functions in price are downward-sloping. This is not the 'standard' case textbooks examine when discussing price competition but, as we shall see, it is of practical importance in analysing the merger of providers of complementary inputs.

In such cases, whether a marginal reduction in the price of a subset of s firms will increase or reduce their profits will depend on the size of the subset relative to the number of the outside firms. Rather than derive the results formally, we simply outline here how our previous argument can be modified for the case of price competition.

A forced marginal reduction in the price of any firm in the subset would have no effect on its profit if the prices of the other firms did not change, since it is already optimizing with respect to its own price. But by assumption, $s - 1$ of those other prices will decrease and $n - s$ of those prices will increase. Assume the goods are complements in the sense that higher prices on the part of the other firms reduce the amount one's own firm is asked to supply. If $s = n$, all of the prices will decrease and this reduction will unambiguously raise profits. If, on the other hand, $s = 1 < n$ then all of the other prices will rise and this will unambiguously reduce profits. For intermediate values of s a marginal reduction in the price of firms in the subset could increase or decrease profits.

This explains Cournot's discovery in comparing monopoly and duo-poly provision of perfect complements – in his case zinc and copper producers selling to bronze makers. In a pricing game among sellers of complements,[7] he proved that the monopolist ($n = s$) would find it optimal to charge less in total than the sum of the prices charged by the oligopolists! This seemingly odd result occurs because the monopolist would internalize the effect that a higher price would have on reducing demand at the other firms.

The above analysis has relied on the assumption of downward-sloping reaction functions in both the quantity-competition case and the price-competition case. But what if we were dealing in either case with *strategic* complements (upward-sloping reaction functions)? The analysis is then quite straightforward: an exogenous marginal change in the strategic variable of a subset of s firms will induce a marginal change in the same direction in the strategic variable of the $n - s$ other firms and therefore the effect on profit will not depend on the relative size of s.[8] Thus, in the case of quantity competition with substitutes in demand, an exogenous marginal contraction in output will always be profitable to the s firms in the subset. Similarly, if the firms compete in price with the goods comple-ments in demand, an exogenous marginal reduction in price will always be profitable to the s firms in the subset.[9]

3   LOSSES FROM EXOGENOUS MERGER

In this section we first discuss the implications of the comparative-static property of the previous section for exogenous mergers.[10] We then analyse two distinct kinds of mergers involving strategic substitutes. In both cases, since reaction functions are downward-sloping, the profitability of the exogenous merger depends on the size of the merged entity relative to the size of the industry. In the first example we consider a merger of oil extractors producing perfect substitutes and engaged in quantity compe-tition. In the second example we consider a merger of railroads producing perfect complements (transport on adjoining tracks) and engaged in price competition.

The merged entity is assumed to choose the levels of the strategic variables (quantities in Cournot competition or prices in Bertrand compe-tition) of the merged firms in order to maximize their joint profits, given the choices of the firms outside the merger. If the goods are substitutes (complements) in demand and the firms compete in quantities (prices), it will want to reduce the outputs (the prices) of the subset of firms which is being merged in an attempt to increase its profits. If in fact none of the outside firms were to change its output (its price), this would result in greater joint profits for the merged entity. But, with downward-sloping reaction functions, the best reply of each of the outside firms will be an increase in output (price). As a result, the net effect on the profit of the merged firms is unclear and the possibility exists of losses from an exogenous merger.

This is clearly a consequence of the comparative-static property discussed in the previous section and the results derived there can be applied. Consider the case of quantity competition. If s is the number of firms being merged, a contraction of outputs *in a neighbourhood of the initial equilibrium* will result in losses to the merged group whenever s exceeds the adjusted number of outside firms, $\alpha (n - s)$, by less than one. Let us assume that equilibrium profits of each individual firm in the merged subset is a concave function of its own output. It then follows that, if $s - \alpha (n - s) < 1$, any reduction of output – even a non-local one – will reduce profits and any exogenous merger is unprofitable to the merged firms.

If the merger is to be profitable, the number of firms involved must therefore exceed the adjusted number of outsiders by more than one. In that case a *marginal* reduction of output is profitable, as was shown in the previous section. But since a merger involves a *non-marginal* reduction in output, this condition is not sufficient. It must instead be verified that:

$$\pi(q^M, Q^M_{-i}) \geq \pi(q^*, Q^*_{-i}), \tag{6.8}$$

where q^* is the output of firm i (and Q^*_{-1} is the aggregate output of the other $n - 1$ firms) in the pre-merger equilibrium (that is, $\bar{q} = q = q^*$); similarly, q^M is the output of firm i (and Q^M_{-i} is the aggregate output of the other $n - 1$ firms) in the post-merger equilibrium. Let $q(x)$ denote the equilibrium output of an outsider if each merged firm produces x. Consider the roots defined implicitly by the following equation:

$$P(s\gamma + (n - s)q(\gamma))\gamma - C(\gamma) = P(nq^*)q^* - C(q^*). \tag{6.9}$$

Assuming the left-hand side is strictly concave in γ, there will be two real roots – one trivial and one non-trivial. The trivial root will be: $\gamma_1 = q^*$. The non-trivial second root will be smaller than q^* if and only if $s - \alpha(n - s) > 1$. Profitability of an exogenous merger therefore requires both $s - \alpha(n - s) > 1$ and $q^* > q^M > \gamma_2$.

Exactly the same type of argument holds for price competition with complements in demand. Even though a marginal reduction in the price of each merging firm would be profitable, there will exist a critical price (denoted below as γ_2^p) such that, if each insider charges less in the post-merger equilibrium, the merger is unprofitable.

The following examples will help clarify the implications of exogenous mergers in those two cases.

3.1 Merging under Quantity Competition with Perfect Substitutes

Consider the case of an industry composed of n identical firms engaged in the activity of oil extraction. The oil extracted by any given firm is viewed by consumers as a perfect substitute for the oil produced by any of the $n - 1$ other firms. The individual firm outputs can therefore be summed to give the total industry output of oil. Assume, for simplicity, that the inverse demand curve for oil is linear. By proper choice of units, it can always be written $P = \beta - Q = \beta - (q + Q_{-i})$, where, as before, q is the output of individual firm i and Q_{-i} is the aggregate output of the $n - 1$ other firms, Q being the total industry output. Assume also that each firm can extract oil at no cost.[11]

If one of the firms were to increase its output of oil, the best reply on the part of each of the other firms is a reduction in output. We thus have strategic substitutes (downward-sloping reaction functions).

Now suppose a subset of s of those n firms is forced to merge. The question arises as to whether this exogenously-imposed merger will increase the equilibrium profit per firm of those s oil producers. As has already been pointed out in the previous section, with a linear demand and constant marginal costs, we have $\alpha = 1$ in equation (6.6). Therefore, if the merger is to raise profits, the merged subset must outnumber the unmerged subset by more than one; that is, $s > n - s + 1$. This is the local profitability condition, which guarantees that an exogenous marginal contraction of output is profitable. But, since the merger will result in a non-marginal reduction of output, this condition is not sufficient to assure that the post-merger equilibrium profit will in fact exceed the pre-merger equilibrium profit of the merged oil producers. In addition, it must be verified that q^M, the post-merger output per merged firm, exceeds γ_2, the critical level output defined by equation (6.9). This may be referred to as the global profitability condition.

It is straightforward to verify that the pre-merger symmetric Nash-equilibrium output per firm in an n-firm industry, when the inverse demand is linear and marginal cost is zero, will be $q^* = \beta/(n+1)$. Each firm's equilibrium profit is then $P(nq^*)q^* = \beta^2/(n+1)^2$. If we substitute in (6.9), we find that γ must satisfy:

$$\left(\beta - s\gamma - (n - s)\frac{\beta - s\gamma}{n - s + 1} \right) \gamma = \frac{\beta^2}{(n + 1)^2} , \qquad (6.10)$$

where $(\beta - s\gamma)/(n - s + 1) = q(\gamma)$, the equilibrium output of each outside firm when each merged firm produces γ.

Equation (6.10) is a quadratic in γ with two real roots. The first root is trivial: $\gamma_1 = \beta/(n + 1)$. The second root is the one we seek:

$$\gamma_2 = \frac{n - s + 1}{s} \frac{\beta}{n + 1}.$$

It is straightforward to verify that $\gamma_2 < q^*$ if and only if $s > n - s + 1$. Now the post-merger output per merged firm will be $q^M = \beta/s(n - s + 2)$.[12] The global necessary condition for profitability of the merger ($q^* > q^M > \gamma_2$) yields:

$$\frac{\beta}{s(n - s + 2)} > \frac{n - s + 1}{s} \frac{\beta}{n + 1} \qquad (6.11)$$

or, equivalently:

$$(n - s + 1)^2 - s < 0. \qquad (6.12)$$

Salant, Switzer and Reynolds (1983, p. 193) show that (6.12) requires $s > 0.8n$.[13] In other words, with a linear demand curve and constant marginal costs, the exogenous merger will be profitable only if it includes at least 80 per cent of the firms in the industry.[14]

Thus, in this example, if $s \leq (n + 1)/2$, no reduction of output, even marginal, from its pre-merger Cournot-equilibrium level can increase the profits of the s affected firms and a non-marginal reduction will definitely decrease it. Such mergers will cause losses to the merged firms. If $(n + 1)/2 < s < 0.8n$, the merged producers would benefit from a joint *marginal* contraction of their outputs from the pre-merger level. But the actual reduction of output which a merger would induce is so large that the merger would result in losses for the merging firms.

We have so far restricted our attention to the *private* profitability of mergers. But what can be said about the *social* value of mergers in this example? Define social welfare as the sum of all the firms' profits and of consumer surplus.[15] With the firms producing at no cost, this is simply the area under the inverse demand curve up to equilibrium industry output. Since a merger of any number of firms will reduce aggregate industry output,[16] and thereby increase price, it is easy to see that it will always reduce social welfare.[17]

3.2   Merging under Price Competition with Perfect Complements

Picture a railroad track running from a coal mine to the market and assume that different segments of the track are owned by different companies. For simplicity, assume that initially each of n companies owns a single segment of track and that the companies set fares on their segments simultaneously.[18] Then a coal shipper would have to pay the fare on each of the segments to ship to market. For simplicity, we assume that the demand for coal is a linear function of the cost of transporting it: $Q = \beta - P = \beta - (p + P_{-i})$. Here P is the aggregate price paid by the shipper, p is the price charged on segment i and P_{-i} is the aggregate price charged on the $n - 1$ other segments. As in the previous example, we assume that both the fixed and the variable costs of operating each of the n segments of track are zero.

To the coal shipper, however, costs are not zero. An increase in the fare on the ith segment would raise the shipper's costs and would shift leftward his demand for shipping on all of the other segments. In contrast to the usual case of substitutes, an increase in the fare of the other firms is therefore *bad* for i's business. The best reply to an increase in the sum of the rivals' prices is a reduction in one's own price. Hence perfect complements in demand give rise to downward-sloping reaction functions.

There is obviously a very close similarity between the mathematical structure of this example and that of the previous example. In fact, as shown in Sonnenschein (1968), there exists a dual relationship between the two formulations. In our context, this implies that the results concerning the private profitability of mergers under quantity competition with perfect substitutes can be applied to this example of merger under price competition with perfect complements simply by interchanging the role of prices and quantities. Hence the pre-merger equilibrium price per segment is $p^* = \beta/(n + 1)$ and the equilibrium profit of each railroad is $p^*Q(np^*) = \beta^2/(n + 1)^2$. Note that what we previously derived as the formula for the equilibrium quantity of an individual firm is in the current context the formula for a firm's equilibrium price; moreover the expression for the equilibrium profit of an individual firm is the same under price competition as it was under quantity competition. The post-merger price per segment after a forced merger of s railroads is $p^M = \beta/s(n - s + 2)$. Hence we get exactly the same expression as before for γ_2^p, where γ_2^p now represents the critical price level below which the non-marginal price reduction causes a loss.

Thus merging a subset of s railroads competing in prices will increase their profits only if they constitute more than 80 per cent of the firms in the pre-merger equilibrium. As in the previous example, if the merger includes less than 80 per cent of the railroads, it will inflict losses upon the merged firms, either because no price reduction would be beneficial ($s \leq (n + 1)/2$) or because the equilibrium price reduction induced by the merger is too large to be profitable ($(n + 1)/2 < s < 0.8n$).

Where this example differs markedly from the previous one, however, is with respect to the effect of a merger on social welfare. In the example of quantity competition with substitutes, any merger *reduces* welfare. But in our railroads example, where the goods are complements in demand and competition is in price, a merger will always reduce the aggregate price and, as a result, will always *increase* social welfare. Therefore some socially profitable mergers are privately unprofitable and would presumably not occur if the decision to merge were endogenized. We will examine this issue further in the next section.

Before moving on to consider a model of endogenous merger, a word should be said about merging under strategic complements. As noted in the last section, with strategic complements the equilibrating adjustment by outsiders will always reinforce an exogenous move by insiders. Hence the private profitability of mergers will be independent of the number of firms included in the merger. Since merger to monopoly is always profitable, smaller mergers must also be profitable. This explains the finding of Deneckere and Davidson (1985) that, given their assumptions, the merged firms always gain from merger when competition is in prices. Their result comes not from their assumption of price competition but instead from their assumption of upward-sloping reaction functions. As our railroad example shows, there exist important cases of price competition where the reaction functions in price space are downward-sloping. In such cases there can be losses from the exogenous merger of firms engaged in price competition.

4 A MERGER GAME

Recently Kamien and Zang (1990) have developed a two-stage merger game.[19] In the first stage, each of n players simultaneously selects an n-tuple: a bid for the other $n - 1$ firms and an asking price for its own firm. If the highest bid for a firm exceeds the asking price of that firm, it is sold to the highest bidder for the price he bids (if two or more bids tie, a tie-breaking rule determines the identity of the acquiring firm). The new market structure is then observed before the second-stage game begins.

In the second stage, some of the original n players have sold out and no longer control any technology. The remaining players may own one or more technologies. Kamien and Zang assume each of the remaining players selects the outputs of the firms under its control to maximize his joint profits – taking as given the outputs of the firms under the control of others.[20]

In the case of constant marginal costs and zero fixed costs, the cost of producing a given aggregate output is independent of the interfirm distribution of this output. It follows that whatever aggregate output a player controlling more than one firm chooses to produce can be provided at least cost by a single firm. Hence Kamien and Zang exploit the trick in Salant, Switzer and Reynolds and assume that a multi-firm player sets to zero the output of all but one firm.

Kamien and Zang's model endogenizes what we have so far treated as exogenous: the decision to merge. Using their model, we can now ask whether mergers which have been characterized as beneficial or harmful from either a social or a private point of view will in fact occur. In what follows we extend their analysis by considering in addition a price game played by sellers of perfect complements. As in the output game, an indeterminacy arises in the case of constant marginal costs and zero fixed costs. Hence, in the railroad example of the previous section, a player operating more than one segment of the track is indifferent as to vectors of fares set on the segments under its control as long as the components of each vector add to the same aggregate price. It will be convenient to assume in such cases that the player sets to zero all but one of the prices.

We also depart from Kamien and Zang by introducing fixed costs. There are really two sources of fixed costs in either oligopoly model: costs which can be avoided only by producing zero output (for example, costs of maintaining an oil pipeline or a railroad bed) and costs which can be avoided only by charging a zero price (for example, costs of collecting fares from buyers on a given segment). When analysing quantity competition, we typically ignore the latter type of fixed cost. This omission is inconsequential when analysing mergers under Cournot competition since the (common) price paid to each component of a merged entity is positive before and after the merger. Symmetrically, when discussing price competition, we will ignore the former type of fixed cost. This omission is inconsequential when analysing mergers under Bertrand competition since the (common) usage of each segment of track owned by the merged entity is positive before and after the merger. Henceforth, when we mention fixed costs in the context of quantity competition, we mean costs which can be avoided only at a zero output. When we mention fixed costs in the context of price competition, we mean costs which can be avoided only at a zero price.

In the case of output competition with constant marginal costs and positive fixed costs, setting to zero the output of all but one firm is the *unique* cost-minimizing solution to providing a given aggregate output.

Similarly, in the case of price-competition with perfect complements, setting to zero all but one of the prices is the unique least cost way of collecting a given aggregate price.

Merger behaviour in the first stage of Kamien and Zang's model depends on the profits which each player anticipates receiving in the Nash equilibrium of each second-stage subgame. The profits in each second-stage subgame are particularly easy to characterize when marginal costs are constant and equal. This is true whether the strategic variable in the second stage is quantity or price and the following discussion applies to both cases. If marginal costs are constant and equal, each player operating at least one firm receives an equilibrium profit before deduction of fixed costs which is a function of the number of such players. Denote this function $\hat{\pi}(z)$. Thus, if z players each control at least one firm at the end of the first stage, then each will receive $\hat{\pi}(z) - F$ in the second stage, where F denotes the fixed cost per firm.

Certain conditions must hold if, in a subgame perfect equilibrium of the two-stage game, one of the n players (denoted i) in the original industry acquires the firms of $s - 1$ of the other players, while the remaining players each operate one firm. First, each of the $s - 1$ players which sells its firm must receive at least $\hat{\pi}(n-s+2) - F$. If any did not receive that much, it would be more profitable to ask unilaterally an infinite price, operate solo, and earn $\hat{\pi}(n - s + 2) - F$. Hence, to acquire these $s - 1$ firms, player i must bid at least $\hat{\pi}(n - s + 2) - F$ for each of them.

Second, in an equilibrium player i must not pay so much for the $s - 1$ acquired firms that it would be strictly preferable for it to unilaterally drop some of those firms by bidding zero for them. Suppose player i considered dropping x firms and retaining the rest. Suppose it bid $B_j (j = 1,\ldots,s - 1 - x)$ for the firms it considers retaining. Since it must have bid at least $\hat{\pi}(n - s+2) - F$ for each of the firms it considers dropping, its net profit if it retains all of the $s - 1$ firms is no larger than $\hat{\pi}(n - s + 1) - F - x(\hat{\pi}(n - s + 2) - F) - \sum_{j=1}^{s-1-x} B_j$.

If instead player i bids zero for x of the $s - 1$ firms, its resulting profits will depend on which of two possibilities arises in the next stage: (1) the strategic variable of at least one of the dropped firms might be set to zero or (2) the strategic variable of each of the dropped firms might be set to the common non-zero level of the other firms. It is clear that the former possibility cannot arise in equilibrium. For, if the strategic variable of any firm player i acquires should be set to zero if it were dropped, then player i would not acquire that firm in the first place. It would not care whether it or some other player was responsible for setting the firm's strategic variable to zero and would prefer to avoid the cost of acquiring the firm. In equilibrium, therefore, player i knows that, if it were to drop some firms, their strategic variables would be set to the common non-zero level of the other firms in the market. The net profits it can anticipate after unilaterally deviating by dropping x firms are therefore $\hat{\pi}(n - s + x + 1) - F - \sum_{j=1}^{s-1-x} B_j$. It follows that, if the situation where player i acquires the $s - 1$ firms is an equilibrium, then, for all $x = 1, \ldots, s - 1$, the following inequality must hold:

$$\hat{\pi}(n - s + 1) - F - x(\hat{\pi}(n - s + 2) - F) - \sum_{j=1}^{s-1-x} B_j$$

$$\geq \hat{\pi}(n - s + x + 1) - F - \sum_{j=1}^{s-1-x} B_j \qquad (6.13)$$

or, equivalently, for all $x = 1, \ldots, s - 1$:

$$\hat{\pi}(n - s + 1) - x(\hat{\pi}(n - s + 2) - F) \geq \hat{\pi}(n - s + x + 1). \quad (6.14)$$

Otherwise player i would choose to drop the x firms.

It is a consequence of (6.14) that, if for some $x = 1, \ldots, s - 1$:

$$\hat{\pi}(n - s + 1) - x(\hat{\pi}(n - s + 2) - F) < \hat{\pi}(n - s + x + 1), \quad (6.15)$$

then one of the necessary conditions is violated and the acquisition of the $s - 1$ firms by player i cannot be an equilibrium outcome.

We can use this result to demonstrate that *none* of the unprofitable exogenous mergers identified in Salant, Switzer and Reynolds arises endogenously in Kamien and Zang's merger game. Recall that Salant, Switzer and Reynolds showed that, if in an n-firm oligopoly a subset of s firms is forced to merge ($s \geq 2$), then the collective profits of that subset may fall. This occurs if, for given n and s:

$$\hat{\pi}(n - s + 1) - F < s(\hat{\pi}(n) - F) \qquad (6.16)$$

or, equivalently:

$$\hat{\pi}(n - s + 1) - (s - 1)(\hat{\pi}(n) - F) < \hat{\pi}(n). \qquad (6.17)$$

But, since $\hat{\pi}(z)$ is a strictly decreasing function of z (Kamien and Zang, 1990; Gaudet and Salant, 1991c), we have $\hat{\pi}(n - s + 2) \geq \hat{\pi}(n)$ for $s \geq 2$. Therefore, if (6.17) holds, the following also holds:

$$\hat{\pi}(n - s + 1) - (s - 1)(\hat{\pi}(n - s + 2) - F) < \hat{\pi}(n), \qquad (6.18)$$

which is simply (6.15) with $x = s - 1$. Since a condition necessary for the merger to arise endogenously is violated, no such merger would occur. Privately unprofitable mergers do not occur in this model; indeed, some privately *profitable* mergers do not occur. Unprofitable mergers do not occur because parties to the merger anticipate getting more if they unilaterally defect than they would get if the merger occurred. This same anticipation ensures that some profitable mergers do not occur either.[21].

Assume condition (6.14) holds for all $x = 1, \ldots, s - 1$. Then there must exist a subgame perfect equilibrium in which one player acquires the firms of $s - 1$ other players and each of the remaining $n - s$ players independently operates one firm. We can verify this claim by constructing such an equilibrium. Consider the following strategy combination in the first stage: player i bids $\hat{\pi} (n - s + 2) - F$ for each of the $s - 1$ firms it acquires and bids zero for each of the firms it does not acquire; every other player bids zero for all firms; finally, the $s - 1$ players which sell their firms each ask $\hat{\pi}(n - s + 2) - F$, while each of the $n - s + 1$ other players (including player i) asks infinity. Then, under the rules of the game, player i would acquire the firms of $s - 1$ other players. It is left to the reader to verify that no player could increase its profits by unilaterally deviating.

We are now in a position to address the two central questions in the theory of mergers. Can socially unprofitable mergers occur endogenously? Can socially profitable mergers fail to occur? To illuminate both questions, we endogenize the merger decision in the two examples of the previous section.

4.1   The Quantity Competition Example

Consider first the example of quantity competition with perfect substitutes developed in the previous section. If s oil extractors in our n-firm oil industry were forced to merge, then, by equation (6.16), the merger would increase the joint profits of the merged firms if and only if:

$$\frac{\beta^2}{(n - s + 2)^2} - F > s \left[\frac{\beta^2}{(n + 1)^2} - F \right]. \tag{6.19}$$

The threshold value of fixed costs for private profitability – that which equates both sides of (6.19) – is therefore:

$$F_p = \left[\frac{s}{(n + 1)^2} - \frac{1}{(n - s + 2)^2} \right] \frac{\beta^2}{s - 1}. \tag{6.20}$$

If, for given n and s, F is larger than F_p, then the merger is privately profitable. The merger is privately unprofitable if F is smaller than F_p.[22]

From the Kamien and Zang model, we know that such a merger can occur endogenously only if:

$$\frac{\beta^2}{(n - s + 2)^2} - (s - 1)\left[\frac{\beta^2}{(n - s + 3)^2} - F\right] \geq \frac{\beta^2}{(n + 1)^2} \tag{6.21}$$

Let F_0 denote that value of fixed costs for which the equality holds in (6.21), that is:

$$F_0 = \left[\frac{1}{(n + 1)^2} + \frac{s - 1}{(n - s + 3)^2} - \frac{1}{(n - s + 2)^2}\right]\frac{\beta^2}{s - 1}. \tag{6.22}$$

Then if, for given n and s, F is smaller than F_0, the merger will fail to occur. If F is larger than F_0 there may exist an equilibrium in which one firm acquires $s - 1$ other firms.[23]

Consider finally social surplus. In a z-firm quantity game with the linear inverse demand and zero marginal cost, aggregate profits net of fixed costs are $z(\beta/(z + 1))^2 - zF$ and net consumer surplus is $0.5(z\beta/(z + 1))^2$. Hence the sum of producer and consumer surplus is given by:

$$\frac{z(z + 2)}{2(z + 1)^2}\beta^2 - zF.$$

The merger of s firms will therefore increase social welfare if:

$$\frac{(n - s + 1)(n - s + 3)}{2(n - s + 2)^2}\beta^2 - (n - s + 1)F > \frac{n(n + 2)}{2(n + 1)^2}\beta^2 - nF \tag{6.23}$$

and the threshold value of fixed costs for social profitability of the merger is:

$$F_s = \left[\frac{n(n + 2)}{2(n + 1)^2} - \frac{(n - s + 1)(n - s + 3)}{2(n - s + 2)^2}\right]\frac{\beta^2}{s - 1}. \tag{6.24}$$

If, for given n and s, F is larger than F_s, then the merger is socially valuable. It will be socially harmful if F is smaller than F_s.

It can be verified that $F_p \leq F_0$ for all admissible n and s. This implies for the case of linear demand that, if a merger occurs endogenously, it must be privately profitable – a proposition we proved in another way for any demand curve at the beginning of this section.

It can also be verified that F_s is positive for all admissible n and s. This implies that, in the absence of fixed costs, all mergers in quantity competition are socially undesirable. Intuitively such mergers result in lower aggregate output and higher prices with no compensating change in costs. With fixed costs, however, there will be a social cost saving equal to the private cost saving of $(s - 1) F$ from merging s firms. If F is large enough this may render the merger socially profitable, just as it may render privately profitable an otherwise privately unprofitable merger.

4.2 The Price Competition Example

Consider now the railroad example of price competition with perfect complements. With the costs and demand assumptions of the previous section, we will have $\hat{\pi}(z) = \beta^2/(z + 1)^2$. This is the same expression for equilibrium profits as in the quantity competition example. Consequently the conditions remain the same for the non-occurrence (6.15) and the private unprofitability (6.17) of a merger; it follows that the expressions for F_0 and F_p given by (6.22) and (6.20) respectively apply as well to the example with price competition and complements.

However the expression for social welfare will now be different. In the quantity competition example, the goods are perfect substitutes and consumers pay an equilibrium price $\beta/(z + 1)$ for an aggregate quantity $z\beta/(z + 1)$; in the price competition example, the goods are perfect complements, so the consumers pay an aggregate price $z\beta/(z + 1)$ for an equilibrium quantity $\beta/(z + 1)$. In either case, producer surplus net of fixed costs will be $z(\beta/(z + 1))^2 - zF$. However consumer surplus in the two cases will differ. In the case of Cournot competition, consumer surplus is

$$\frac{1}{2}\left[\beta - \frac{\beta}{(z + 1)}\right]\frac{z\beta}{z + 1}$$

whereas, in the case of Bertrand competition, consumer surplus is

$$\frac{1}{2}\left[\beta - \frac{z\beta}{z + 1}\right]\frac{\beta}{z + 1}.$$

Consequently, in the case of price competition, net social surplus in a z-firm industry will now be:

$$\frac{2z + 1}{2(z + 1)^2}\beta^2 - zF.$$

By equating pre- and post-merger equilibrium social welfare, we can solve for the threshold value of fixed costs for a merger to be socially beneficial in our example of price competition with perfect complements. This yields:

$$F_s^p = \left[\frac{2n + 1}{2(n + 1)^2} - \frac{2(n - s + 1) + 1}{2(n - s + 2)^2} \right] \frac{\beta^2}{s - 1}. \tag{6.25}$$

If, for given n and s, F is larger than F_s^p, then the merger in the price game will increase social welfare. Social surplus will fall if F is smaller than F_s^p.

It can be verified that F_s^p is always negative for admissible values of n and s. This implies that merging is always socially beneficial in this example – even in the absence of fixed costs.[24] A merger will lower the aggregate price and will thereby increase demand. In the absence of fixed or variable costs, the induced output expansion must raise social surplus.

4.3 Policy Implications

We are now able to resolve the two questions posed at the outset. Can socially undesirable mergers occur endogenously? Can some socially desirable mergers fail to occur?[25]

Socially undesirable mergers can occur under quantity competition. A simple example is the merger of Cournot duopolists ($n = 2$, $s = 2$). In that case, it can be verified from (6.20), (6.22) and (6.24) that $F_p = F_0 < 0 < F_s$.[26] Hence, if the two firms had zero fixed costs, a merger to monopoly would be profitable enough to occur endogenously but would be socially harmful.

Of course not all socially disadvantageous mergers need be of concern. We know mergers will not occur when they are unprofitable and, in linear examples, will be unprofitable if they involve less than 80 per cent of the industry. A merger of two firms in a three-firm industry ($n = 3$, $s = 2$) illustrates this case. It is easily verified from (6.20), (6.22) and (6.24) that $0 < F_p = F_o < F_s$.[27] Hence, if firms had zero fixed costs, the merger would not only be socially harmful but would harm the merging parties themselves and would not occur endogenously. The intuition for why the merger would not occur is as follows: the acquired firm would insist on at least $\beta^2/16$, since that is the profit it would expect by operating solo in a three-firm industry. But this exceeds the gain in profit ($\beta^2/9 - \beta^2/16$) which the acquiring firm would expect from operating in a two-firm rather than a three-firm industry.

In fact some socially disadvantageous mergers will not occur even though they are privately profitable. Consider a merger of all three firms in the same three-firm industry ($n = 3$, $s = 3$). It is easily verified in that case from (6.20), (6.22) and (6.24) that $F_p < 0 < F_o < F_s$.[28] Hence, if firms had zero fixed costs, the merger to monopoly would be socially undesirable but – although profitable – would not be *sufficiently profitable* to arise endogenously. The merger would not occur for the following reason: each of the two acquired firms would insist on at least the duopoly profit – in aggregate at least $2\beta^2/9$ – since that is the profit each would expect if it operated solo in a two-firm industry. But the acquiring firm would not offer this amount since it exceeds the gain in profit $(\beta^2/4 - \beta^2/16)$ which it would expect from operating in a one-firm rather than a three-firm industry.

Some socially desirable mergers will not occur endogenously without government intervention. In the context of quantity competition with fixed costs, Salant, Switzer and Reynolds (1983, p. 195) showed that some socially profitable mergers are privately unprofitable. To illustrate, consider a merger of two-firms in a four-firm industry ($n = 4, s = 2$). It is easy to calculate from (6.20), (6.22) and (6.24) that $0 < F_s < F_p = F_o$.[29] Hence, for any $F \in (F_s, F_p)$, such a merger is socially profitable but privately unprofitable and of course will not occur in the Kamien and Zang model.

In fact, even some socially and privately profitable mergers may not occur. Consider the case of a three-firm merger in the same four-firm industry ($n = 4, s = 3$). It can be verified that $0 < F_p < F_s < F_o$.[30] Therefore for $F \in (F_s, F_o)$ we have a merger which is both socially and privately profitable but will fail to occur.

Socially beneficial mergers may also fail to occur in the case of price competition among providers of complements. In fact in that case examples are particularly easy to construct since, as already pointed out, all mergers are then socially desirable, even in the absence of fixed costs ($F_s^p < 0$). To illustrate such failure to occur, consider the case of the merger of two railroads on a rail line with three independent companies ($n = 3, s = 2$). It can be verified that $F_s^p < 0 < F_p = F_o$.[31] If each firm had zero fixed costs, therefore, the merger would be socially beneficial but would be unprofitable and would not occur. Intuitively the merger would not occur since it involves less than 80 per cent of the industry and would therefore be unprofitable. But, since it would result in lower prices and increased output, it would be socially beneficial.

In fact, under price competition with perfect complements some mergers may fail to occur which are both socially and privately profitable. Consider a merger of all three firms in the same three-firm industry ($n = 3, s = 3$). It can be verified in this case that $F_s^p < F_p < 0 < F_o$.[32] If firms have zero fixed costs, therefore, such a merger is clearly both socially and privately profitable. But it will nonetheless fail to occur endogenously. To review the argument which by now should be familiar: each of the two acquired firms would insist on at least the duopoly profit $(2\beta^2/9)$ since it expects that it would get that amount by unilaterally raising its asking price and operating solo in a two-firm industry. But the acquiring firm will not pay this since the amount exceeds the gain $(\beta^2/4 - \beta^2/16)$ to it from turning the three-firm industry into a monopoly.

5   CONCLUDING REMARKS

In this chapter we have reviewed some recent contributions to the theory of horizontal mergers. After explaining a property of oligopoly models on which merger theory is based, we discussed the private and social implications of exogenous mergers. Finally we summarized a model of endogenous mergers.

The reader will surely have noticed (both from the dates on the papers we have cited and from the roughness of the ideas) that the theory of horizontal mergers is still in its infancy. Until Kamien and Zang's two-stage game, no one had built and analysed a model of endogenous mergers. Their paper constitutes an instructive beginning. Nonetheless, as they would surely be the first to admit, it omits important aspects of the merger decision (such as the behaviour of shareholders in determining whether a merger occurs). Future papers will presumably analyse more realistic merger games.

We have tried in this chapter to emphasize points which will remain important in future research. Thus future models will surely be based on the comparative statics discussed in Section 2. And, while they will presumably make different predictions from those of Kamien and Zang about which mergers will occur endogenously, attention will ultimately return to the two issues we have emphasized: the avoidance of socially injurious mergers which would occur endogenously and the promotion of socially beneficial ones which would not occur endogenously.

NOTES

1. This section is based on Gaudet and Salant (1991a).
2. See Gaudet and Salant (1991b) and note 4.
3. For details, see Gaudet and Salant (1991a, p. 660).
4. This pair of inequalities is closely related to the sufficiency conditions for existence and uniqueness of a pure strategy 'Cournot' equilibrium. See assumptions A. 4 and A. 5 of Gaudet and Salant (1991b).
5. For example, α would be smaller if we instead had a strictly convex inverse demand curve and constant marginal cost or, alternatively, a linear inverse demand curve and a strictly increasing marginal cost.
6. In the standard case, $n = 2$ and $s = 1$. But then $s - \alpha(n - s) = 1 - \alpha < 1$ for *any* $\alpha > 0$. Hence $d\pi/d\bar{q} > 0$. Thus, for this over-studied special case, the comparative-static results are independent of curvature assumptions.

7. Cournot was dead by the time Bertrand erroneously criticized him for omitting discussion of price as a strategic variable.

8. Since $dq/d\bar{q} > 0$, equation (6.5) implies that $dQ_{-s}/d\bar{q}$ is always positive – regardless of the size of s. But equation (6.4) then implies that $d\pi/d\bar{q} < 0$, regardless of how many firms are in the subset whose output is contracted exogenously.

9. We restrict our attention in this chapter to cases of substitutes in demand when discussing quantity competition and complements in demand when discussing price competition. But the analysis can of course be extended to cover complements in quantity competition and substitutes in price competition. See Gaudet and Salant (1991a, Appendix) as well as Gaudet and Salant (1989).

10. This section is based on Salant, Switzer and Reynolds (1983).

11. Or, alternatively, that marginal cost is constant and P measures price net of this constant marginal cost. We of course neglect here all issues related to exhaustibility of the oil resource stock. To account for exhaustibility, the full cost should include the opportunity cost of extracting the oil today rather than leaving it in the ground for future extraction.

12. The aggregate output of the newly merged entity will be sq^M, which maximizes the joint profits of the s firms given the equilibrium output of the outsiders. Notice that this is the Cournot-equilibrium output of each firm in an $(n - s + 1)$-firm industry. Since marginal costs are constant (zero) and there are no fixed costs, the equilibrium distribution of the aggregate output of the merged entity between its s constituent firms is indeterminate: it will be indifferent, for example, between having each produce q^M or having one produce sq^M and the $s - 1$ others produce zero.

13. The left-hand side of (12) has two roots in s. One of them is inadmissible, since it requires $s > n$. The admissible root is $s = (2n + 3 - \sqrt{(4n + 5)})/2$, which attains its minimum value of 4 when $n = 5$.

14. Zachau (1987) has worked out a particularly striking example of losses from merger due to failure to meet the global condition. He shows that, with a quadratic cost function and a constant elasticity demand curve of the form $p = bQ^{-1}$, the only profitable merger is a merger to monopoly ($s = n$). The reason is that for $1 < s < n$, the merger results in a reduction of output so large that $q^M < \gamma$. This occurs even though, for $s > n - s + 1$, a marginal contraction of output in the neighbourhood of the initial equilibrium still results in a gain.

15. In a recent paper, Farrell and Shapiro (1989) show how the external effect of a merger on consumers and non-participant firms can be used to provide sufficient conditions for privately profitable mergers to raise social welfare.

16. The change in industry output will be $\Delta Q = (n - s + 1)sq^M - nq^* = -(s - 1)q^*/(n - s + 2)$, which is negative for $1 < s \leq n$.

17. This may change when there are positive fixed costs, which we will introduce in the next section.

18. For an investigation of four major end-to-end mergers see Vellturo (1988) and the references therein.

19. This section extends Kamien and Zang (1990).

20. They also consider a second model in which a subset of acquired firms is operated independently in a decentralized manner. For an analysis of this 'decentralized game', see Kamien and Zang (1990).

21. In contrast, Salant, Switzer and Reynolds (1983, p. 198) briefly sketch an endogenous merger game with different rules. In their game, a unilateral defection by any prospective party to the merger means that the merger would fail to occur and that each firm would collect its pre-merger profit. This alternative approach eliminates from the equilibrium set *only* the unprofitable mergers. It eliminates no profitable mergers.

22. We will restrict our attention, in our examples, to levels of fixed costs which leave initial equilibrium profits positive; that is, levels of F which satisfy $\beta^2/(n + 1)^2 > F$. It is easy to verify that $\beta^2/(n + 1)^2 > F_p$ for all n and s. Therefore there are values of F which simultaneously leave profits positive and exceed the threshold level F_p.

23. Condition (6.21) is condition (6.14) with $x = s - 1$. Although necessary, it is not by

itself sufficient for the endogenous merger of the s firms to constitute an equilibrium of the two-stage game. For this reason, F greater than F_o is not sufficient for the merger to be an equilibrium. A sufficient condition for the merger to be an equilibrium is that (6.14) holds for all $x = 1, \ldots, s - 1$. To illustrate, if $s = 2$ then the range of x degenerates to $x = 1$ and condition (6.21) is necessary and sufficient for existence of an equilibrium with endogenous merger.

24. The presence of fixed costs associated to charging a positive price makes mergers in price competition with complements more socially desirable and also more likely to occur.

25. As Vellturo (1988) discusses, the US government was unable for decades to induce railroads adjoining end-to-end to 'consolidate' despite the efficiency gains which such mergers would have created.

26. In particular, $F_p = F_o = -0.0278\beta^2$ and $F_s = 0.0694\beta^2$. In this case, $F > F_o$ is sufficient for the existence of an equilibrium with merger (see note 23).

27. In particular, $F_p = F_o = 0.0139\beta^2$ and $F_s = 0.0243\beta^2$.

28. In particular, $F_p = -0.0313\beta^2$, $F_o = 0.0174\beta^2$ and $F_s = 0.0469\beta^2$.

29. In particular, $F_s = 0.0113\beta^2$ and $F_p = F_o = 0.0175\beta^2$.

30. In particular, $F_p = 0.0044\beta^2$, $F_s = 0.0178\beta^2$ and $F_o = 0.0269\beta^2$.

31. In particular, $F_s^p = -0.0590\beta^2$ and $F_o = F_p = 0.0139\beta^2$.

32. In particular, $F_s^p = -0.0781\beta^2$, $F_o = 0.0174\beta^2$ and $F_p = -0.0313\beta^2$.

7. New Dimensions of the Patent System

Manfredi La Manna

---

1 INTRODUCTION

The last few years have witnessed a renewed and sustained interest in the economics of patents by theoretical economists. Unfortunately this interest has been due more to the opportunity to apply to patents concepts developed in other fields (notably game theory, and especially bidding games and multi-stage games) than to a genuine interest in the specific – and often intriguing – features of the patent system.

In this chapter we will not consider models of patent races, not because they have already been surveyed elsewhere,[1] but for the deeper reason that much of the literature has extended the basic patent race model in directions that ignore some of the very characteristics of patents. Partha Dasgupta, a leading contributor to the new economics of R&D, has admirably captured the underlying structure of patent races models, as follows:

> N players ($N \geqslant 2$) bid for an indivisible object valued by each at V (> 0). All bids are forfeited. The highest bidder wins the object. If there are K ($\leqslant N$) highest bidders each of these (K) players wins the object, with probability $1/K$. (Dasgupta, 1986, pp. 535–6)

Undoubtedly the analogy of patent races with bidding games is a powerful one and has furnished many interesting insights, but at a price – the neglect of some of the distinctive features of patents and their relationships with R&D.

The criticism advanced in this chapter is not the sterile one of 'unrealism': as Dasgupta has pointedly reminded economic theorists of R&D, a model should be judged, among other things, with respect to its intended use and, given a specific purpose, the more 'economical' the model, the better. The point is that many models of patents abstract from issues that ought to be of fundamental importance in designing a 'good' (if not optimal) patent system, such as: *What* should patents be awarded to? How

159

restrictive should patent protection be? Could patents be used to alter the allocation of resources *between* research and development?

It cannot be denied that the literature on patent races has shed light, for instance, on factors that induce either persistent technological dominance by the market leader(s), or leap-frogging, or catching up by their rivals; on the effects of the type of product–market competition (either Cournot or Bertrand) on competition in R&D and so on. However, in general, very little attention has been paid to the fact that a patent is not simply a pot of gold to be awarded to the fastest sprinter, but also a policy instrument, whose many dimensions can be manipulated to affect the R&D process.

Taking a multi-dimensional view of the patent system has also the advantage of highlighting the interdependence of the modelling of patents and the modelling of R&D: the richer the articulation of R&D behaviour, the larger the number of patent policy instruments. Thus, as soon as it is recognized that in some instances the outcome of R&D is a horizontally differentiated product, the issue of the breadth of patent protection becomes an interesting policy problem (see Section 3). Similarly, by treating research and development as two different stages, one can address the issue of *what* is patentable (either research prototypes or developed products) (see Section 6).

In an attempt to redress the balance in the literature this chapter will ignore the specifically game-theoretic issues involved in patent races and explore instead models that in some way suggest new ways of analysing the patent system. In Section 2 the standard patent life model will be sketched and examined as a 'patent regulation game'. In Section 3, in addition to patent life, new dimensions will be brought in so as to consider the optimal patent duration–breadth mix. Section 4 explores yet another facet of the patent system by considering the determination of the optimal minimum patentability standard and offers a novel version of the standard patent regulation game. Sections 5 and 6 address two fundamental and yet neglected issues in the economics of patents, namely how the patent system can be used to alter the 'Schumpeterian trade-off' between static and dynamic efficiency and how patentability standards can be manipulated so as to alter the allocation of resources *between* research and development.

2   THE PATENT REGULATION GAME AND OPTIMAL PATENT LIFE

Consider the simple case of a linear inverse market demand curve and constant marginal cost:

$$P(Q) = A - Q \tag{7.1}$$

$$C(Q) = c_0 Q \tag{7.2}$$

Supposing that, prior to innovation, production of the good is marginally unprofitable,[2] two types of innovation can make it profitable: (1) a 'product innovation' that, by making the good more appealing, shifts $P(Q)$ rightwards; and (2) a 'process innovation' that shifts marginal cost c_0 downwards. For a given shift, irrespective of which type of innovation takes place, the post-innovation situation is as depicted in Figure 7.1.

Turning now to the innovation-producing technology, suppose that the extent of innovations, x, is related to the amount of R&D inputs, R. For simplicity, let the resulting innovation possibility frontier belong to the iso-elastic family:

$$x(R) = (\frac{R}{\theta})^\alpha \text{ or, alternatively, } R(x) = \theta x^\alpha, \ \theta > 0, \ \alpha > 0. \tag{7.3}$$

In its simplest version the patent regulation game (PRG) is played by only two players: the innovator, who maximizes profits, and the patent officer (PO), whose task is to maximize the sum of consumers' surplus and industry profits, net of R&D costs. The PO's problem is to induce the innovator to invest the 'right' amount in R&D by granting him an exclusive property right in his innovation (that is, a patent) lasting T periods. Setting $\tau \equiv (1 - e^{-rT})$, the PO's and the innovator's maximands can be written respectively as

$$W(x,\tau) = \{C(x) + G(x) + L(x)\}\frac{1}{r} - L(x)\frac{\tau}{r} - R(x) \tag{7.4}$$

$$\pi(x,\tau) = \frac{\tau}{r} G(x) - R(x), \tag{7.5}$$

where r is the social (and private) rate of discount and $C(x)$, $G(x)$ and $L(x)$ stand respectively for consumers' surplus, gross profits and deadweight loss, as depicted in Figure 7.1. (7.4) implies that, at the end of T periods, the innovation becomes freely available and thus price falls to marginal cost. The term in curly brackets is the discounted stream of gross benefits from the innovation and $L(x)\tau/r$ is the discounted loss of welfare for the duration of the patent. It turns out that it is more convenient to use τ as choice variable, rather than T; thus we shall refer to τ as 'patent life'. (Notice that, as T ranges from 0 to ∞, τ ranges from 0 to 1.)

The traditional version of the PRG can be described as follows: the innovator maximizes profits by setting his control variable x and taking patent life τ as a parameter, whilst the PO maximizes welfare by setting patent life and taking as given the reaction function determined by the innovator's profit-maximization exercise. The innovator's reaction function $\hat{x}(\tau)$ can be interpreted as an 'innovation contract' which specifies the extent of the innovation, x, for any given patent life, τ. Using (7.1)–(7.3), the innovator's profits and reaction function can be written as:

$$\pi(x,\tau) = \frac{\pi x^2}{4r} - \theta x^{1/\alpha} \tag{7.6}$$

$$\hat{x}(\tau) = (\frac{\alpha\tau}{2\theta r})^{\alpha/(1-2\alpha)}. \tag{7.7}$$

Using (7.1)–(7.3), the PO's welfare function (7.4) can be written as

$$W(x,\tau) = \frac{4-\tau}{8r}x^2 - \theta x^{1/\alpha}. \tag{7.8}$$

Substituting (7.7) into (7.8) and maximizing w.r.t. to patent life τ, the (unique) solution of the traditional PRG for a new product $(\hat{x}, \hat{\tau})$ can be seen to be

Figure 7.1 *Post-innovation consumers' surplus, gross profits and welfare loss*

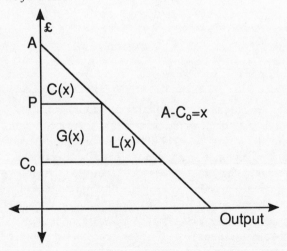

$$\text{for } \alpha < 1/4 \quad \hat{\tau} = \frac{8\alpha}{1+4\alpha} \quad \hat{x} = [\frac{4\alpha^2}{(1+4\alpha)\theta r}]^{\alpha/(1-2\alpha)} \tag{7.9}$$

$$\text{for } \alpha \geqslant 1/4 \quad \hat{\tau} = 1 \qquad \hat{x} = [\frac{\alpha}{2\theta r}]^{\alpha/(1-2\alpha)}. \tag{7.9'}$$

Note

1. If innovations are 'easy' (that is, $1/4 \leqslant \alpha < 1/2$), the granting of a patent is not an effective way of counterbalancing the output-restricting behaviour of an innovator–monopolist. The PO hits the constraint $\tau \leqslant 1$ (patent life cannot be 'more' than infinite) when the marginal benefit of a patent life extension is still positive (that is, $W_\tau(x, \tau) > 0$)[3]. Notice that, when innovations are 'easy', the innovator is able to attain his first-best optimum: $(\hat{x}, \hat{\tau})$ is precisely the pair that an unconstrained monopolist would choose.
2. When innovations are 'difficult' (that is, $\alpha < 1/4$), short-lived patents are an effective means to check the propensity to over-invest in R&D by the innovator–monopolist (assuming $\alpha = 0.1$, patent life is less than six (three) years if $r = 10$ per cent (20 per cent)). Somewhat surprisingly, patents seem to be more effective in curbing potentially excessive innovation than in promoting it.

3 THE OPTIMAL PATENT DURATION – BREADTH MIX

Tandon (1982) has extended the basic Arrow–Nordhaus[4] model of patenting by introducing a second policy instrument in addition to patent life; that is, a compulsory royalty rate. Consider the model examined in the previous sub-section and assume that the innovator is required to license his innovation at a royalty rate ρ that is a fixed percentage of the extent of the innovation, x (that is, the unit royalty rate is ρx). The net present value of his royalties will be

$$\pi(x; \rho, \tau) = \rho(1 - \rho)x^2\tau - \theta x^{1/\alpha}. \tag{7.10}$$

Notice that, if the innovator is allowed to set his own royalty rate – as implicitly assumed in section 2 – he will set $\rho = 1/2$ and (7.10) will be identical to (7.6). The role assignment is the same as in the previous sub-section, with the innovator being the follower and the PO the leader and maximizing welfare function (7.12) w.r.t. τ and ρ, subject to the constraint given by the innovator's reaction function (7.11):

$$\bar{x}(\rho,\tau) = [\frac{2\rho(1-\rho)\alpha\tau}{\theta r}]^{\alpha/(1-2\alpha)} \tag{7.11}$$

$$W(\rho,\tau) = [\bar{x}(\rho,\tau)]^2(1-\rho^2\tau)\frac{1}{2r} - \theta x^{1/\alpha}. \tag{7.12}$$

Tandon shows that the solution of the above problem is to set $\tau = 1$ (infinite patent life) with ρ determined by the following equation:[5]

$$\frac{4\alpha-1}{\alpha}\rho^2 - 3\rho + 1 = 0. \tag{7.13}$$

Recently Gilbert and Shapiro (1990) have shown that Tandon's result is a special case of a more general proposition on the trade-off between the length and the breadth of patent protection. They do not specify the precise meaning of 'breadth' of patent protection and work instead with a reduced-form specification that identifies breadth with the flow rate of profit for the patentee, π (that is, a wider breadth means a higher π). The social problem is then to maximize the present value of sum of consumers' surplus and profits, subject to the patentee earning a reward of V ($=$ present value of the stream of πs).[6] Their main result is that, if welfare is concave in π (that is, patent breadth is increasingly costly in terms of welfare losses), then the optimal patent life is infinite.

In order to illustrate the logic of this argument, we shall draw on an important paper by Klemperer (1990) who resorts to what is perhaps the most natural way of specifying the breadth of patent protection; that is, by referring to a model of (horizontal) product differentiation. In fact, if goods are horizontally differentiated, a patent, in addition to the duration of protection from imitation, must specify how different a competitor's good must be in order not to infringe the patent. Thus determining the breadth of patent protection is equivalent to fixing the boundaries of the market for the patented good.

The introduction of product differentiation implies that the monopoly power conferred upon the patent holder carries *two* types of welfare losses:

1. *'forced travel loss'*: this is the loss of consumers' surplus incurred when consumers who would have bought the patented good, if it was priced

competitively, are forced to 'travel' and buy the less preferred unpatented variety;

2. *'forced abstinence loss'*: this is the loss of consumers' surplus incurred when the high (monopoly) price of the patented good forces consumers to switch out of the product altogether (whether patented or not).

In the terminology of the 'address' model discussed in Chapter 4, by buying 1 unit of a variety located at a distance w, the jth consumer derives net utility equal to $m_j + r_j - p - t_j w$, where m_j, r_j and t_j are respectively consumer j's income, reservation price for his/her preferred variety, and unit transport (or 'mismatch') cost.

The problem faced by the Patent Office can be summarized as follows:

1. choose the patent 'breadth' w such that the welfare loss/profit ratio $L(w)/\pi(w)$ is lowest;
2. set patent life T such that the innovator is (just) willing to undertake the R&D investment required to produce the new product variety; that is:

$$V = \pi(w)(\frac{1 - e^{-rT}}{r}). \qquad (7.14)$$

The trade-off facing the PO is between 'narrow' but 'long' patents (w is small and T is large) and 'wide' but 'short-lived' ones (w is large and T is small). If $w = \infty$, obviously no consumer can 'travel' to the market boundary to buy the unpatented good and thus only the 'forced abstinence loss' need be taken into account. Conversely, if $w = 0$ consumers can always choose between the patented and the unpatented variety and thus only the 'forced travel loss' matters. We shall consider this latter case in more detail, providing an example in which a very narrow patent breadth ($w \approx 0$) coupled with a very long patent life ($T \approx \infty$) is most efficient. If all consumers have identical unit transport costs the patent holder will have to set his/her price so that no consumer would want to 'travel' (if one did, so would all others). Since setting $w \approx 0$ involves no 'forced abstinence loss', we only need to check that a narrow patent breadth minimizes the 'forced travel loss' – profit ratio. The narrower w is the lower is the price that the monopolist would have to charge so as to attract customers away from the (close) unpatented variety. We can now show under what conditions the 'forced travel loss' – profit ratio increases when the price is increased, thereby proving the proposition that $w \approx 0$ is optimal, with reference to Figure 7.2.

The figure depicts three demand curves for the patented variety: ABC is linear, ABC' is (very) convex, and ABC" is concave; marginal cost is normalized at 0. We want to establish that, provided demand is not 'too' convex, the welfare loss–profit ratio is lower at $p°$ than at $2p°$. For the benchmark linear demand case the relevant ratio is $ABG/OGBP°$ at $p = P°$ and ACF/OFC $(2P°)$ at $p = 2P°$; in terms of the shaded areas λ, δ, π it is easy to see that

$$\frac{\lambda}{(\pi + \delta)} < \frac{2\lambda + \delta}{2\pi}. \tag{7.15}$$

Inequality (7.15) follows immediately noting that $\delta = 2\lambda$. *A fortiori* a similar inequality holds for the concave demand curve $ABC"$. However, if demand is 'very' convex, as ABC' is, the welfare loss–profit ratio would be *lower* at the higher price $2P°$.

Therefore, provided demand is not too convex, a very narrow patent breadth would minimize the welfare loss per unit of profit; and consequently, in order to make the production of a new variety worthwhile for the patent holder, patent life must be extended as much as required (so that (7.14) is satisfied). More generally, Klemperer (1990) has found that, under fairly robust conditions, the optimal patent breadth–length mix depends on the relationship between the distribution of reservation prices across consumers and the distribution of their transport (or 'mismatch') costs.

Figure 7.2   Demand functions and optimal patent breadth

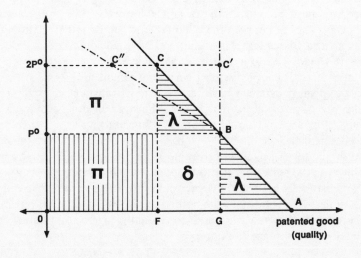

· 4 PATENT LIFE AND MINIMUM PATENTABILITY STANDARDS[7]

In the previous sections we have briefly reviewed the standard theory of optimal patent life, as formulated by Nordhaus (1969) and Scherer (1972) and more recently extended to include a compulsory royalty rate (Tandon, 1982) and patent 'breadth' (Gilbert and Shapiro, 1990; Klemperer, 1990). This section addresses another dimension of the patent system, namely the game-theoretic implications of the optimal determination of patent life v. a *minimum patentability standard*. Unlike a duopoly game, in which both control variables (such as prices, output levels) and the players' strategic roles (follower, leader) are exogenously determined, in the context of a patent game it is one of the players – the Patent Office – that sets the rules of the game; that is, how patents are applied for and granted. Thus a fully optimizing patent officer (PO) has to solve a double assignment problem, choosing both his/her role (either F(ollower) or L(eader)) and control variables (either minimum patentability standard, x, or patent life, T). All models of optimal patent life implicitly assume that welfare is always maximized under the game in which the PO leads and optimizes over T. However it seems obvious that the solution of the above game selection exercise will in general depend on demand and technology conditions; and this is, in fact, the conclusion reached here – more specifically this section shows that, when innovations are not 'difficult', leadership is irrelevant and setting patentability standards is more efficient than setting patent life.

4.1 Patent Games

As in the PRG the very rules of the game can be manipulated by the PO simply by setting the appropriate procedures for filing and granting patents, he/she can select any of the six patenting arrangements shown in Table 7.1. In Table 7.1 a typical entry (Rz, Sy) is to be interpreted as the game in which the innovator (the PO) plays role R (S) and optimizes over control variable z (y); of course there are no entries for the double leadership case.

The notion of minimum patentability standard can be easily quantified as the 'extent' of the innovation, x (see (7.3)); that is, the extent by which either the demand curve is shifted outwards or marginal cost is reduced.

The present value of the innovator's per-period profits and the PO's welfare function have already been introduced (see (7.4) and (7.5)) and are reproduced here for ease of reference:

$$\pi(x,T) \equiv \frac{\tau}{r} G(x) - R(x) \tag{7.16}$$

$$W(x,T) \equiv [C(x)+G(x)]\frac{1}{r} + L(x)\frac{e^{-rT}}{r} - R(x), \tag{7.17}$$

where, as usual, $\tau \equiv 1 - e^{-rT}$.

The six games the PO can choose from, described in Table 7.1, can be grouped in three classes: $\{(Fx, FT), (Lx, FT)\}$, $\{(FT, Fx), (LT, Fx), (FT, Lx)\}$ and (Fx, LT), with each class yielding a distinct equilibrium, as shown below.

Proposition 1

Irrespective of the Innovator's strategic role, followership by the PO combined with optimization over τ yields the economically trivial $(0,0)$ equilibrium (no innovation, zero patent life).

Proof. In both the (Fx, FT) and the (Lx, FT) games the PO's reaction function obtained from the first-order condition for the maximization of (7.17) is degenerate and coincides with the x-axis. ∎

Proposition 2

Irrespective of the innovator's strategic role, optimization over x by the PO yields the $(x^*, 1)$ equilibrium; that is, patent life is infinite $(\tau = 1)$ and the minimum patentability standard x^* is determined by $\tau^{PO}(x^*) = 1$, where $\tau^{PO}(x)$ is the PO's reaction function.

Proof. Consider first the (LT, Fx) game which, it may be noted, is the mirror-image of the traditional optimal patent-life model; whereas in the

Table 7.1   Alternative patent arrangements, classified by control variable and strategic role

| | | | Patent officer | | | |
| | | | Follower | | Leader | |
			x	T	x	T
Innovator	Follower	x	—	Fx, FT	—	Fx, LT
		T	FT, Fx	—	FT, Lx	—
	Leader	x	—	Lx, FT	—	—
		T	LT, Fx	—	—	—

latter the PO plays the leader role, here she chooses to follow and, in contrast with the conventional model, allows the innovator to determine patent life.

The innovator–leader's problem is:

$$\max_{\tau \leqslant 1} \pi(\tau) = \frac{\tau}{r} G(\psi(\tau)) - R(\psi(\tau)), \tag{7.18}$$

where $\psi(\tau) \equiv \tau^{PO-1}(x)$ and, from (7.17) the PO's reaction function is

$$\tau^{PO}(x) = \frac{1}{L_x}(C_x + G_x + L_x - rR_x). \tag{7.19}$$

It is simple to show that $\pi_\tau(\tau) > 0$, and thus the patent-life constraint is binding ($\tau = 1$) and the minimum patentability standard x^* is determined by $\tau^{PO}(x^*) = 1$:

$$\pi_\tau(\tau) = \frac{G}{r} + \psi_\tau(\tau)\{\frac{\tau}{r}G_x - R_x\} > 0. \tag{7.20}$$

Inequality (7.20) follows from the fact that the quantity in curly brackets equals $-\{C_x(x) + (1-\tau)[L_x(x) + G_x(x)]\}/r < 0$ and $\psi_\tau(\tau)$ is the reciprocal of the slope of the PO's reaction function, which from the second-order condition for the maximization of (7.17) is negative.

Under both the *(FT, Fx)* and *(FT, Lx)* games the innovator's first-order condition ($[1 - \tau]G_x = 0$) yields a degenerate reaction function (that is, the best-reply level of τ is a constant) which coincides with the $\tau = 1$ line. Therefore both games yield the $(x^*, 1)$ equilibrium, with infinite patent life and x^* determined by the intersection of $\tau = 1$ and the PO's reaction function (see point A, Figure 7.3). ∎

So far we have shown that, out of six possible patent games, two *((Fx, FT)* and *(Lx, FT))* yield the economically insignificant solution of no innovation, three *(FT, Lx)*, *(FT, Fx)*, and *(LT, Fx))* are feasible and all sustain the same equilibrium, characterized by an infinite patent life and by a minimum patentability standard, x^*, lying on the PO's reaction function.

The interesting question, of course, is whether the latter equilibrium can yield a higher level of welfare than the traditional version of the patent game, in which the PO acts as a leader and optimizes w.r.t. patent life τ (that is, the *(Fx, LT)* patent game examined in Section 2). In this respect we can now prove the following.

Theorem
The set of cost and demand parameters such that the (Fx, LT) patent game
yields lower welfare levels than under the alternative game (LT, Fx) is non-
empty.

Proof. As the second-order conditions for the maximization of (7.16)
and (7.17) guarantee that the innovator's and the PO's reaction functions
are respectively upward- and downward-sloping, to prove the theorem it
suffices to show that they cross at a point where $\tau > 1$, or, equivalently,
that $\{\tau^{PO}(x^*) = \tau^I(\bar{x}) = 1\} \Rightarrow (x^* > \bar{x})$, as at point B in Figure 7.3. This implies
not only that the alternative patent game (*LT, Fx*) performs better than
the traditional (*Fx, LT*) game whenever the latter calls for an infinite
patent life, but also (deploying a continuity argument) that there exists a
set of cost and demand parameters such that the two games yield the same
level of welfare $W(\hat{x}, \hat{\tau}) = W(x^*, 1)$, with $\hat{\tau} < 1$, as shown in Figure 7.3.
Therefore the (*LT, Fx*) game performs strictly better than the classic (*Fx,
LT*) game whenever demand and cost parameters are such that the latter
game calls for an optimal patent life τ^0, $\hat{\tau} < \tau^0 \leqslant 1$.

The innovator's reaction function is as follows:

$$\tau^I(x) = r\frac{R_x(x)}{G_x(x)}. \tag{7.21}$$

Let $\tau^{PO}(x^*) = 1$; that is, $C_x(x^*) + G_x(x^*) - rR_x(x^*) = 0$,

then

$$\tau^I(x^*) = \frac{C_x(x^*) + G_x(x^*)}{G_x(x^*)} > 1. \tag{7.22}$$

Define $\bar{x}$ as $\tau^I(\bar{x}) = 1$, then, as $\tau_x^I(x) > 0$, $\bar{x} < x^*$.

The above result has been proved under fairly general conditions;
additional insights can be gained by using the parametrization used in
Section 2 to compute optimal patent life $\hat{\tau}$ and the optimal extent of the
innovation (or patentability) standard $\hat{x}$ for the traditional (*Fx, LT*) game
(see (7.9) and (7.9′)). For the parametrization (7.1)–(7.3) under the 'new'
(*LT, Fx*) scheme the equilibrium patent life is, of course, $\tau^* = 1$ and the
minimum patentability standard x^* turns out to be

$$x^* = (\frac{3\alpha}{4\theta r})^{\alpha/(1-2\alpha)}. \tag{7.23}$$

Computing the levels of welfare associated with the equilibrium of each
of the two patent games, namely $W(\hat{x}, \hat{\tau})$ and $W(x^*, 1)$, for all values of α

Figure 7.3 Optimal patent life vs optimal patentability standards

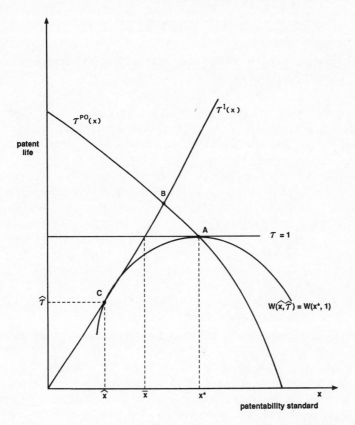

reveals that the alternative (LT, Fx) game yields an improvement on the conventional (Fx, LT) game not only when innovations are easy (that is, $1/4 \leqslant \alpha < 1/2$), but also when they are 'not too difficult' ($1/7 \leqslant \alpha < 1/4$).

This shows rather dramatically that the presence of a binding constraint on the control variable set by the leader may reverse the benefits of being a leader at all. The reason for this intriguing fact can be better understood if player j's reaction function $\tau^j(x)$ is interpreted as an 'innovation contract' which specifies the minimum patentability standard x required to be granted a patent term τ. When innovations are not 'difficult' the social benefit flowing from the ability to set a 'high' minimum patentability standard x^* more than offsets the cost of letting the innovator choose an infinite patent life.

Finally it is interesting to note that, when innovations are 'easy', the alternative version of the PRG outperforms Tandon's regime in which the PO–leader is endowed with *two* policy instruments (patent life and a compulsory royalty rate), thus suggesting that the welfare losses associated with being a leader are indeed significant.

5 THE SCHUMPETERIAN TRADE-OFF AND PATENTABILITY STANDARDS

Suppose that a monopolist, faced with the prospect of being granted a patent generating a profit of £π should invest £x_1 in R&D and charge a price of p_1 for the patented good. Consider now the alternative arrangement under which each of n firms is allowed to patent the same good: each firm would earn less than £π/n (unless collusion is perfect), would invest £x_n ($< x_1$) in R&D and charge p_n ($< p_1$). Which market structure is socially preferable? A huge literature (admirably surveyed by Kamien and Schwartz, 1982, and Baldwin and Scott, 1987) has attempted to model and investigate empirically the trade-off underlying the above problem. The so-called 'Schumpeterian trade-off', of course, is between 'dynamic efficiency' (related to the allocation of resources to R&D) and 'static efficiency' (related to the allocation of resources, for given levels of R&D): a monopoly generates a higher rate of technological progress ($x_1 > x_n$), but also higher welfare losses due to higher prices ($p_1 > p_n$).

It may come as a surprise to note that the immense literature of Schumpeterian competition (Baldwin and Scott cite 340 references) has failed to highlight the role of the patent system in altering the above trade-off.

In this section, which draws on La Manna *et al.* (1989), we shall consider a model in which the patent officer can manipulate the *novelty* criterion of patentability, thereby allowing for more than one patent to be granted within a given class of new products. The general structure of the model follows that of Dasgupta and Stiglitz (1980): all firms strive to invent a new product with well-defined characteristics (that is, the 'extent' of the innovation is fixed) and each firm follows a different research route (research routes are independent and equally effective). There is uncertainty regarding the *timing* of innovation: by investing £x in R&D at time 0, a firm cannot determine with certainty the date of discovery. Unlike Dasgupta and Stiglitz, who use a Poisson distribution of invention times, we can afford the luxury of generality and write $P(t_1, t_2, \ldots t_n)$ as the density function that the first discovery occurs t_1 periods after time 0, the second after t_2 periods and so on.

We shall consider two alternative patent regimes:

1. *Strict regime*: the first firm to invent receives a patent lasting for T_s

periods and in each period collects a profit of £π_1. For the duration of the patent no other firm is granted a patent and so cannot produce. After the expiry of the patent, there is free entry and profits are driven to zero.

2. *Permissive regime*: the novelty requirement for patenting is relaxed so that all genuine inventors who apply within T' periods of the first claimant receive a patent. After T_p periods the patent on the earliest invention expires and thus becomes public knowledge, rendering all subsequent patents economically worthless. In view of the current administrative lag between applying for and being awarded a patent (on average, two years), a simple way of implementing the above scheme is to grant patents to all applications received up to the award of the earliest patent, the details of which are kept secret until then. If there are n patentees, each earns $\pi_n \leqslant \pi_1/n$ (with strict equality for $n = 1$): this implies that if there are two or more firms, they cannot engage in full collusion.

Then it can be proved that:

Proposition 3
If patent life is a policy variable, the permissive regime is welfare-superior to the strict regime if there are constant returns to scale in the production of the new good and market demand is not 'too' convex (linear, constant-elasticity and so on).

Proof. Given the same patent life, the permissive regime will always sustain more firms than the strict regime, for, under it, the first firm to invent faces a positive probability that, within the lifetime of its patent, it will have to share the market with other firm(s), thus reducing expected profits. The general form of the proof is to show that, by increasing patent life under the permissive regime, so that both regimes at a free-entry equilibrium sustain the same number of firms n, the permissive regime generates greater social benefits. Under a strict and a permissive regime, respectively, a free-entry equilibrium is defined by:

$$E\{P(t_1, t_2, \ldots t_n)\,\pi_1\,g\,(t_1)\} - nx = 0, \tag{7.24}$$

where

$$g(t_1) \quad \begin{cases} \equiv 1/r[e^{-rt_i} - e^{-r(t_i + T_s)}] & i = 1 \\ \equiv 0 & \forall i > 1. \end{cases}$$

$$E\{P(t_1,t_2,\ldots t_n) \sum_{i=1}^{n} i\pi_i f(t_i)\} - nx = 0, \tag{7.25}$$

where

$$
\begin{array}{lll}
\equiv 1/r[e^{-rt_i} - e^{-rt_i+l}] & t_1 + T' > t_{i+1} & i \geq 1 \\
f(t_i) \equiv 1/r[e^{-rt_i} - e^{-r(t_i+T_p)}] & t_{i+1} > t_1 + T' > t_i & i \geq 1 \\
\equiv 0 & t_i > t_1 + T' & i > 1.
\end{array}
$$

From (7.24) and (7.25) we obtain

$$E\{P(t_1,t_2,\ldots t_n)\ \{\ [f(t_1) - g(t_1)] + \sum_{i=2}^{n} f(t_i)\ i\cdot\pi_i/\pi_1\}\} = 0. \tag{7.26}$$

Consider now the welfare effects of a switch in regimes. Aggregate social efficiency (the sum of consumer surplus and industry profits net of R&D costs) is clearly maximized when price equals marginal cost. Thus actual welfare can be expressed as the difference between this maximum level of welfare W^*, and D_i, the temporary welfare loss incurred for the duration of the patent. It follows that social welfare under the two regimes can be written respectively as

$$E\{W^s\} \equiv E\{P(t_1, t_2, \ldots t_n)[(W^*/r)e^{-rt_1} - D_1 g(t_1)]\} - nx. \tag{7.27}$$

$$E\{W^p\} \equiv E\{P(t_1,t_2,\ldots t_n)[(W^*/r)e^{-rt_1} - \sum_{i=1}^{n} D_i f(t_i)]\} - nx. \tag{7.28}$$

These equations take into account that, when the first patent expires, the deadweight loss is zero. Repeating the previous argument, a switch from the strict to the permissive regime is welfare-improving if

$$E\{P(t_1,t_2,\ldots t_n)\{[f(t_1) - g(t_1)] + \sum_{i=2}^{n} f(t_i)D_i/D_1\}\} < 0. \tag{7.29}$$

From (7.27) and (7.29) it is clear that a switch to a permissive regime raises welfare if

$$i\pi_i/\pi_1 > D_i/D_1, \quad \forall i \leqslant n. \tag{7.30}$$

It is simple to show that (7.30) holds if demand is linear or of constant elasticity (or indeed, not 'too' convex).[8] ■

The key to the proof and to the economic rationale of Proposition 3 is that the Patent Office is free to set patent life at the required level: optimal patent life in the strict regime is shorter than under the permissive regime, but the additional length of time before price is driven to marginal cost is more than offset by the lower deadweight losses associated with the larger number of active firms. Proposition 3 shows that, if the Patent Office, by a suitable choice of patent life and novelty standards, can alter the Schumpeterian trade-off, it will do so in an anti-Schumpeterian fashion, trading off a slower rate of technical progress for the 'static' benefits associated with more output. Of course, Proposition 3 may not hold if there are economies of scale in the production of the new good and, more interestingly, if patent life is beyond the control of the Patent Office, as would be the case if succeeding waves of technical change render existing discoveries obsolete before the expiry of patents (see Propositions 2 and 3 in La Manna *et al.*, 1989).

6 RESEARCH, DEVELOPMENT AND PATENTS

With very few exceptions, patent races end with, unsurprisingly, the awarding of a patent: after that the winner(s) are assumed to collect their rewards in terms of profit earned on the production of the patent good without incurring further expenses. This assumption is strikingly counter-factual: under the present patent system, all patents require some form of 'development' to be turned into useful blueprints for production. This brings out an unfortunate effect of treating R&D merely as 'bids', namely the failure to distinguish in a meaningful way between research and development. Few authors are as candid as Brander and Spencer (1983), who openly admit that, in their model of R&D, 'R&D' could be replaced with 'lumpy investment' without changing in any way the substance and the details of the model. To argue that this is a defect rather than a virtue, one has to show that the failure to distinguish *between* research and development deprives the patent system of potentially significant features. In this section we will provide a simple characterization of research and development as two *distinct* stages and will draw the policy implications for the optimal design of the patent system.

Before sketching our model, it may be instructive to consider two of the very few models available in the literature that draw a distinction between research and development. In Reinganum (1985) the distinguishing feature of research is that the first firm to complete it has the option of becoming a Stackelberg leader in the development stage – the difference between research and development is purely strategic and patents play no role in it. Indeed Reinganum, in line with most models of patent races, sees patents merely as the reward for the combined R&D programme and assumes that the outcome of the research stage becomes rapidly common knowledge (that is, it is not patentable). As a result her model makes fascinating reading as an application of game theory to a two-stage model in which patents are merely incidental.

Grossman and Shapiro (1987) distinguish between research and development purely in terms of timing: R and D are two identical processes divided by an 'intermediate result' the successful completion of which allows firms to move from 'research' to 'development'. Even this tenuous distinction between R and D allows Grossman and Shapiro to consider an interesting option in patent policy, namely whether to grant patents to the 'intermediate outcome' or to the outcome of the combined R&D programme. However they make two key assumptions that deprive patents of much of their significance: firms are assumed to be able to monitor perfectly and costlessly the state of progress of research of their rivals and market structure is assumed to be independent of patenting policy.

In the model sketched below, by relaxing these two assumptions, we can assign to patents the role of signals of the state of research progress and endow the Patent Office with a further instrument to alter industry structure and the allocation of resources to R and D.

6.1 Patents as Early-warning Signals[9]

In our model firms take three decisions:

1. whether to pay a research fee, φ, that yields a probability p of producing a successful prototype of a new product/process (*research stage*);
2. to what extent, x, to develop their research prototypes or, equivalently, how much to invest in development inputs, v – the extent of development being a continuous function $x(v)$ of v (*development stage*);
3. how much final output, Q, to produce (*output stage*).

Having thus distinguished between R and D, we can consider a new dimension of the patent system in addition to the choice between a strict and a permissive regime examined in the previous section, namely the option to grant patents to either research prototypes (*ideas-based regime*) or to fully-developed products (*product-based regime*). Combining the novelty criterion with the workability criterion we obtain a 2 × 2 matrix of

Table 7.2   Patent regimes, classified by novelty and workability criteria

		Workability criterion	
		Ideas-based	Product-based
	Permissive	PI	PP
Novelty criterion			
	Strict	SI	SP

patent regimes (Table 7.2). As with any multi-stage game that uses a subgame perfect equilibrium as solution concept (see Chapter 1, Section 4), our three-stage game is solved 'backwards', starting with the final stage.

Assuming that the research lottery has been entered by firm j and has resulted in success for k firms (including firm j), the Nash equilibrium level of output for firm j, Q_j^* is defined in terms of the level of investment in development inputs by firm j, v_j, and by all other $k-1$ firms, v_{-j}, $Q_j^* \equiv Q_j^*(v_j, v_{-j})$ and the resulting gross profits (that is, net profits plus development costs) can be written as $\gamma(v_j, v_{-j}; k)$.[10]

Let $\mu(p, m, j)$ be the probability that $(j-1)$ out of m firms succeed in producing a working research prototype (or, alternatively, as the probability that, conditional on one firm out of m having succeeded, j others also succeed):

$$\mu(p, m, j) \equiv \binom{m-1}{j} p^j (1-p)^{m-1-j}. \tag{7.31}$$

Of course, under a strict regime (when only one patent is awarded), success at the research stage does not guarantee the award of the patent; thus if j firms succeed at the research stage, each has a $1/j$ chance of being granted the patent. Thus the probability of a successful inventor being awarded a patent if there are m firms is:

$$\xi(p, m) \equiv \sum_{j=0}^{m-1} \mu(p, m, j) \frac{1}{j+1}. \tag{7.32}$$

For further reference, notice that, letting $q \equiv (1-p)$:

$$p \, \xi(p, m) \equiv \frac{1-q^m}{m}. \tag{7.33}$$

Finally we can define the zero-expected-profit free-entry condition under each of the four patent regimes.

Strict, ideas-based regime (SI)

$$E\{\pi^{SI}\} \equiv p\, \xi(p,\, N) \max_{v} [\gamma(v;\, 1) - v] - \varphi. \tag{7.34}$$

Using (7.33), (7.34) can be written as

$$E\{\pi^{SI}\} \equiv \frac{1-q^{N}}{N} \max_{v} \{\gamma(v;\, 1) - v\} - \varphi. \tag{7.35}$$

We can already see the key feature of an ideas-based patent regime: as the (single) patent is awarded to a research prototype, development expenditures are undertaken *under certainty*. This is why profits from development are given by $\max_{v} [\gamma(v;\, 1) - v]$. As p is the probability of success and ξ the probability of being awarded the patent if successful, the first term in (7.35) is expected profit from research, while the last, φ, is the cost of research.

Strict, product-based regime (SP)

$$E\{\pi^{SP}\} \equiv p \max_{v} [\xi(p,\, n)\, \gamma(v;\, 1) - v] - \varphi. \tag{7.36}$$

Using (7.33), (7.36) can be written as

$$E\{\pi^{SP}\} \equiv \frac{1-q^{n}}{n} \max_{v} \{\gamma(v) - \frac{pn}{1-q^{n}}v\} - \varphi. \tag{7.37}$$

A comparison between (7.34) and (7.36) brings out the distinguishing feature of a product-based regime: (successful) inventors have to commit resources to the development of their prototypes *before* the identity of the patentee is known. This explains why, under an SP regime, v is chosen so as to maximize $[\xi(p,\, n)\, \gamma(v;\, 1) - v]$; that is, as compared with an SI regime, an SP regime generates uncertainty.

Permissive, ideas-based regime (PI)
Let

$$\pi(j) \equiv \max_{v_i} [\gamma(v_i,\, v_{-i};\, j) - v_i]; \tag{7.38}$$

therefore $\pi(j)$ are the profits made at a (symmetric) Nash equilibrium in a

$(j+1)$-firm oligopoly where each firm chooses its level of development expenditure non-cooperatively. Then

$$E\{\pi^{PI}\} \equiv p \sum_{j=0}^{N-1} \mu(p, n, j)\pi(j) - \varphi. \qquad (7.39)$$

Notice that, under a PI regime, resources are committed to development when the structure of the final-output market is known with certainty.

Permissive, product-based regime (PP)

$$E\{\pi^{PP}\} \equiv p \max_{v} \left[\sum_{j=0}^{n-1} \mu(p, n, j)\, \gamma(v, j) - v \right] - \varphi. \qquad (7.40)$$

Comparing an SP and a PP regime, it can be seen that, whereas in the former the identity of the (single) patentee is unknown at the time of committing resources to development, in the latter it is the *number* of patentees (and thus the structure of the final-output market) that is unknown.

Using this taxonomy of patent regimes, the analysis of the previous section can be seen as a special case of the comparison of the SP and PP regimes. In what follows we shall focus on welfare considerations affecting the choice between ideas- and product-based patent regimes.

Starting with the comparison between the simpler SI and SP regimes, it is easy to show that:

Proposition 4
A strict, ideas-based regime is unambiguously welfare-superior to a strict, product-based regime (provided the number of firms can be treated as a continuous variable).

Proof. The criterion used to determine which patent regime is more beneficial is net expected welfare $E\{W\}$ defined as the sum of expected consumer surplus CS and industry profits Π:

$E\{W\} \equiv$ [probability of at least one discovery] × [gross social welfare under certainty] − [expected industry development costs] − [industry research costs].

Applying the above definition to the SI and SP regimes, we obtain

$$E\{W^{SI}\} \equiv (1 - q^N)\{CS(v^{SI}) + \Pi(v^{SI}) - v^{SI}\} - N\varphi. \tag{7.41}$$

$$E\{W^{SP}\} \equiv (1 - q^n)\{CS(v^{SP}) + \Pi(v^{SP})\} - npv^{SP} - n\varphi. \tag{7.42}$$

If the integer constraint associated with the indivisibility of firms is ignored,[11] and research costs, φ, are such that $E\{\pi^{SI}\} = E\{\pi^{SP}\} = 0$, then Proposition 4 is easily proved:

$$E\{W^{SI}\} \equiv (1 - q^N)CS(v^{SI}) > (1 - q^n)CS(v^{SP}) \equiv E\{W^{SP}\}. \tag{7.43}$$

The above inequality follows by noting that, from the FOCs for the maximization of (7.35) and (7.37), we obtain respectively $\gamma_v = 1$ and $\gamma_v = pn/(1 - q^n)$; as $\gamma(\cdot)$ is concave in v and $pn/(1 - q^n) > 1$, an SI regime yields 'more improved' products/processes ($v^{SI} > v^{SP}$) and hence a higher consumer surplus (as $CS(\cdot)$ is increasing in v). Moreover, as $\gamma(\cdot)$ is increasing in v, the two regimes cannot sustain the same number of firms at a zero-profit equilibrium, for if $N = n$, then $E\{\pi^{SI}\} > E\{\pi^{SP}\}$. Then, at a zero-profit equilibrium, the SI regime will support more firms ($N > n$), since $(1 - q^m)/m$ is decreasing in m. ∎

The economic intuition behind Proposition 4 is clear: under a strict regime, the structure of the final-output market is known by all firms at the start (as only one patent is awarded, a monopoly will inevitably arise); however, in the case of more than one firm being successful at the research stage, under a product-based scheme, *all* successful firms will have to commit resources to development expenditure before knowing the identity of the lucky patentee. As a result, development expenditure (and cost reductions/product improvements) will be lower; as the expected net benefits from developing a research prototype are lower under a SP regime, fewer firms will enter the combined research–development programme, thus lowering the probability of a discovery being made at all. Therefore, compared with a strict, product-based regime, an SI regime generates both a higher rate of technical change and a higher probability of technical change taking place.

Before comparing ideas- and product-based regimes under a permissive scheme, it is worth examining in some detail the characteristics of a permissive, ideas-based regime (PI). A PI regime is the complete opposite of the popular winner-takes-all model of R&D races (in our terminology, an SP regime). In fact, in an SP regime, the value of the race prize (the patentee's monopoly profits) does not depend on the number of entrants, but the probability of success does, whereas, in a PI regime, the probability of discovery is independent of market structure, but the value of the prize is not.

Consider first the simpler case of no uncertainty ($p = 1$) and exogenously determined number of entrants, N. Then, using the following parametrization:

$$P = P_0 - \sum_{i=1}^{m} Q_i ; \qquad m = n, N, \tag{7.44}$$

$$C = (c_0 - x_i)Q_i + v_i , \tag{7.45}$$

$$x_i = \theta v_i^\alpha , \tag{7.46}$$

it is simple to show that increased entry (in a comparative-statics sense) will produce three effects:

1. *higher industry research costs*: in the absence of uncertainty, entry by an additional firm does not yield any benefits as far as research efforts are concerned;
2. *lower rate of technical change*: that is, $dv/dN < 0$; cost reductions are lower the larger the number of active firms;
3. *larger output*: that is, $dNQ/dN > 0$; entry always raises industry output.[12]

The fact that opposing forces are at work suggests that entry may *reduce* welfare; and indeed it can be shown that entry may be both feasible and socially detrimental.[13]

Finally we can introduce an endogenously determined number of entrants and uncertainty ($p \neq 1$). Tedious substitution reveals that, for the parametrization (7.44)–(7.46), net expected social welfare can be written as

$$E\{W^{PI}(N)\} = \sum_{i=1}^{N} \binom{N}{i} p^i q^{N-i} v^{PI} \frac{2 + i(1 - 4\alpha)}{4\alpha} - N\varphi. \tag{7.47}$$

Even by resorting to the parametrization (7.44) – (7.46) $E\{W^{PI}\}$ does not simplify to a well-behaved function; however some interesting results can be obtained by comparing the welfare characteristics of a N-firm free-entry oligopoly as compared to a $(N-1)$-firm oligopoly. For this purpose let $\Delta(p,N)$ be the change in welfare brought about by the Nth firm entering the industry; that is,

$$\Delta(p,N) \equiv E\{W^{PI}(N)\} - E\{W^{PI}(N-1)\}. \tag{7.48}$$

Obviously for any given N, $\Delta(p,N) = 0$ defines all the pairs (φ, p) such that the marginal expected gross social benefit derived from the Nth firm is equal to φ, the cost of research.

We are interested in the relationship between $E\{\pi^{PI}(N)\} = 0$ and $\Delta(p,N) = 0$; the former determines the number of firms active at a free-entry equilibrium and the latter helps establish whether such equilibrium sustains too few or too many firms. It should be clear that, unlike the traditional winner-takes-all patent race (in which social welfare is monotonically decreasing in the number of entrants), under a PI regime a free-entry equilibrium may well sustain *too few* entrants. This is because entry has three conflicting effects on research and development: if discoveries are 'difficult' and research costs are not 'too' high, a large number of research units may be beneficial in so far as it generates a high probability of a discovery being made at all; however a large number of successful inventors will produce two further effects: on the one hand it will yield a high level of final output, but on the other will generate a low level of cost reduction (or product improvement). By balancing these three effects one can define the second-best number of firms, N^w, which need not coincide with the free-entry equilibrium number of entrants, N.

Figure 7.4 depicts $\Delta(p,N) = 0$ and $E\{\pi^{PI}(N)\} = 0$ for $\alpha = 0.1$ (the average value of the development cost elasticity according to the empirical literature on R&D); it can be seen that the (φ, p) plane can be divided into three zones:

ZONE A $N^w > N$. When discoveries are 'difficult' relative to the cost of research, a free-entry equilibrium does not generate enough research units.

ZONE B $N^w = N$. Social welfare cannot be improved by imposing restrictions to entry.

ZONE C $N^w < N$. Although the rugged contours of Zone C do not allow us to draw clear-cut conclusions, it can be seen that, when discoveries are 'easy' and the cost of research 'low', a free-entry equilibrium sustains *too many firms* (and thus any policy change that makes entry less profitable may improve welfare).

From the preceding analysis it has emerged that, especially when discoveries are 'easy' and research costs are 'high', a PI patent regime may generate *excessive research* and *too little development*. The rationale for this result and a possible suggestion for improving social welfare by a change of patent regime can be understood by viewing patents as information signals. Unlike the traditional model of patent rates which, by defining patents as the reward of the *combined* R&D effort, deprives the patent system of any informational role, in our model patents can alter the allocation of resources between research and development by taking on the role of 'early warning signals' in the sense that, by a suitable choice of patentability criteria (ideas- or product-based), patents may be used either to convey or to withhold valuable information before resources are committed to developing research prototypes into finished products/processes.

It should be clear that, in deciding on the (second-best) optimal patentability criteria, a key role is going to be played by the effects on *entry* of the chosen criterion. In fact, for any exogenously given number of entrants $\bar{m}$, it is easy to see that a PI regime will always outperform a PP regime. Research expenditures will be the same but development expenditures will be lower under a PP regime.[14] Of course if there is free entry the two regimes cannot sustain the same number of entrants and the PP regime will always induce *fewer* firms to enter.

The question may be asked as to whether a change from a PI regime to a more demanding regime (in terms of workability standards) may not improve social welfare in those cases in which a PI regime yields too much research and too little development, bearing in mind that, under a PP regime, firms will always invest more in development as compared to a PI regime.

Figure 7.4   Second-best and free-entry industry structure under a permissive ideas-based patent regime

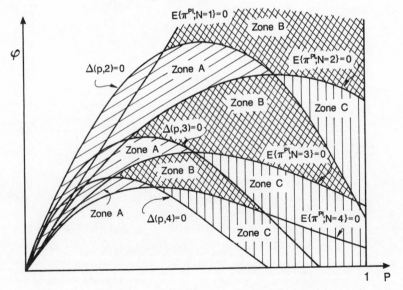

The answer turns out to be affirmative: using the parameterization (7.44)–
(7.46) one can produce examples in which there exists a range of values of the
parameters (p, α) such that a PP regime is socially preferable to a PI regime.
Figure 7.5 depicts the levels of net expected social welfare in a duopoly under
a PP regime, $E\{W^{PP}(n=2)\}$, and in a triopoly under a PI regime,
$E\{W^{PI}(N=3)\}$. It can be seen that, when discoveries are 'easy' $(p > \hat{p})$, a switch
from the entry-inducing PI regime to the concentration-inducing PP regime
may in fact yield a welfare improvement. On reflection, this is in line with
intuition: when the probability of each firm being successful at the research
stage is 'high', the advantage of the PI regime of generating a higher overall
probability of success may be more than offset by the more extensive development of research prototypes under a PI regime.

Figure 7.5   Permissive product- vs ideas-based patent regimes

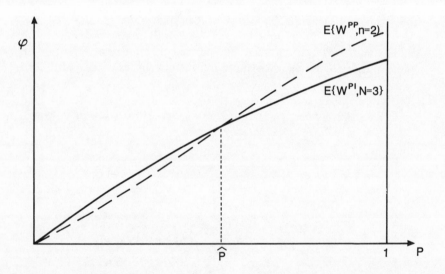

CONCLUSIONS

That there is an urgent need for the reassessment of the current patent
regime is confirmed by the increasing dissatisfaction felt in many industries with respect to patent law. A glaring example is provided by the
biotechnology industry: current patent law is singularly ill-suited to deal
with the very concept of patenting 'life forms' and recent attempts to
modify it lack any theoretical underpinnings.[15] The recent developments
in the economics of patent reform surveyed in this chapter could provide a

fruitful theoretical foundation on which empirical investigations could be based with the aim of forging a patent system suited to meet the needs of the twenty-first century.

NOTES

1. For an excellent survey of technological competition within a sequential setting, see Beath, Katsoulacos and Ulph (1989); see also Kamien and Schwartz (1982), Chapter 4.
2. 'Marginally unprofitable' means that, prior to innovation, $A = c_0$. Of course nothing of substance hinges on this notation-saving assumption.
3. Subscripts indicate the argument with respect to which differentiation is carried out.
4. See Arrow (1962); Nordhaus (1969); Kamien and Schwartz (1982), Chapter 2; Baldwin and Scott (1987), Chapter 2.
5. Tandon's equation (18) is a cubic in ρ, but factoring out the economically meaningless solution $\rho = 1$ one obtains (7.13).
6. Gilbert and Shapiro do not consider the issue of the optimal amount of R&D and thus can take V as exogenous.
7. This section draws on La Manna (1992).
8. For details see La Manna *et al.* (1989), pp. 1432–3 and Appendix C.
9. This section draws on La Manna (1991).
10. For example, using the parametrization (7.44)–(7.46), it is simple to confirm that

$$\gamma(v_j, v_{-j}; k) = [\frac{k}{k+1} \theta v_{-j}^\alpha - \frac{1}{k+1} \sum_{i \neq j}^{k} \theta v_i^\alpha]^2 - v_j.$$

11. This is not an altogether innocuous assumption, for it can be shown that there are circumstances under which the integer constraint does reverse the welfare inequality postulated in Proposition 3. For details, see La Manna (1991).
12. Using (7.44)–(7.46) it is easy to confirm that, in order for entry to be profitable for the $(N+1)^{th}$ firm, $\frac{1}{2(N+1)} > \alpha$ and that industry rises with entry if $\frac{1}{N+1} > \alpha$.
13. For details see La Manna (1991).
14. It is simple to show that v^{PI} is a linear combination of the profit-maximizing levels of v under certainty, whereas v^{PP} is a convex combination.
15. For a bold attempt to reform patent law in the field of biotechnology that relies more on casual empiricism than on an explicit theoretical foundation, see Commission of the European Communities (1988).

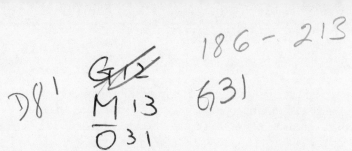

8. Entrepreneurship: A Model of Risky Innovation under Capital Constraints

Mark Casson

1 INTRODUCTION

The main problem in analysing entrepreneurship is to decide what it means. Some people identify it with a personality attribute revealed in business life – such as flair – while others identify it as a specific role, such as that of the self-employed owner–manager of a firm. Because of its elusiveness, entrepreneurship is usually analysed in purely qualitative terms. The most significant attempt to build a formal algebraic model is by Kihlstrom and Laffont (1979) who focus on the role of the employment contract in allocating risk between the employer (the entrepreneur) and the employee. They borrow this idea from Knight (1921), although it is more appropriately attributed to Cantillon (1755), as indicated below.

This chapter develops a model which synthesizes this risk-bearing idea with other long-established insights – notably those of Schumpeter (1934, 1939) on innovation and the Austrian school on the market process (Hayek, 1937; Kirzner, 1973, 1979; von Mises, 1949).

The model offers new theoretical advances too. First, it provides an exact method of measuring the economic rents that accrue to the entrepreneur. Secondly, it integrates transaction costs into the theory of the entrepreneur, along the lines suggested in Casson (1982). Finally, it demonstrates the crucial importance of capital constraints on the intensity of entrepreneurial activity. The analysis of capital constraints helps to elucidate the influence of the banking system on long-run structural change in the economy.

2 A REVIEW OF THE THEORY

From an economic point of view entrepreneurship is best considered as a function. The entrepreneur *is* what the entrepreneur *does*, in other words.

The contractual status of the entrepreneur – whether he is owner, manager or middleman – can then be analysed in terms of a division of labour which specializes this function in certain roles. The problem is that the literature suggests several quite distinct functions, as indicated below.

2.1 Risk Bearing

Cantillon, an Irish economist of French descent, was the first to demonstrate that contracts reallocate risk. A merchant who purchases supplies at a price which is fixed independently of resale value insures the seller against subsequent fluctuations in price. If the merchant could resell the product forward at the same time that he purchased it then risk could be avoided, but, as a service to customers, sales are normally effected spot, at the customer's convenience, from goods held in stock. Thus the merchant becomes a specialized bearer of risk. A manufacturer can also become a bearer of risk (Azariadis, 1975) by purchasing a worker's labour before he sells the product of that labour. In this way Cantillon's scheme of thought divides society into two main classes – the risk-taking entrepreneurs, and the non-entrepreneurial consumers and workers.

2.2 Arbitrage

For Austrian economists the entrepreneur is the key figure in the market process. In a continually changing environment he moves the economy towards equilibrium through speculation and arbitrage. From a subjectivist standpoint, markets provide individuals with information on what other people think resources are worth. This allows people to buy or sell according to whether their own subjective valuations are greater or less than the weight of opinion, as reflected in the market price. The price discovery function is specialized with entrepreneurs who pass on their information through free price quotations. Their motivation for price discovery is the prospect of a temporary monopoly gain from arbitrage. Freedom of entry ensures that the marginal entrepreneur receives only a normal rate of profit, once his costs of discovery are allowed for. The most alert entrepreneurs may attain positive rents because of the scarcity of this attribute of alertness, however.

2.3 Innovation

Schumpeter's heroic vision of the entrepreneur combines a romantic view of human motivation with technological optimism and an unconventional view of monetary economics. The Schumpeterian entrepreneur is an innovator who carries out new combinations – introducing a new technology or product, discovering a new export market, exploiting a new source of raw material supply, or creating a new type of institution, such as a joint stock company, cartel or trust. The entrepreneur is not an inventor – he does not generate technology himself – but merely identifies its commercial potential. Nor does he carry financial risk – that is the role of the banks. Banks extend credit to new ventures by sacrificing liquidity to expand advances. The resultant expansion of bank deposits stimulates a mild inflation which raises the costs of traditional producers competing with the innovation and hastens their obsolescence. The innovation, if successful, encourages imitators who eventually over-expand the new industry and create a crisis of confidence which precipitates depression, as a result of which further innovation is postponed. The entrepreneur's role is to persuade the bank to back the new technology. His motivation is not primarily pecuniary. He is driven by 'the dream and the will to found a private kingdom', 'the will to conquer' and 'the joy of creating'. Nevertheless the realization of the dream depends on convincing hard-headed bankers that the project will be a commercial success.

3   JUDGEMENTAL DECISION MAKING

The most sophisticated literary analysis of entrepreneurship is due to Knight, who extends Cantillon's insights using a subjectivist Austrian perspective. His starting-point is a distinction between risk and uncertainty. Risk, according to Knight, is measurable, because it relates to situations which have many precedents and where, as a consequence, the odds of success can be calculated quite accurately. Many individual risks are statistically independent of one another and hence insurable. Knight regards the joint-stock conglomerate corporation as an important device for providing individual insurance through the pooling of risks.

Situations without precedent create uncertainty. The decision maker must employ subjective probabilities rather than objective relative frequencies in this case. Different people may form different probability estimates. A confident individual who recognizes that his own beliefs differ from the common view may perceive an opportunity for speculation. In particular, if he is more optimistic than others, he can exploit an opportunity that others do not recognize. Their pessimistic evaluation discourages them from competing with him. From his own point of view, their ignorance acts as a barrier to entry – though of course, if their beliefs turn out to be right, it is his over-confidence that leads him into losses instead.

Knight's ideas may be extended by noting that there are many issues that cannot be decided by objective methods, in the sense that there is no obviously correct decision rule that can be implemented given available information. Decisions of this kind call for judgement. Judgement may be defined by exclusion – it is a service which enhances the quality of decisions in novel, complex and ambiguous situations which require an urgent decision (Casson, 1990).

Schumpeterian innovation is a classic example of a judgemental decision. The synthesis of incomplete data on product demand, factor supply and technological possibilities calls for a high level of judgement. A lower level of judgement is involved in Austrian-type speculation and arbitrage too. The concept of judgement, applied to the discovery of monopolistic opportunities, is thus a common theme in both Austrian and Schumpeterian theories. There is a difference of emphasis, of course; the Schumpeterian entrepreneur typically creates a new market through large-scale investment in a long-run monopoly protected by patents, whilst the Austrian entrepreneur equilibrates an established market through small-scale arbitrage of an essentially transitory nature. But once they are adjusted for the degree of novelty, the scale of activity and the time period involved, the underlying phenomenon is the same.

It is important to note that successful judgement does not necessarily imply accepting every proposal. Innovation and arbitrage are not always the right decisions to make. Sometimes it is important not to innovate or arbitrage because the opportunity is illusory: it is the 'fools that rush in' where the more deliberate decision makers fear to tread. Focusing on judgement therefore emphasizes that it is the responsibility for the decision, rather than the outcome of the decision, that is crucial.

4 OWNERSHIP, MANAGEMENT AND THE PLACE OF THE ENTREPRENEUR WITHIN THE FIRM

A firm may be regarded as a nexus of contracts established by an entrepreneur to facilitate the exploitation of his ideas. While an entrepreneur could, in principle, subcontract every aspect of the implementation of a project, it is not normally economic to do so. Transaction costs are minimized by substituting long-term open-ended contracts for explicit spot contracts (Coase, 1937). For example, interlocking employment contracts can be created in which the occupant of one role is subordinated to the occupant of another role in respect of a particular class of decisions. The relations between different roles create a hierarchy which is governed by the entrepreneur in accordance with the constitution of the firm (Aoki, Gustafsson and Williamson, 1990).

The differentiation of roles within the firm reflects the application of the principle of the division of labour to the function of decision making. It is a special case of the division of *intellectual* labour envisaged by Babbage (1832). This division of labour creates a problem, however, of identifying where exactly entrepreneurship is located within the firm.

There are three aspects to this problem. The first is to tackle the entrenched but misleading view that entrepreneurship is unitary, in the sense that there can only be one entrepreneur per firm. Kaldor (1934) suggests, for example, that entrepreneurship is a fixed factor in every firm because there can only be one brain which ultimately makes any decision. But when a committee makes a democratic decision, for example, it is clear that everyone participates in the decision by deciding how to cast their vote.

The idea that entrepreneurship is unitary is a special case of the more general belief that where there is a division of labour the entrepreneur should be distinguishable from other people by his *complete* specialization in the function concerned. If judgemental decision making is taken as the defining function, however, then it is clear that few business people do nothing but take decisions all day. But, on closer examination, it turns out that, although the actual time involved in taking a decision may be quite brief, a large amount of time is devoted to complementary activity of gathering relevant information – consulting colleagues in committee, being briefed by subordinates through reading their reports, and so on. Moreover most organizations effect a quite clear distinction between those roles where decision making is primarily judgemental, because no decision rule is prescribed, and those where it is purely routine. It is those roles where decision making is relatively more judgemental than others that are the entrepreneurial ones, and typically these roles will be found close to the top of the hierarchy.

The third problem is whether the entrepreneur is the owner or the manager of the firm. Clearly this problem does not arise with small owner-managed firms, where it is natural to regard the owner–manager as the entrepreneur. But the separation of ownership and control in the modern large corporation has led Knight and others to take the view that a choice must be made between the competing claims of owners and managers.

According to Knight, no one who bears financial responsibility for a situation will voluntarily allow someone else to take a decision that affects the outcome. Since the shareholders carry financial responsibility, they must therefore take the key decisions. The key decision is to select the chief executive, argues Knight. By choosing a person who will implement appropriate management procedures, all other decision making is rendered routine. The shareholders bear the risks and take the only decision that matters, and so are the entrepreneurs.

There is clearly something unsatisfactory about the idea that the thousands of small shareholders in a large firm collectively act as an entrepreneur. The flaw in Knight's argument is his view that decision making cannot be delegated. Delegation is perfectly feasible if the delegate can be trusted. Both the competence and integrity of the delegate are important in this respect. The chief executive is the shareholders' delegate, and he in turn can delegate to board members, and indeed much further down the pyramid of authority. At each stage confidence in the delegate can be reinforced by incentives. Thus in the long run a manager's salary will reflect his opportunity earnings, which in turn reflect his reputation in the capital market. A good track record of stewardship and judgement will bring its own pecuniary rewards, and there may be non-pecuniary emotional satisfactions too. Wherever decision making is delegated, together with discretion to exercise judgement, both the delegator (the 'principal') and the delegate (the 'agent') can share the entrepreneurial role. Contrary to Knight's argument, it may be noted that the shareholders have only an intermittent role in the selection (normally the annual reselection) of the chief executive, while the chief executive himself has daily involvement in judgemental decisions on the shareholder's behalf, so that on normal criteria it is the chief executive who is best regarded as the entrepreneur.

5   A SIMPLE MODEL

Key aspects of the theories reviewed above can be encapsulated in a simple model. In this model entrepreneurial activity leads to the creation of a new industry. Entrepreneurship therefore involves innovation and structural change, as emphasized by Schumpeter. The outcome of investment in the new industry is uncertain, so there is risk in the sense of Cantillon. Only the other (traditional) industry yields a certain output. In later versions of the model there are divergent opinions about the probability of success, so that there is Knightian uncertainty too. Finally, one entrepreneur may have a temporary monopoly of information about the opportunity, so that Austrian insights are encapsulated as well.

Consider therefore an economy comprising two categories of people: merchants and workers. There is a fixed number of each type. Workers are totally risk-averse. They are initially all attached to the traditional industry, where they are self-employed. Production in the traditional industry is risk-free. Workers will only move into the new industry if they are fully insured against risks relating to the new product.

The new product is a perfect substitute for the old one. Everyone knows that if the new product industry is successful then one unit of the new product will exchange for $p > 0$ units of the mature one; this is because everyone's tastes exhibit the same constant marginal rate of substitution between old and new. If the new product is unsuccessful, however, because of technical or design failures, for example, or for whatever reason, then it is worthless. All the new product produced in any time period achieves the same success, so that the elimination of individual risks through pooling is not possible; in other words, all risk is essentially systematic risk.

Workers obtain insurance through a contract of employment offered by merchants in the new industry. The contract guarantees each worker a fixed wage $w > 0$, independently of whether production is successful. There is such a large number of workers that each worker constitutes an infinitesimal proportion of total labour supply. It is assumed for simplicity that each worker has the same physical productivity in the new industry (so that the number of workers is effectively measured in units of labour supplied to this industry).

Workers differ in their personal comparative advantage; a worker's physical productivity in the old industry is given by the worker-specific parameter a, which is uniformly distributed amongst the working population between the limits a_1 and a_2 in accordance with the distribution function

$$F(a) = (a - a_1)/(a_2 - a_1) \qquad 0 \le a_1 \le a \le a_2. \tag{8.1}$$

Each worker's utility is directly proportional to the value of consumption (measured in units of mature product). Maximizing utility subject to the no-risk constraint shows that workers will move to the new industry if and only if

$$w \ge a. \tag{8.2}$$

It follows from (8.1) and (8.2) that the supply of labour to the new industry, n^s, is

$$n^s = (w - a_1)/(a_2 - a_1). \tag{8.3}$$

A merchant's utility depends upon both the expected return from the new industry and the standard deviation of the return. Although tolerant of risk, the merchant is more averse to it than he is disposed towards it, so that while the expected return carries a positive weight in his utility function the standard deviation carries a negative one. For simplicity the coefficient on the expected return is normalized to unity. This gives the utility function

$$u = (\mu - b\sigma)n^d, \tag{8.4}$$

where μ is the expected value of profit per worker in the new industry, σ is the corresponding standard deviation, $b \geq 0$ is the coefficient of risk aversion shared by all merchants, and n^d is the merchant's demand for labour, as reflected in the employment contracts offered. With a perceived probability of success π $(0 \leq \pi \leq 1)$,

$$\mu = p\pi - w \tag{8.5}$$

$$\sigma = p(\pi(1 - \pi))^{1/2}. \tag{8.6}$$

With homogeneous perceptions of π, and free entry, competition between merchants will eliminate economic rents,

$$u = 0 \tag{8.7}$$

giving a total demand for labour n^d which is infinitely elastic at the wage

$$w_0 = p\pi - b\sigma. \tag{8.8}$$

Substituting (8.8) into (8.3) and using the equilibrium condition

$$n^d = n^s = n^e \tag{8.9}$$

gives the equilibrium outcome

$$w^e_0 = w_0 \tag{8.10a}$$

$$n^e_0 = (p\pi(1 - b((1/\pi) - 1)^{1/2}) - a_1)/(a_2 - a_1). \tag{8.10b}$$

Suppose that the true probability of success is π^*. *Ex post* all uncertainty relating to the new industry is resolved. Thus the true expected value of *ex post* utility is the true expected value of profit which, when normalized with respect to the number of employees, is

$$\mu^*_0 = (p(\pi^* - \pi) + b\sigma). \tag{8.11}$$

This suggests that, *ex post*, innovating merchants benefit from group pessimism ($\pi < \pi^*$) and from a high perception of risk, as measured by σ. Merchants as a group do not benefit to the same degree, however, because pessimism and subjective uncertainty discourage some merchants from participating altogether.

If one merchant alone is optimistic of success then that merchant will enjoy monopsony power over labour entering the new industry. Suppose for simplicity that all merchants except one are totally pessimistic. Maximizing utility (8.4) subject to (8.3), (8.5) and (8.9) gives the new equilibrium

$$w^e_1 = a_1 + (a_2 - a_1)n^e_1 \tag{8.12a}$$

$$n^e_1 = n^e_0/2, \tag{8.12b}$$

where n^e_0 is given by (8.10b). Comparing (8.10) and (8.12) shows that both the wage rate and employment are reduced by the exercise of monopsony power.

The competitive equilibrium is illustrated in Figure 8.1 and the monopsony equilibrium in Figure 8.2. The real wage is measured vertically and

Figure 8.1   Competitive equilibrium

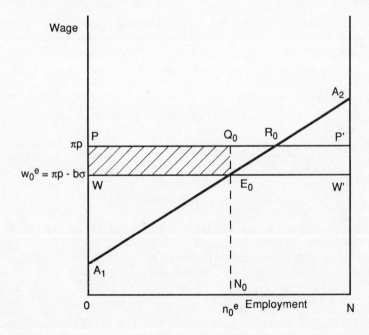

employment horizontally. The total size of the labour force is indicated by the width of the horizontal axis ON. If merchants were risk-neutral their demand for labour in the new industry PP' would be infinitely elastic at the real wage OP, equal to the expected value of the new product, but because of risk aversion demand is shifted down to WW', whose intercept OW measures the risk-adjusted expected value of the product. The upward slope of the labour supply curve for the new industry, A_1A_2, reflects the increasing comparative disadvantage of additional labour drawn into the new industry.

Equilibrium is at the intersection E_0 of WW' and A_1A_2, giving a wage OW and employment ON_0. The area of the quadrilateral $OA_1E_0N_0$ measures the opportunity earnings of labour in the new industry, while the area of the triangle A_1WE_0 measures workers' economic rent. The shaded area of the rectangle WPQ_0E_0 measures the expected profit accruing to merchants, which is their reward for risk bearing, and corresponds to the merchant's profit described by Cantillon. The output of the traditional industry is measured by the area of the quadrilateral $E_0A_2NN_0$. The total value of the economy's output is reduced by the area of the triangle $E_0Q_0R_0$ on account of merchant's risk aversion.

In the monopsonistic equilibrium illustrated in Figure 8.2 the solitary

Figure 8.2   Monopsony equilibrium

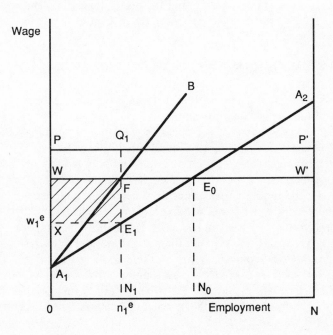

active merchant faces a marginal cost of labour schedule A_1B, whose slope
is twice that of the supply curve A_1A_2. The steeper slope reflects the fact
that a monopsonist incorporates the rising supply price of labour into his
calculation of marginal cost whereas a competitor does not. There is no
corresponding market power in the product market because, by assumption, the old product is a perfect substitute for the new one. Equilibrium is
where the risk-adjusted expectation of marginal revenue, OW, is equal to
the marginal cost, as measured by the height of A_1B; that is, at the
intersection F of WW' and A_1B.

The monopsonist's expected profit is measured by the area of the
rectangle PQ_1E_1X. After deducting the compensation for risk, this leaves a
pure monopsony profit equal to the area WFE_1X. By restricting employment in the new industry to $ON_1 < ON_0$, the exercise of monopsony
power reduces social welfare (measured in units of the traditional product)
by the area of the triangle E_0E_1F.

An Austrian would argue, however, that the relevant comparison is not
with the competitive equilibrium, which represents an unattainable ideal,
but rather with the absence of any innovation at all. Were it not for the
optimism of the monopsonist, no innovation would have occurred, and all
labour would have remained allocated to the traditional industry. From this
perspective the monopsonist increases social welfare (after adjustment for
risk) by the area of the quadrilateral A_1WFE_1. The monopsonist appropri-
ates some of this as pure profit, and the rest, measured by the area of the
triangle A_1XE_1, accrues to employees in the new industry as economic rent.

6   SUPERVISION AND THE SIZE OF FIRM

The preceding model affords only a limited role to the firm. Because a
merchant may simultaneously employ several workers, the merchant himself qualifies as a 'nexus of contracts' in the sense of Section 4. But what
exactly determines the number of employees? While the size of the industry is determinate, the allocation of employees between merchants is not –
except in the case of monopsony, where industry and firm coincide. In
particular, the model above cannot predict, for a competitive industry,
how many firms of what size will operate in the industry.

An important influence on the size of firm is the cost of supervision. The
demand for supervision arises in the present model because of the nature
of the employment contract. When workers are insured against variations
in the value of their output, they have an incentive to slack. If a positive
cost of effort is introduced into the worker's utility function, his rational
response to a fixed wage will be to slack. (This incentive does not exist in

the traditional industry because, by assumption, workers are self-employed there.)

There are two main methods by which a merchant can motivate worker's effort. One is familiar to economists and the other is not. The familiar approach is to monitor the workers by appointing one of them as a supervisor to report on the others. Those who slack are fined by loss of pay. The merchant does not supervise himself, it is assumed, but appoints a supervisor for this task. The merchant's role is simply to 'supervise the supervisor' and since the merchant has only a single supervisee it is assumed for simplicity that this is a costless task.

The average cost of supervision varies according to the span of supervision, which is determined by the number of workers in the production team. It is assumed that the productivity of each worker is independent of the size of the team. Thus team size is governed solely by the cost of supervision. Each team has a single supervisor, and so the supervisor constitutes an indivisible resource. It is assumed for simplicity that any worker can be appointed a supervisor and in this capacity receives the same wage as his supervisees. As team size $z > 0$ increases so the effectiveness of supervision declines (team size is measured exclusive of the supervisor himself). The proportion of time each worker is idle under supervision is

$$g = \alpha_1 z/(1 + \alpha_1 z), \tag{8.13}$$

which is increasing in z for $\alpha_1 > 0$. Each unit of output now requires $1 + \alpha_1 z$ workers, in addition to an imputed proportion $1/z$ of the supervisor's time.

Supervision is a labour-intensive activity with a standardized technology and so the average cost of supervision is simply the sum of these two cost components, namely

$$c = w(\alpha_1 z + (1/z)). \tag{8.14}$$

In a free-entry competitive industry a firm must minimize (8.14) in order to survive.

The new industry expands by the replication of teams of optimal size. It is assumed that each merchant operates a single team (that is, all firms are single-plant) and that there are sufficient merchants to sustain all the replication required. Dividing industry output by optimal team size determines the number of firms involved.

Differentiating (8.14) with respect to z and equating to zero shows that the optimal team size is

$$z^e = \alpha_1^{-1/2} \tag{8.15}$$

so that the minimum attainable average cost is

$$c^e = 2w\alpha_1^{1/2}. \tag{8.16}$$

The break-even condition (8.7) implies that wages will be bid up to

$$w_2{}^e = (p\pi - b\sigma)/(1 + 2\alpha_1^{1/2}) \tag{8.17}$$

whence from (8.3)

$$n_2{}^e = (w_2{}^e - a_1)/(a_2 - a_1). \tag{8.18}$$

Equilibrium employment $n_2{}^e$ is divided between supervisors and supervisees in the ratio $1 : z$.

The equilibrium is illustrated in Figure 8.3. The left-hand quadrant determines the minimum average cost of supervision and the optimal size of team, whilst the right-hand quadrant feeds these results into the determination of employment in the new industry as a whole. The height of the average cost curve in the left-hand quadrant reflects the wage rate determined in the right-hand quadrant. It is this that ensures the cost factor OS in the left-hand quadrant coincides with the cost factor WX in the right-hand quadrant.

In the left-hand quadrant the average fixed cost due to the supervisor's wage is indicated by the hyperbola FF', whilst the increasing average cost of slacking is indicated by the straight line OV. Overall average cost TT' is minimized at J, which determines the optimal team size z^e.

In the right-hand quadrant the risk-adjusted value of new industry output, net of slacking cost $OS = WX$, is given by OX. The infinitely elastic demand for labour XX' intersects the labour supply schedule A_1A_2 at E_2, giving employment ON_2. This consists of OY workers and YN_2 supervisors. The cost of supervision is measured by the area of the vertically hatched rectangle E_2N_2YH, whilst the cost of output lost from slacking is measured by the area of the horizontally hatched rectangle $WGHX$. Given the assumed pattern of slacking (8.13), the cost of optimal supervision is equal to the cost of the optimal degree of slacking, as reflected in the fact that the hatched areas are equal. Given the reduced level of employment, the risk premium accruing to merchants is reduced to the area of the rectangle PQ_2GW. Workers' economic rent is reduced to the area of the triangle A_1XE_2.

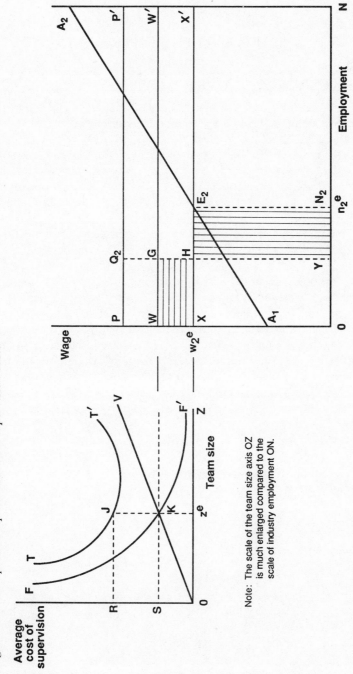

Figure 8.3 Competitive equilibrium with supervision costs

Note: The scale of the team size axis OZ is much enlarged compared to the scale of industry employment ON.

7   LEADERSHIP AND THE ENTREPRENEUR

An alternative to supervision is leadership. Leadership, though widely
used in practice, is largely ignored by economists. It involves influencing
workers' preferences in order to neutralize the cost of effort. The leader's
personal example, backed by his moral rhetoric, emphasizes the importance of commitment to the task (Casson, 1991). Workers anticipate self-
inflicted non-pecuniary penalties – guilt, loss of self-esteem, and so on – if
they slack. When these emotional penalties outweigh the material benefits
of slacking, workers will work hard even though they are not supervised.

It is assumed that, while anyone can act as a supervisor, only a few
people are capable of exercising leadership. The potential leaders are all
merchants in this model, though in real life many workers (notably trade
union leaders, and industrialists with shop-floor origins) have leadership
qualities too. It is assumed that exercising leadership (for the few who
have the necessary qualities) is no more difficult than supervising the
supervisor, which in the present model makes it a costless activity.

Leadership, it is assumed, is most effective in small groups. The incidence of slacking increases faster with the span of control under leadership than it does under supervision. The ability of the leader to influence
workers by personal example, and to relate his rhetoric to the personal
attitude of each worker, requires more face-to-face contact than does the
relatively impersonal method of supervision.

The incidence of slacking under leadership is measured by

$$g_2 = \alpha_2 z/(1 + \alpha_2 z) \qquad\qquad \alpha_2 > \alpha_1 \tag{8.19}$$

and so, with no fixed costs associated with a supervisor's wage, the
average cost of leadership is simply

$$c_2 = \alpha_2 wz. \tag{8.20}$$

Substituting

$$\mu = w - c_2 \tag{8.21}$$

into (8.4) and maximizing utility gives the team size

$$z = (((p\pi - b\sigma)/w) - 1)/2\alpha_2. \tag{8.22}$$

Two types of equilibrium are possible. In the first there are sufficient
leaders to replace supervisors entirely. Given a fixed number of leaders, m,

the total demand for labour is then mz, and equilibrium with supply is achieved at the wage

$$w^e_3 = k_1 + (k_1^2 + 4k_2)^{1/2}, \tag{8.23}$$

where

$$k_1 = \alpha_1 - ((m/2)(1 - (\alpha_1/\alpha_2))) \tag{8.24a}$$

$$k_2 = (m/2)(1 - (\alpha_1/\alpha_2))(p\pi - b\sigma). \tag{8.24b}$$

The corresponding level of employment in the new industry is

$$n^e_3 = (w^e_3 - a_1)/(a_2 - a_1) \tag{8.25}$$

and the optimal team size is

$$z_e = n^e_3/m. \tag{8.26}$$

It can be shown that both wages and employment vary directly with the number of leaders m and inversely with the incidence of slacking under leadership α_2. Because the number of leaders influences the wage rate, the optimal size of team depends on the wage rate too.

A somewhat more interesting and relevant equilibrium occurs when specialization in leadership is incomplete. This typically occurs when the number of leaders is very small. When leaders and supervisors operate side by side in the industry the wage and employment levels are determined by the marginal costs of supervision, in accordance with (8.17) and (8.18) above. Substituting (8.17) into (8.22) shows that the optimal size of team is

$$z^e = \alpha_1^{1/2}/\alpha_2. \tag{8.27}$$

Thus the optimal size of team under leadership depends on the relative and absolute incidence of slacking under leadership and supervision and is independent of the expected value of output and the wage.

The ability of a leader to avoid the cost of supervision allows him to obtain an economic rent. The rent per leader under incomplete specialization is

$$u^e = (p\pi - b\sigma)((1 + \alpha_1^{1/2})/(1 + 2\alpha_1^{1/2}))\alpha_1^{1/2}/\alpha_2. \tag{8.28}$$

Thus the leader's rent varies directly with the incidence of slacking under supervision and inversely with the incidence of slacking under leadership.

The determination of leadership rent in this second case is illustrated in Figure 8.4. The demand for labour under supervision is infinitely elastic at a wage OX, as in Figure 8.3. The leader's demand for labour is indicated by the downward-sloping schedule WL. The downward slope arises because under leadership both marginal and average cost rise continuously with team size, and it is impossible to replicate additional teams of optimal size. The intersection D of WL and XX' determines the numbers of workers operating under leadership, OM. Total employment in the industry is determined at the intersection E_3 of XX' and A_1A_2, exactly as in Figure 8.3. Employment under supervision is MN_3.

Supervisory firms earn no economic rent, whereas leaders do. The expected rent, net of risk, is given by the shaded area WXD. This rent reflects the fact that leadership avoids the fixed costs of supervision incurred by the other firms. Leadership does not avoid slacking problems, however; the value of output lost by slacking under leadership is measured by the area WCD.

Figure 8.4   Competitive equilibrium with leadership as well as supervision

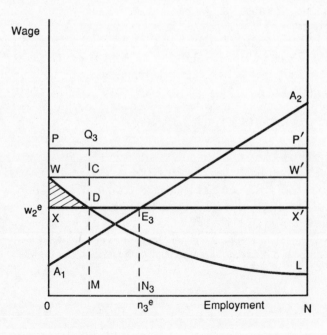

8   CAPITAL CONSTRAINTS

It is the merchant's doubts about the effort of workers that create the demands for supervision and leadership noted above. But the converse is also possible: workers may doubt the merchant's promises as spelt out in the contract of employment. There is the question of integrity – will the merchant actually pay up when wages are due (net of any fines for slacking) – and also the question of competence – will the merchant be able to pay up, even if he wants to, if production turns out unsuccessfully? It is this second question of competence that is the focus of attention here.

Workers who are totally risk-averse will need to be assured that the merchant can meet his wage obligations in the 'worst case' scenario. If the worst case is that the output is, say, worth only half the wage bill, then the other half of the wage bill must be covered by the merchant's own capital. In the present model the worst case is that the output is completely valueless, which means that the entire wage bill must be covered by merchant's capital. Thus workers' demand for insurance creates a demand for capital which means that, if merchants are capital-constrained, the expansion of the new industry may be impaired.

If the capital is actually paid out in advance of production, and production takes time, then it is equivalent to 'working capital' or a 'wages fund' (Cannan, 1893). In the analysis here, however, capital is merely kept in reserve and paid out at the same time that revenues (if any) are generated. This eliminates analytical complications arising from the role of time preference and the influence of the real rate of interest on the overall cost of production.

Assume for simplicity that the capital of the economy consists of stocks of the mature product. This is a totally durable good. It does not assist production (as capital does in conventional multi-factor production functions) but mainly exists for future consumption. The capital is distributed between merchants and workers in the proportions $s: 1 - s$. Being totally risk-averse, the workers will not make the capital available to merchants except through banks (whose role, for the moment, is ignored).

Given a wage w, and total wealth y, the sustainable level of labour demand is

$$n^{d'} = sy/w. \tag{8.29}$$

This constraint need not be binding, in which case the equilibrium is determined exactly as before. But, where it is binding, the equality of (8.3) and (8.29) gives the equilibrium

$$w^e_4 = (a_1 + (a_1{}^2 + 4(a_2 - a_1)sy)^{1/2})/2 \tag{8.30}$$

$$n^e_4 = sy/w^e_4 \tag{8.31}$$

which, in the special case $a_1 = 0$, reduces to

$$w^e_4 = (a_2 s)^{1/2} \tag{8.32}$$

$$n^e_4 = (sy/a_2)^{1/2}. \tag{8.33}$$

The equilibrium is illustrated in Figure 8.5. To simplify the figure, monitoring problems connected with supervision and leadership have been ignored. This is not a serious omission, for, although supervision costs may determine *whether* the capital constraint is binding, they do not determine wages or employment *given that it is*. The equilibrium is determined at the intersection E_4 of the capital constraint YY' and the supply of labour schedule A_1A_2. The equilibrium wage is OL and equilibrium employment ON_4. A pure economic rent, measured by the area of the shaded rectangle WKE_4L, accrues to the merchants as owners of capital. This is an addition to the reward they receive for risk-bearing (measured by the area of the rectangle PQ_4KW). The pure rent to capital confirms the

Figure 8.5   Competitive equilibrium with capital constraints

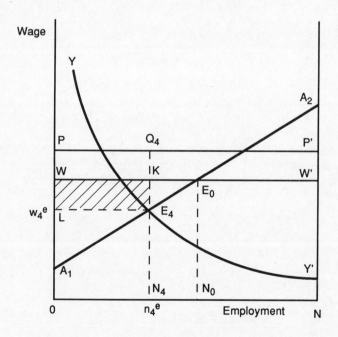

popular view (refined by Marxist economists) that access to capital, as well as tolerance of risk, explains the profits earned by the entrepreneur.

9   HETEROGENEOUS EXPECTATIONS

The preceding analysis does not really do full justice to the subjectivity of expectations emphasized by Hayek and Knight. When expectations differ it is the most optimistic, as well as the least risk-averse, who are inclined to innovate, and the ultimate distribution of income between individuals will be governed by whether or not this optimism is justified.

To capture the effect of optimism as clearly as possible it is useful to abstract from risk aversion by assuming that all merchants are risk-neutral ($b = 0$). To further simplify the analysis, supervision issues and bank lending are again ignored. Thus merchants are obliged to rely upon their own capital in guaranteeing wage payments.

With heterogeneous expectations, different merchants evaluate employment contracts using different values of π. The distribution function $F(\pi)$ specifies the proportion of all merchants whose perception of the probability of success is less than π. It is assumed that the degree of optimism, as reflected in the value of π, is distributed independently of personal wealth. This means that $F(\pi)$ can also be interpreted as the proportion of all merchant wealth in the hands of those who perceive the probability of success to be less than π.

Each merchant for whom

$$\pi \geq w/p \tag{8.34}$$

will offer employment contracts up to the limit of his wealth. Hence the total demand for labour at wage w will be

$$n^d = (sy/w)(1 - F(w/p)). \tag{8.35}$$

Assuming, for simplicity, a uniform distribution of subjective beliefs,

$$F(\pi) = \pi, \tag{8.36}$$

the demand for labour reduces to

$$n^d = sy((1/w) - (1/p)). \tag{8.37}$$

Equating demand to supply using (8.3) and (8.37) gives a rather complex expression for the equilibrium, but setting $a_1 = 0$ (that is, the labour supply schedule has zero intercept) gives the simpler results

$$w^e_5 = j((1 + (2p/j))^{1/2} - 1) \tag{8.38}$$

$$n^e_5 = (sy/2p)((1 + (2p/j))^{1/2} - 1), \tag{8.39}$$

where

$$j = a_2 sy/2p. \tag{8.40}$$

This equilibrium is illustrated in Figure 8.6. The downward-sloping demand for labour DD' reflects the heterogeneity of merchants' beliefs and the amount of wealth at their disposal. The vertical intercept of the demand curve OD is given by the price of successful output, p. Demand intersects supply OA_2 at E_5, where the marginal merchant is just sufficiently optimistic to offer the marginal worker employment in the new industry.

If optimism is justified then *ex post* the optimists earn a profit measured by the area of the rectangle PQ_5E_5X, whereas, if pessimism is appropriate,

Figure 8.6   Equilibrium with heterogeneous expectations

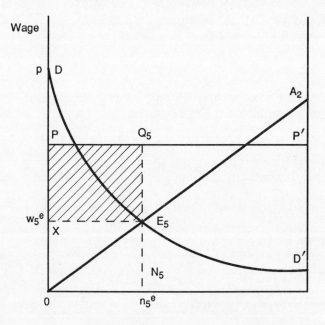

the optimists make a loss measured by the area of the rectangle OXE_5N_5 instead. The value of non-participation is, of course, zero in either case.

Let π^* once again represent the true probability of success; then it pays, on balance, to participate if

$$\pi^* \geq (j/p)((1 + (2p/j))^{1/2} - 1). \tag{8.41}$$

Thus optimists gain *ex post* if (8.41) is satisfied, but otherwise they lose. It then pays to be pessimistic simply to avoid being lured into a loss-making situation.

10 QUALITY OF JUDGEMENT AND THE SCREENING ROLE OF BANKS

It was noted in Section 3 that in the long run entrepreneurial reward will reflect quality of judgement because it is judgement that is the ultimate scarce input where decision making is concerned. A simple case of reward to judgement was illustrated in Figure 8.2, where the monopsony reward to the innovator reflects a rent to superior assessment of the probability of success. The example in Section 9 also demonstrates the point by showing how a positive reward can be obtained by relatively optimistic people whose optimism is, on average, justified.

Neither of these examples considers the most sophisticated form of judgement, though. A merchant with perfect judgement would only invest in the new industry when he knew in advance that success would occur. If merchants with perfect judgement could be identified then it would be possible to channel funds selectively in their direction.

One possibility is that banks have a skill of this kind. If they do have such skills then they may be able to mobilize workers' wealth to fund the sophisticated entrepreneurs. In particular, if banks have perfect judgement of who is a sophisticated entrepreneur, then bank investments become effectively risk-free. This means in turn that, provided banks are honest, even totally risk-averse workers can afford to leave their money on deposit with the banks.

The rent accruing to perfect judgement depends crucially upon the uniqueness of this judgement. If several individuals have perfect judgement they will always be competing against each other for the resources required to back their judgement, and the rents will accrue to the owners of resources (specifically to the owners of resources in inelastic supply) instead. This point is emphasized in Casson (1982), where it is shown that, when rents accrue to superior judgement, bargaining skills are needed to maximize the rents involved.

Suppose, therefore, that there is a single sophisticated merchant who has been identified by several banks, and that they compete to lend to him. The merchant is not constrained by problems relating to supervision and leadership, so his demand for funds is limited only by the influence of the wage on his cost of production. It is assumed that he has no personal wealth of his own.

Because the merchant is competing for labour against unsophisticated merchants he does not have absolute monopsony power. Nevertheless he is a sufficiently 'big player' for him to be able, in principle, to influence the wage. But when the capital constraint set by bank lending is quite tight, he may not wish to exploit this monopsony power. In other words, his demand for labour is constrained by the size of the 'wages fund' to below the level to which it would be reduced, in the absence of capital constraints, in order to exercise monopsony power. The size of this wages fund is determined by the workers' wealth which is on deposit with the banks.

When the capital constraint is binding the merchant will need to be sure to exercise monopsony power against the banks, though. It is assumed for simplicity that, when the banks compete, the cost of borrowing, as measured by the real rate of interest, will be bid down to zero. This zero cost reflects the fact that the merchant's perfect judgement eliminates normal business risk. It also reflects the complete confidence of the banks (and their depositors) in their judgement about the borrower's qualities. It also means that the banks are unconcerned about the fact that, in lending to someone with no personal wealth, they are fully insuring him against the consequences of a bad decision. This implies that either they have complete confidence in the borrower's integrity as well as his judgement, or they believe that the quality of his judgement is independent of the amount of deliberation and effort involved.

To exercise his monopsony power against the banks, the merchant must restrict his demand for borrowing to no more than the maximum the banks are able to lend. Otherwise he will begin to compete against himself. The rate of interest will rise until the cost of capital is so high that the merchant only just breaks even, and all the merchant's economic rent is dissipated. When the banks are in turn competing for workers' deposits, the rent will accrue to the workers instead.

The simplest case to analyse algebraically is one in which the supply of labour is infinitely elastic at a wage w^*:

$$a_1 = a_2 = w^*. \tag{8.42}$$

Provided capital constraints prevent the sophisticated merchant from hiring everyone (so that the inelastic economy-wide supply of labour constrains him) the infinite elasticity of labour supply eliminates any monopsony power. His demand for labour is determined simply by his capital constraint. He exploits his monopsony power against the banks simply by requesting no more funds than they actually have available. This means that, in effect, he voluntarily restricts his demand for funds to the value of worker's wealth.

The unsophisticated merchants, it is assumed, have heterogeneous expectations, as in Section 9, which they back using their personal wealth. Banks do not lend to unsophisticated merchants, and unsophisticated merchants do not put wealth on deposit with the banks. (It is easy to relax this assumption by supposing that those who choose not to participate at the wage w^* will deposit their funds with the banks instead.) The profitability of merchants' participation is not affected by the option of investing in bank deposits so long as bank deposits earn a zero return, so the demand for labour from unsophisticated merchants is exactly the same as before.

Given the elastic labour supply, the total demand for labour is also the equilibrium employment. It is readily deduced that equilibrium employment is

$$n^{e_6} = (s(1 - (w^*/p)) + (1 - s)\beta)(y/w^*), \tag{8.43}$$

where $\beta = 1$ if the next new industry project will be successful and $\beta = 0$ otherwise. The first component of (8.43) represents the familiar demand from unsophisticated merchants with heterogeneous expectations and the second component the demand from the sophisticated one.

The equilibrium is illustrated in Figure 8.7. (If the new industry is going to be unsuccessful, then the sophisticated merchant does not participate and so the equilibrium is the same as in Figure 8.6.) When the sophisticated merchant does participate, he enters the labour market with a demand $D_2 D_2'$ determined by his borrowing constraint. (In the absence of a borrowing constraint his demand would be infinitely elastic at a wage OD_1, as indicated by the schedule $D_1 F$). His demand is superimposed on the demand from unsophisticated merchants $D_1 D_1'$ (corresponding to the schedule DD' in Figure 8.6) giving an aggregate demand for labour, obtained by horizontal summation, $D_2 D_3$.

The infinitely elastic labour supply to the new industry is represented by the schedule $A_1 A_2$. Equilibrium employment is determined at the intersection E_6 of $D_2 D_3$ and $A_1 A_2$. Employment offered by unsophisticated merchants is ON_u and by the sophisticated merchant ON_s. Profit per employee for the sophisticated merchant is measured by QM, and his total profit is measured by the area of the shaded rectangle $D_1 QMA_1$.

Given an expected frequency of successful outcomes π^*, the ability to avoid all loss-making through perfect judgement produces an expected reward per employee $\pi^*(p - w)$, compared to the equivalent reward $\pi^*p - w$ earned by an ordinary optimist and a zero reward earned by a pessimist. The premium attributable to perfect judgement compared to ordinary optimism is therefore $w(1 - \pi^*)$ per employee.

11 THE WIDER ISSUES

In the analysis of banking it was assumed that banks have a reputation for selecting entrepreneurial projects with unerring judgement. This implies that only those individuals with demonstrably perfect judgement can borrow from banks because banks can screen out everyone else. This in turn implies that entrepreneurial failures occur only because merchants who have personal wealth can avoid screening by banks. This is, of course, a very extreme view, which is untenable in practice. Banks do, of course, lend to entrepreneurs with less than perfect judgement, and occasionally serious banking failures do occur. The analysis nevertheless highlights some significant issues. In particular:

Figure 8.7   Equilibrium with a sophisticated merchant financed by the banking system

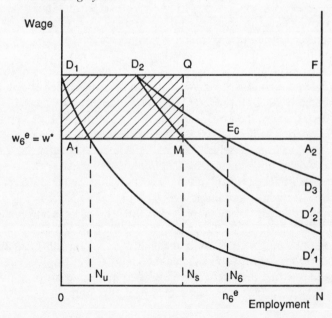

1. What determines the quality of entrepreneurial judgement? Are some entrepreneurs systematically better than others, or is better than average performance simply the result of a run of good luck?
2. If there are systematic factors promoting good judgement, is it possible to identify these factors in order to single out talented entrepreneurs? Can entrepreneurial potential be developed through suitable training and life-experience?
3. Is there any reason to believe that banks are better at making lending decisions than ordinary individuals? Is it really advantageous for individuals to deposit funds for banks to re-lend, rather than to lend themselves – for example, through direct investment in equities?

Casson (1982) argues that good judgement is partly a product of life-experience. A wide range of employment experience, based on a career 'spiral' through varied jobs of increasing difficulty, is useful in giving the entrepreneur practice in synthesizing information from diverse sources. Migration may also provide a similar kind of varied experience.

Personality is important, too. A high degree of confidence helps the entrepreneur to cope with the stresses of decision making, whilst perseverance and ascetic life-style may be useful in surviving setbacks. Where high-level entrepreneurship is concerned, a rational scientific systems view is useful as well.

High norms encourage achievement. People with low norms may perceive few problems and so develop few skills in decision making. The moral content of norms is particularly important, as the discussion of leadership in Section 7 indicated. An entrepreneur with a reputation for personal integrity is more likely to be looked up to as an employer, and to receive information freely from his employees. He is also more likely to be trusted by lenders, and to find access to capital easier.

This suggests that education can improve entrepreneurship both by providing technical instruction – showing how to cope with complexity by adopting a 'systems view', for example – and by instilling moral values. It is sometimes suggested that the cultivation of individualism is an important moral factor, but this needs to be qualified by the fact that entrepreneurs frequently need to operate in a group situation. They not only need to lead social groups, such as teams of production workers, but also to participate in groups alongside political leaders, bankers and other entrepreneurs – for example, in coordinating national industrial policies. Excessive individualism can disrupt such group behaviour. What really seems to be required is an ethic of *voluntary association*, a willingness to choose between alternative group affiliations, but to develop commitment and loyalty to a group once it has been joined.

It is quite possible, in principle, to screen for qualities of this kind. Life histories can be obtained and checked (a common recruitment procedure), attitudes can be sampled through interview, and even participation in simulated problem situations can be invoked. The main danger is that the candidate knows the qualities being screened for and can outwit the assessor. Such astuteness is by no means universal, however. Moreover the problem may not be so acute as it seems, since the ability to discover and then impersonate the qualities other people want is a kind of entrepreneurial ability itself.

One obvious reason why banks may develop expertise in screening is that they have a wide range of relevant experience. Although a bank may lack technical expertise in the area in which the entrepreneur has formulated his project, it may be able to substitute personality assessment for assessment of the project itself (Harper, 1990). Repeated use of personality assessment may allow bank managers to form quite sophisticated judgements about borrowers. Equity investors, by contrast, normally have to rely on media commentaries and annual reports for their information, although professional investors may use stockbrokers' reports as well. Thus the view that bank deposits are safer than equity investments because they benefit from access to greater expertise may well be true. Moreover bank investments are more likely to be protected by government rescue in the event of failure than are personal equity stakes.

12   CONCLUSION

Some of the greatest thinkers in the social sciences – Cantillon, Hayek, Knight and Schumpeter, amongst others – have contributed to the development of the economic theory of the entrepreneur. Until recently the theory has been articulated mainly in verbal terms. This chapter has attempted to show how many of the insights can be captured in a simple model. As with all economic models, drastic simplifications are made in order to purify the analysis of all but the key effects. The model is nevertheless sufficiently versatile to encompass several important dimensions of entrepreneurship.

It has been argued that the key service supplied by entrepreneurs is quality of judgement. A capacity for absolutely correct judgement is often unique, and affords monopoly or monopsony rents to the entrepreneur. Other successful entrepreneurs may simply be individuals disposed to optimism in a situation where optimism is on balance justified. Optimists who are willing to venture their own capital can, on average, earn a profit because pessimists do not compete with them for the use of resources.

Even where expectations are homogeneous, entrepreneurs can earn a reward because of their greater tolerance of risk. In the model above, the expected reward of the marginal entrepreneur is just sufficient to compensate him for the risk involved.

In an idealized world entrepreneurial ideas could simply be licensed through competitive bidding to other people who would exploit them. But the limitations of the patent system are such that the licensing of ideas is impracticable. Entrepreneurs must exploit their own ideas, and this draws them into the management of teams. The firm comes into being as a nexus of contracts, notably, though not exclusively, contracts of employment. The entrepreneur must choose between leadership and supervision as a method of motivating the firm's employees. The entrepreneur becomes more than just a speculator or arbitrager – he becomes a leader and a manager as well.

It has been emphasised that the model developed in this chapter is a very flexible one. It is, therefore, a suitable tool for the entrepreneurial academic who wishes to adapt it to analyse issues besides the ones addressed here. It is particularly suitable for researchers in the recently revitalized areas of small firm growth, industrial policy, and international competitiveness, as well as for scholars seeking stronger intellectual foundations for business and economic history. It is therefore to be hoped that further extensions of the model will be developed in due course.

9. Oligopoly Pricing: Time-varying Conduct and the Influence of Product Durability as an Element of Market Structure

Ian Domowitz

---

1 INTRODUCTION

The student of oligopoly faces a bewildering array of issues. Important sub-topics include entry deterrence, degree of product differentiation, non-cooperative output, pricing, and investment policies, and the relationship between collusion and information structure.[1] To complicate matters, appropriate research methodologies in the field have themselves become an issue.[2] There is no single or dominant 'theory of oligopoly' even to the extent of providing a unifying framework for empirical study, as noted by Fisher (1989).

Nevertheless, within whatever boundaries are imposed for theoretical discussion, oligopoly theory should provide predictions with respect to the relationship between market structure, firm conduct and performance, as measured by the behaviour of prices and price–cost margins (Shapiro, 1989b). This chapter is devoted to the empirical analysis of such behaviour at the industry level, adopting a set of rather eclectic views along the way.

Even those who argue the value of game theory in the analysis of oligopoly pricing in particular, and industry behaviour more generally, agree that game-theoretic analysis teaches the importance of the context within which a firm must operate. Strategic behaviour in terms of investment that affects costs and tactical behaviour in terms of pricing do not occur in a vacuum. The latter is well understood even in the context of one-shot static games, while the former demands some dynamic structure. At the level of an industry, the state of the macroeconomy forms an important part of the environment, in addition to individual industry and regional demand conditions.[3] One focus of this chapter is on empirical predictions of dynamic games that purport to shed light on the cyclical

214

behaviour of prices and associated price-cost margins in industries with varying degrees of market power.

Attributing observed departures of price from marginal cost to generic descriptions of 'imperfect competition' or 'market power' can be seriously misleading.[4] Stiglitz (1984), for example, provides explanations of positive mark-ups in perfectly competitive settings that depend on effects ranging from changing elasticities of demand over the business cycle to imperfect information with respect to product quality. The degree of rigidity of prices and mark-ups and the nature of the cyclical effect are traceable to changes in the elasticity of demand in the first case and to increases in the real rate of interest in the second. Another potential determinant of price rigidities and cyclical behaviour is the second focus of this chapter, namely differences in the durability of goods as an important additional element of market structure in explaining inter-industry differences in mark-up cyclicality and price rigidity.[5] There are no theoretical counterparts to the oligopoly supergame models that motivate the first look at the cyclical behaviour of mark-ups in this examination of differences in performance across durable and non-durable goods sectors.[6] The approach taken here is unabashedly empirical, and it is hoped that the results presented will be a stimulus to further theoretical work in the area.

It is found that price rigidity and the cyclicality of both prices and the mark-up of price over marginal cost strongly depend upon conduct in the form of tacitly collusive behaviour on the part of oligopolies. The degree of price rigidity and both the degree and direction of cyclicality of prices and mark-ups vary with market structure in the sense of durable versus non-durable goods production, and this effect is independent of industry conduct. Explanations of the first set of results are to be found within dynamic oligopoly pricing theory, but such theory is silent with respect to the durable/non-durable goods distinctions found in the data.

The focus on the empirical investigation of the implications of repeated games and the role of durability precludes discussion of some other game-theoretic based empirical work on oligopoly pricing, in part because of space constraints, but also on philosophical grounds.[7] The basic quarrel is not simply over the value of industry 'case' studies as opposed to inter-industry investigations (for example, Bresnahan, 1989), but over the value of empirical conclusions based on static one-shot game formulations. Even in his defence of the value of game-theoretic reasoning in industrial organization against Fisher's (1989) attack, Shapiro (1989a) labels static theory as a straw man and says that 'the whole point ... is that static models are inadequate'. Papers purporting to differentiate between possible game forms played by firms in an industry or to test conduct (for example, monopoly behaviour versus Cournot) are predicated almost exclusively on restrictions based on static equilibrium.[8] Time-series data often are used without regard for possible equilibrium dynamics or for potential non-stationarity in the industry environment.[9]

This chapter begins with a discussion of three oligopoly pricing models that have implications for time-varying conduct in response to changes in economic conditions. The predictions of the three models agree as to the feasibility of promotion and maintenance of tacitly collusive pricing behaviour, but differ with respect to the cyclical nature of prices and mark-ups. One model also links rigidities with cyclical behaviour. Mark-ups of price over marginal cost are examined in Section 3, modelling the mark-ups themselves as unobservable time-varying parameters in a simple production-function setting. Prices are examined directly in Section 4 in the context of a simple mark-up model with dynamic adjustment. It is possible to examine nominal price rigidities directly in such a context, and the resolution of the behaviour of mark-ups with that of prices is discussed in the context of the three models which motivate the work presented here.

2   COLLUSION, CYCLICALITY AND RIGIDITIES IN OLIGOPOLY SUPERGAMES

The importance of dynamics in the problem of tacit collusion by a group of oligopolists has been recognized since Stigler (1964) examined the relationship between information and collusion.[10] Modern theory has formalized oligopolistic interaction over time as a study of stationary environments in which agents play a repeated game over an infinite number of periods.[11] Such games are called supergames, and agents set price or output in each of the repeated games in such a way as to respond to rivals' choices. History matters basically because the individual participants decide that it should and condition actions upon past developments.[12] This view of the importance of history in repeated games stems directly from the stationarity of the environment in which each game is played. In a world in which there is no change in the competitive environment, feasible strategies and expected payoffs are identical at each stage of the supergame.

Supergames in such stationary environments have proved to be ideal for the analysis of tacit collusion on the part of oligopolists. The ability of oligopolists to maintain a tacitly collusive scheme in which profits are elevated above non-cooperative levels depends on the ability to detect defections from such an 'agreement' and credibly punish firms that deviate. The fundamental conclusions from analysis of oligopoly supergames are simple to state.[13] Collusive outcomes can be sustained as non-cooperative equilibria if the oligopolists do not discount future payoffs too much. Strategies that bring about such outcomes specify that any defecting firm be punished, generally by having other firms in the industry revert to a non-cooperative strategy for some period of time (possibly forever). The scope for tacit collusion is greatest when oligopolists can quickly (and with certainty) observe defections of rivals. Supergames in stationary environments reveal that collusive outcomes are equilibria independent of economic conditions (such as demand) and the number of firms, so long as detection of cheating and rapid punishment are possible. Thus the lower 'threatened punishment' prices are never observed.

These results depend heavily on the stationarity of the economic environment and the stability of industry conduct patterns. The problem of tacit collusion is much more interesting in the more realistic case of changing environmental conditions. From a policy perspective, models capable of explaining oligopoly pricing over the business cycle and with respect to demand shifts are of particular interest.

One such model is the trigger strategy formulation of Green and Porter (1984).[14] In their quantity-setting supergame model, firms cannot observe the level of industry demand perfectly in each period or stage of the game, nor can a firm perfectly observe the output choice of competitors. Shifting demand makes it difficult to discriminate between unexpected drops in demand, say, and cheating on the part of firms. The model posits discrete shifts in conduct between collusive and non-cooperative pricing regimes, via a trigger strategy. If the market price remains above the tacitly agreed-upon trigger price at the time production decisions are made, firms produce at a collusive level. If the price drops below the trigger price, all firms agree to revert to a static Cournot equilibrium for some period of time. Any firm which considers a secret expansion of output above the collusive level must trade off immediate profit gains against the increased probability that the market price may fall below the trigger price, increasing the likelihood of an industry reversion and lowering profits. Reversionary episodes could occur simply because of low demand, however. Porter (1983) uses this formulation to study the behaviour of the Joint Executive Committee, a cartel that controlled freight shipments from the East Coast of the United States at the end of the nineteenth century.

The Green-Porter model offers a testable prediction concerning the cyclical behaviour of prices and price–cost margins, although it was not meant to explain cyclical behaviour. Output is fixed unless a reversion occurs, and if all demand shocks are unobservable, prices and margins should be procyclical. Permitting partial responses with respect to output, that is, allowing output to be mildly procyclical, would not change this basic prediction. Domowitz, Hubbard and Petersen (1987a) note that, while changes in cost are not considered in the Green–Porter formulation, economy-wide inflation should not affect the collusive output level, so long as the nominal level of the trigger price is updated, Shocks which increase costs will reduce profit margins until the collusive output is updated, but prices will continue to be procyclical.[15]

The goal of Rotemberg and Saloner (1986) explicitly is to explain oligopoly pricing and price-cost margin behaviour over the business cycle. Tacit collusion in their supergame model takes place in the presence of observable temporary shifts in demand. Shocks to demand are serially uncorrelated; thus demand conditions carry no information about the future. Firm payoffs are non-stationary because of these shocks. Since the shocks are observable, decisions are made based on known states of demand. In periods of high demand, firms agree to choose a price low enough for the rewards from defection to be sufficiently reduced to keep cooperation the optimal strategy. The most difficult time to maintain collusion is during a boom period, because the discounted loss from cheating is independent of current demand (serially uncorrelated shocks), which in turn implies that the gain from defection is increasing in the level of current demand.

The empirical implication of the Rotemberg–Saloner analysis is that oligopolies reduce the spread between price and marginal cost to lower the per unit gain from cheating during booms. Price-cost margins are counter-cyclical. If marginal cost is procyclical, prices are countercyclical as well.[16]

An important feature of business cycle analysis is that future demand depends to some extent on current demand. The assumption of serially uncorrelated demand shocks in the Rotemberg–Saloner supergame is not innocuous. The properties of collusive pricing over the business cycle when demand is subject to cyclical movements are investigated by Halti-wanger and Harrington (1991). The pricing strategy profile calls for pricing at collusive levels (characterized as a price path), with deviations punished by reversion to single-period Nash equilibrium strategies. As in other supergame models, the authors find that the joint profit-maximizing outcome can be sustained as a subgame perfect equilibrium if the discount factor is sufficiently high, but they also reach an interesting additional conclusion relevant to pricing over the cycle: collusion is much more difficult to sustain in an environment in which demand is subject to cyclical variations relative to a stationary environment. In contrast to Rotemberg and Saloner, Haltiwanger and Harrington find that the most difficult time to collude is during what is typically classified as a recession.

Unlike the Rotemberg–Saloner model, such a finding does not pin down the cyclicality of prices or price-cost margins in a model with cyclical demand. Cyclical pricing by firms depends on the cyclical behaviour of the joint profit-maximizing price path and the degree to which firms discount future payoffs. Simulation results presented by Haltiwanger and Harrington suggest that price behaviour is not simply characterized with respect to cyclicality, and also show some evidence of price rigidity in periods of falling demand. An interesting feature of some of the simulation evidence is maintenance of procyclical profits in the face of countercyclical prices that sustain the collusive outcome.

Their results do provide some guidance for empirical investigations of the behaviour of prices and mark-ups over the cycle, however. In addition to indicators of current demand, their analysis strongly emphasizes the potential importance of a measure of future demand as a determinant of the intertemporal price path. They correctly note that such measures have been left out of previous empirical studies. The degree of market concentration is predicted to result in more procyclical pricing. Price rigidity is expected to have the same effect. Higher industry growth rates are also identified as potential contributors to more procyclical pricing behaviour.[17] I now turn to the provision of some empirical evidence on these points.

3 PRICE—COST MARGINS AT THE INDUSTRY LEVEL

Answers to the questions raised above as to oligopoly pricing and mark-up behaviour over the cycle, and to the simple question as to whether observed mark-ups reflect collusive behaviour in terms of magnitude alone, obviously require a measure of the mark-up. Standard price–cost margins calculated from census data are defined with respect to average variable cost, $(P - AVC)/P$, not with respect to marginal cost as required.[18] It is a feature of the 'new empirical industrial organization' literature (Bresnahan, 1989) to disregard accounting measures of the price-cost margin and to treat it as an unobservable to be estimated.

There are, of course, no data on marginal costs for industries. Hall (1988) has suggested a method for estimating the mark-up of price over marginal cost by examining cyclical fluctuations in total factor productivity. This approach is used here, taking into account the extensions suggested by Domowitz, Hubbard and Petersen (1988).

Consider a simple production function in which, for the ith industry in period t, output Q is produced with constant returns to scale from capital K and labour L according to

$$Q_{it} = A_{it} e^{\gamma_i} K_{it} f(L_{it}/K_{it}), \tag{9.1}$$

where γ represents the rate of Hicks-neutral technical progress and A represents a productivity shock.

As noted originally by Solow (1957), if price equals marginal cost and the marginal product of labour equals the real wage, the percentage change in $A (\Delta a)$ can be measured from the data. Let $q = \ln (Q/K)$, and let $l = \ln (L/K)$. The Solow residual is

$$\Delta a_{it} = \Delta q_{it} - \alpha_{Lit}\Delta l_{it} - \gamma_i, \tag{9.2}$$

where α_L represents the labour share in the value of output.

If price exceeds marginal cost, so that the ratio of price to marginal cost is $1/(1 - \beta)$, then (9.2) can be rewritten as

$$\Delta a_{it} = \Delta q_{it} - (1 - \beta)^{-1}\alpha_{Lit}\Delta l_{it} - \gamma_i. \tag{9.3}$$

Hence

$$\Delta q_{it} - \alpha_{Lit}\Delta l_{it} = \gamma_i(1 - \beta) + \beta_i\Delta q_{it} + (1 - \beta_i)\Delta a_{it}. \tag{9.4}$$

It is assumed that the true productivity shock Δa is uncorrelated with aggregate fluctuations.[19] With this identifying assumption, procyclical movements in the Solow residual are generated when $\beta > 0$, that is, when price exceeds marginal cost.

This estimate of the mark-up of price over marginal cost excludes materials in the calculation of marginal cost. If materials' use changes in strict proportion to output, the formula governing the relationship between the ratio of price to marginal cost based on value added (β) and the true mark-up (β^*) is such that

$$\beta^* = \beta(1 - \alpha_M), \tag{9.5}$$

where α_M is the materials share in the value of output.

Let M denote materials, so that $m = \ln (M/K)$. Then

$$\Delta q_{it} - \alpha_{Lit}\Delta l_{it} - \alpha_{Mit}\Delta m_{it} = \gamma_i(1 - \beta^*_i) + \beta^*_i\Delta q_{it} + (1 - \beta^*_i)\Delta a_{it}. \tag{9.6}$$

The parameter β^* is allowed to vary with the level of demand, so that

$$\beta^*_{it} = \bar{\beta}^* + \beta_1 x_t, \tag{9.7}$$

where x is an aggregate demand variable–capacity utilization in manufacturing in the applications considered here.[20]

There are two important issues to be faced in the estimation of equations (9.6) and (9.7). The first concerns the data to be used. The full set of data available is a panel data base of 284 four-digit census manufacturing industries in the United States for the period 1958–81, as described in Domowitz, Hubbard and Petersen (1986a, 1986b). In order to approximate the structural characteristics of the markets modelled by Green–Porter, Rotemberg–Saloner and Haltiwanger–Harrington, a sub-sample of 57 industries is selected; Table II of Domowitz, Hubbard and Petersen (1987a) contains a complete listing. The common characteristics of these industries are: (1) they are 'producer goods' industries;[21] (2) they have been recognized as census industries at least since 1958; (3) they have four-firm (adjusted) concentration ratios above 0.50 in 1972;[22] and (4) they are not listed as 'miscellaneous' or 'not elsewhere classified'. The object of this selection procedure is to examine mature, homogeneous-goods oligopolies operating in well-defined markets. For ease of reference below, this set of industries will be referred to as the 'trigger-strategy group'. The availability of longitudinal data for this group (and for the full sample as well) has a distinct advantage over standard cross-sectional data sets used in most previous work. The omission of individual industry effects not captured by the available information set can bias coefficient estimates and provide misleading results. Unobservable time-invariant industry differences are removed here using a fixed-effects estimator.

The second problem concerns the obvious simultaneity of Δq in equation (9.6) describing the movement of the Solow residual. An instrumental-variables procedure is required, and under the assumption of no common element to productivity disturbances across industries, an aggregate demand variable such as real GNP growth could be used. The use of such an instrument would be invalidated by the phenomenon of 'real business cycles', in which industry productivity movements would be considered highly correlated because of common real shocks. The estimation procedure here employs current and lagged values of the rate of growth of real military purchases as exogenous aggregate instrumental variables.[23] The use of this set of instrumental variables does not require assumptions incompatible with the real business cycle view.

Estimates of equation (9.6) using (9.7) to define the mark-up of price over marginal cost are presented in Table 9.1. The trigger-strategy group has been further partitioned into 'high margin' and 'low margin' industries based on census data.[24] It might be expected that the high-margin industries are most likely to behave in a collusive fashion. As should be the case, parametric estimates of average margins differ radically across the two groups, providing a check on the methodology used here.[25]

It is first of some interest to ask whether average margins ever approach collusive levels. Price reversions in the supergames above are generally to the Cournot level, although Haltiwanger and Harrison predict even more drastic price cuts. In Domowitz, Hubbard and Petersen (1987a) collusive levels were interpreted strictly as price–cost margins in monopoly, and comparisons of Cournot and monopoly margins were made across different levels of the Herfindahl index and elasticities of demand. Elasticities must be quite high for the monopoly price–cost margin to be less than 0.5, while a margin in the Cournot case cannot credibly exceed 0.30. A comparison of such figures with census margins resulted in the suggestion that collusive behaviour in US manufacturing industries was unlikely.

A different conclusion emerges from the results reported here. First of all, collusive behaviour in the real world may not permit fully profit-maximizing monopoly outcomes for a variety of reasons. Observing margins above 0.30, but somewhat below 0.50, can still be an indication of collusive behaviour. The implied (average) margin for the group most likely to exhibit tacit collusion is 0.423. This figure is statistically significantly different at any reasonable level from the average price–cost margin of the remainder of the trigger-strategy sample, measured at 0.283, within the Cournot range.

The results in Table 9.1 also indicate that margins for the high-margin concentrated industries are strongly procyclical, providing support for the implications of the Green–Porter model. Examination of the Haltiwanger–Harrington model requires the addition of expectations to the estimating equation. Results incorporating expected future capacity utilization are reported in Table 9.2.[26] Margins again are found to be

Table 9.1   Concentration, strategic behaviour and cyclical movements in margins (I)

Industries	x	Δq	$x\Delta q$	$\bar{R}^2$	Implied margin
C4A > 0.50, low margin	0.011 (0.019)	0.142 (0.219)	0.170 (0.288)	0.840	0.283
C4A > 0.50, high margin	−0.017 (0.014)	0.225 (0.090)	0.238 (0.115)	0.921	0.423
C4A > 0.50, high margin, non-durables	−0.016 (0.014)	0.082 (0.146)	0.407 (0.185)	0.923	0.421
C4A > 0.50, high margin, durables	−0.017 (0.024)	0.430 (0.073)	−0.004 (0.090)	0.919	0.427

Note: The equations were estimated using instrumental variables, as described in the text. Heteroskedasticity-consistent standard errors are in parentheses. The estimation interval was 1958 to 1981.

procyclical for the high-margin group, although the standard errors are now a bit larger.

It is the set of non-durable goods industries that accounts for this procyclical result, however.[27] This observation is evident in both tables and, therefore, does not rely on expectational considerations in any primary fashion. Point estimates for collusive durable goods industries indicate countercyclical behaviour of the price–cost margin, but the standard errors are large enough for us to infer an acyclical mark-up for durables. The large standard errors may be explained in part by the fact that the durable goods sector is a relatively small sample in this data set. A statistical test of the equality of cyclical effects across durable and non-durable classifications clearly rejects the null hypothesis of equality, despite the high standard error associated with the durables' countercyclical effect.

None of the models discussed can really address this distinction in cyclical behaviour. They must be considered to be models of non-durable goods in the sense that they do not differentiate between implicit rental and sales prices of a durable good.[28] The distinction between rental and sales prices for durable goods implies that transitory demand disturbances will have smaller effects on output prices and margins in the durables sector. Implications of this effect for price rigidity are examined in the next section.

Bils (1987) examines durable goods pricing in the context of monopolistic competition. His model explicitly predicts procyclical mark-ups for non-durable goods and that mark-ups for durable goods are more likely to be countercyclical. His arguments relate more to consumer behaviour

Table 9.2 Concentration, strategic behaviour and cyclical movements in margins (II)

Industries	x	Δq	$x\Delta q$	Ex	$\bar{R}^2$	Implied margin
C4A > 0.50, low margin	0.022	0.123	0.196	−0.023	0.838	0.286
	(0.041)	(0.254)	(0.334)	(0.057)		
C4A > 0.50, high margin	−0.047	0.269	0.173	0.064	0.918	0.413
	(0.028)	(0.089)	(0.116)	(0.042)		
C4A > 0.50, high margin, non-durables	−0.053	0.135	0.330	0.077	0.919	0.410
	(0.027)	(0.134)	(0.171)	(0.048)		
C4A > 0.50, high margin, durables	−0.030	0.454	−0.040	0.033	0.917	0.421
	(0.043)	(0.116)	(0.153)	(0.078)		

Note: The equations were estimated using fixed effects and instrumental variables, as described in the text. Heteroskedasticity-consistent standard errors are in parentheses. The estimation interval was 1958 to 1981.

than to strategic firm rivalry, but the theory is consistent with the empirical results presented here.

Murphy, Shleifer and Vishny (1989) present a model that rationalizes the interpretation of the large standard error on the durables' countercyclical effect as evidence of acyclicality. Again there is no strategic rivalry involved and the results stem from the durability of the good produced, and the assumption that productivity is high at high industry output and low at low industry output, while no individual firm has market power. In their model, the implicit rental rate of the durable is indeed countercyclical. The price of the good is the discounted sum of future rental rates, however. At the peak of a boom, all future rental rates are higher than the current rate. This implies that the price of a durable reaches a low sometime before a peak and then begins to rise. Empirically this effect should mitigate any cyclical movements in observed mark-ups.

Since these theories pertain to settings beyond tacitly collusive behaviour in a supergame context, it is of some interest to examine the robustness of these cyclical findings with a larger sample. The full sample of 284 manufacturing industries is the basis of the results reported in Tables 9.3 and 9.4. Overall mark-ups are procyclical, but the addition of expectations of future demand in Table 9.4 mitigates the degree of procyclical behaviour both economically and statistically. The distinction between results with and without expectations narrows greatly, however, for the case of non-durable goods, in which procyclical mark-up behaviour is pronounced. The degree of procyclicality of mark-ups increases with industry concentration, overall and for non-durable goods. This effect has been noted previously in various studies by Domowitz, Hubbard and Petersen, and is one of the predictions of the Haltiwanger–Harrington model.

Finally, procyclicality of mark-ups is traceable to non-durable goods industries. Since this effect is robust to the inclusion of an additional 227 industries to the trigger-strategy sample, this evidence is consistent with the work of Bils (1987) on monopolistic competition. Furthermore, point estimates for concentrated durable goods industries indicate countercyclical behaviour but again with large standard errors. Unconcentrated industries producing durables exhibit acyclical mark-ups.

4   DURABILITY, NOMINAL RIGIDITY AND CYCLICAL PRICE ADJUSTMENT

An assessment of the cyclical behaviour of prices themselves provides interesting complementary evidence and offers some new testable hypotheses. The relative rigidity of prices is of interest in both industrial organization and macroeconomics. There is some evidence, for example, that price rigidity increases with the degree of concentration in the market.[29] This is counter-intuitive in simple oligopoly pricing models, as noted, for example, by Carlton (1989). As the market becomes more concentrated, static oligopoly models would suggest that the industry group behave more like a monopolist; rigid prices are not a property of monopoly in general. On the other hand, the maintenance of collusive arrangements by non-cooperative equilibria such as those in the three models examined here may entail price rigidities. Hall (1987) presents a related two-sector equilibrium model in which competitive and non-competitive sectors producing different goods coexist. Prices are shown to be more rigid in the non-competitive sector.

Lack of price flexibility has implications for the magnitude of mark-ups and for their cyclical movement as well. Stiglitz (1984) shows that price rigidities may themselves account for positive price–cost margins even in perfectly competitive settings. Rotemberg and Summers (1987) consider a model in which exogenously specified price rigidity accounts for

Table 9.3 Market structure, durability and cyclical movements in margins (I)

Industries	x	Δq	$x\Delta q$	$\bar{R}^2$	Implied margin
All industries	-0.010	0.256	0.136	0.876	0.361
	(0.012)	(0.063)	(0.083)		
Non-durable goods	-0.010	0.199	0.188	0.862	0.355
	(0.011)	(0.078)	(0.101)		
Durable goods	-0.018	0.331	0.085	0.921	0.402
	(0.018)	(0.019)	(0.077)		
C4A < 0.50	-0.010	0.341	0.019	0.874	0.357
	(0.012)	(0.091)	(0.118)		
C4A > 0.50	-0.011	0.121	0.321	0.880	0.388
	(0.015)	(0.094)	(0.121)		
C4A < 0.50, non-durables	-0.011	0.332	0.016	0.857	0.345
	(0.125)	(0.103)	(0.013)		
C4A > 0.50, non-durables	-0.008	-0.021	0.476	0.872	0.375
	(0.014)	(0.013)	(0.162)		
C4A < 0.50, durables	-0.015	0.289	0.120	0.933	0.389
	(0.017)	(0.083)	(0.109)		
C4A > 0.50, durables	-0.031	0.445	-0.024	0.909	0.425
	(0.020)	(0.073)	(0.093)		

Note: The equations were estimated using instrumental variables, as described in the text. Heteroskedasticity-consistent standard errors are in parentheses. The estimation interval was 1958 to 1981.

procyclical movements in productivity, also leading to a positive average mark-up of price over marginal cost. In the context of the oligopoly pricing models considered in this chapter, the Haltiwanger–Harrington model posits greater procyclicality in mark-ups as prices become less flexible. This is a testable implication and is examined below.

A simple dynamic mark-up model of pricing is used to examine some of these themes and to examine differences across industry structure, with special attention now to the distinction between durables and non-durables sectors. Let P denote the industry output price and let C be unit variable cost. The rate of change of industry price is modelled as an adjustment towards target price changes according to

$$\Delta p_{it} = \omega \Delta p^*_{it} + (1 - \omega)\Delta p_{it-1}, \tag{9.8}$$

where lower-case variables denote logarithms, the asterisk denotes the target, and i and t represent the industry and time period, respectively. Such a formulation is consistent with the adjustment mechanism obtained from a problem in which firms maximize the value of the difference

Table 9.4   Market structure, durability and cyclical movements in margins (II)

Industries	x	Δq	$x\Delta q$	Ex	$\bar{R}^2$	Implied margin
All industries	−0.037	0.287	0.090	0.056	0.876	0.362
	(0.022)	(0.070)	(0.091)	(0.031)		
Non-durable goods	−0.041	0.234	0.139	0.062	0.861	0.350
	(0.025)	(0.071)	(0.092)	(0.031)		
Durable goods	−0.030	0.349	0.059	0.028	0.921	0.398
	(0.030)	(0.081)	(0.107)	(0.047)		
C4A < 0.50	−0.037	0.367	−0.017	0.055	0.874	0.353
	(0.024)	(0.099)	(0.130)	(0.033)		
C4A > 0.50	−0.033	0.154	0.273	0.042	0.880	0.381
	(0.026)	(0.084)	(0.111)	(0.032)		
C4A < 0.50, non-durables	−0.039	0.355	−0.016	0.055	0.857	0.342
	(0.024)	(0.107)	(0.138)	(0.034)		
C4A > 0.50, non-durables	−0.039	0.032	0.400	0.064	0.871	0.365
	(0.020)	(0.097)	(0.126)	(0.031)		
C4A < 0.50, durables	−0.028	0.313	0.087	0.037	0.933	0.385
	(0.026)	(0.092)	(0.122)	(0.042)		
C4A > 0.50, durables	−0.028	0.441	−0.018	−0.007	0.908	0.426
	(0.042)	(0.091)	(0.122)	(0.068)		

Note: The equations were estimated using fixed effects and instrumental variables, as described in the text. Heteroskedasticity-consistent standard errors are in parentheses. The estimation interval was 1958 to 1981.

between revenues from sales and the sum of production and price adjust-ment costs (for example, Rotemberg, 1982).

The target output price is given by a mark-up over unit variable costs,

$$P^*_{it} = (1 + \lambda_{it})C_{it}, \tag{9.9}$$

in which the mark-up, λ, may vary over industries and over time. Trans-forming (9.9) into logarithms and differencing, the target growth rate is approximated by

$$\Delta p^*_{it} = \Delta \lambda_{it} + \Delta c_{it}.^{30} \tag{9.10}$$

The mark-up is allowed to vary with the state of demand, as in the last section. A time trend is added in the formulation of the mark-up equation here, consistent with the results in Domowitz, Hubbard and Petersen (1986b):[31]

$$\lambda_{it} = \gamma_0 + \gamma_1 x_t + \gamma_2 t + \eta_{it}, \tag{9.11}$$

where η is assumed to be an industry-specific unobservable with a unit root. Combining (9.8), (9.10) and (9.11) yields the estimating equation

$$\Delta p_{it} = \alpha_0 + \alpha_1 \Delta p_{it-1} + \alpha_2 \Delta c_{it} + \alpha_3 \Delta x_t + e_{it}, \tag{9.12}$$

in which the coefficients are obvious combinations of the parameters in (9.8) and (9.11). These restrictions are not imposed in the empirical work reported here, entailing some loss in efficiency. Although differencing removes any fixed-cost component that may inadvertently enter into the computation of variable cost, the measure of cost is still not perfect and a (unitary) cost coefficient restriction, in particular, may not be appropriate.

Cost obviously is an endogenous variable in this formulation, and Table 9.5 contains the results of instrumental variables estimation of (9.12) for the trigger-strategy sample of industries.[32] Industries in this group exhibit economically and statistically significant price rigidity and countercyclical pricing. The former is obviously consistent with the predictions of pricing behaviour of Rotemberg and Saloner, although their theory also requires that prices fall relative to marginal cost in booms, and procyclical margins were pronounced for non-durable goods. The two findings are reconciled if some of the expenditure on labour is in fact a fixed cost. The fixed cost component of labour was investigated in Domowitz, Hubbard and Peter-sen (1988). It was found that overhead labour is a very important compo-nent of total cost. In fact, given the definitions of 'fixed labour input' as

Table 9.5   Concentration, strategic behaviour and cyclical movements in prices (I)

Industries	Constant	Δp_{-1}	Δc	Δx	$\bar{R}^2$
C4A > 0.50, high margin	0.009	0.169	0.638	−0.010	0.661
	(0.002)	(0.029)	(0.054)	(0.003)	
C4A > 0.50, high margin, non-durables	0.008	0.130	0.694	−0.006	0.682
	(0.002)	(0.028)	(0.048)	(0.003)	
C4A > 0.50, high margin, durables	0.012	0.376	0.340	−0.295	0.680
	(0.003)	(0.054)	(0.089)	(0.054)	

Note: The equations were estimated using instrumental variables, as described in the text. Heteroskedasticity-consistent standard errors are in parentheses. The estimation interval was 1958 to 1981.

primarily managerial labour, the fixed cost component is likely to be understated in the presence of any labour hoarding. The fixed costs attributable to the sum of plant overhead labour and central office expenditures are as large as those attributable to capital for most industry groups. The potential importance of labour hoarding seems clear; see also Hall (1987).

As in the case of price–cost margins, there are major differences in the results that depend on the durable–non-durable goods distinction. Prices are much more rigid in the durable goods industries. This is consistent with the higher margins reported for durable goods earlier, as might be predicted from the work of Stiglitz (1984) and Rotemberg and Summers (1987). Although the degree of countercyclicality of prices is statistically significant for non-durables in this group of presumably collusive industries, it is not economically important, being extremely small in magnitude. The same cannot be said for the durable goods industries. The countercyclical effect in durables is virtually 50 times that in the non-durables sector (as measured simply by the short-run impact effect). The results in this regard support the work of Bils (1987) on pricing in a monopolistically competitive setting.

Evaluation of the data in the light of the Haltiwanger–Harrison model again requires the addition of expected future demand; coefficient estimates are reported in Table 9.6 for the trigger-strategy group. The results vary little between models with and without rational expectations of demand movements, although the countercyclical nature of pricing overall is a bit more pronounced once expectations are taken into account. The results of Table 9.6 cannot be said to support the Haltiwanger–Harrison formulation in general, however. In their model, countercyclical pricing is more likely in industries with low concentration levels and relatively

Table 9.6   Concentration, strategic behaviour and cyclical movements in prices (II)

Industries	Constant	Δp_{-1}	Δc	Δx	$E\Delta x$	$\bar{R}^2$
C4A > 0.50, high margin	0.009	0.197	0.608	−0.006	−0.076	0.678
	(0.002)	(0.035)	(0.053)	(0.035)	(0.054)	
C4A > 0.50, high margin, non-durables	0.009	0.162	0.653	−0.076	−0.102	0.698
	(0.002)	(0.038)	(0.052)	(0.038)	(0.061)	
C4A > 0.50, high margin, durables	0.011	0.431	0.335	−0.292	−0.120	0.700
	(0.003)	(0.054)	(0.085)	(0.057)	(0.084)	

Note: The equations were estimated using fixed effects and instrumental variables, as described in the text. Heteroskedasticity-consistent standard errors are in parentheses. The estimation interval was 1958 to 1981.

flexible prices.[33] The estimates here suggest that the degree of countercyclicality increases with price rigidity.

Some additional insight can be obtained by looking at different subsamples of the full sample. Results are reported in Tables 9.7 and 9.8. One major conclusion regarding cyclical pricing and market conduct emerges from a comparison of these tables with the trigger-strategy group: prices are both rigid and countercyclical in the purportedly collusive group, but exhibit little rigidity and basically acyclical behaviour in the sample

Table 9.7   Market structure, durability and cyclical movements in prices (I)

Industries	Constant	Δp_{-1}	Δc	Δx	$\bar{R}^2$
All industries	0.008	0.019	0.841	−0.011	0.719
	(0.001)	(0.024)	(0.040)	(0.021)	
C4A < 0.50	0.009	−0.014	0.886	−0.022	0.757
	(0.001)	(0.025)	(0.042)	(0.022)	
C4A > 0.50	0.007	0.094	0.745	−0.020	0.666
	(0.001)	(0.023)	(0.043)	(0.029)	
C4A < 0.50, non-durables	0.008	−0.024	0.897	−0.021	0.769
	(0.002)	(0.025)	(0.049)	(0.029)	
C4A > 0.50, non-durables	0.007	0.062	0.791	−0.000	0.695
	(0.002)	(0.024)	(0.038)	(0.033)	
C4A < 0.50, durables	0.020	0.160	0.691	0.087	0.725
	(0.002)	(0.050)	(0.062)	(0.040)	
C4A > 0.50, durables	0.011	0.357	0.409	−0.235	0.676
	(0.023)	(0.042)	(0.066)	(0.039)	

Note: The equations were estimated using instrumental variables, as described in the text. Heteroskedasticity-consistent standard errors are in parentheses. The estimation interval was 1958 to 1981.

Table 9.8   Market structure, durability and cyclical movements in prices (II)

Industries	Constant	Δp_{-1}	Δc	Δx	$E\Delta x$	$\bar{R}^2$
All industries	0.008	0.032	0.824	−0.010	−0.091	0.733
	(0.001)	(0.020)	(0.037)	(0.017)	(0.038)	
C4A < 0.50	0.009	−0.002	0.871	−0.019	−0.010	0.769
	(0.002)	(0.026)	(0.042)	(0.014)	(0.040)	
C4A > 0.50	0.008	0.119	0.709	−0.029	−0.114	0.685
	(0.002)	(0.032)	(0.041)	(0.030)	(0.058)	
C4A < 0.50, non-durables	0.009	−0.013	0.877	−0.017	−0.126	0.761
	(0.007)	(0.025)	(0.045)	(0.013)	(0.043)	
C4A > 0.50, non-durables	0.007	0.090	0.747	−0.009	−0.157	0.714
	(0.002)	(0.035)	(0.038)	(0.034)	(0.065)	
C4A < 0.50, durables	0.009	0.189	0.679	−0.085	−0.081	0.741
	(0.002)	(0.020)	(0.088)	(0.045)	(0.053)	
C4A > 0.50, durables	0.011	0.417	0.369	−0.252	−0.133	0.701
	(0.023)	(0.049)	(0.062)	(0.046)	(0.067)	

Note: The equations were estimated using fixed effects and instrumental variables, as described in the text. Heteroskedasticity-consistent standard errors are in parentheses. The estimation interval was 1958 to 1981.

overall, judging both by the magnitude of the effects and the large size of the standard errors. This conclusion is true even for highly concentrated industries relative to the trigger-strategy group, although price rigidity is found to increase in concentration in the full sample, as tacit collusion models would suggest. If the high-margin trigger-strategy subgroup is indeed characterized by tacit collusion as the three supergame models predict, then price rigidity and cyclicality strongly depend upon conduct.

The exception to this general finding is to be found only in durable goods. The degree of price rigidity and countercyclical pricing behaviour for the full sample is quite similar to that for the trigger-strategy group.[34] This result provides additional support for the Bils (1987) prediction of countercyclical pricing of durables, which did not depend on the type of market structure or conduct which underlies the work of the supergame models. It is interesting to note that non-durables exhibit little price rigidity and acyclical behaviour, regardless of market concentration level, over the full sample of industries.

5   CONCLUDING REMARKS

Industrial organization economists speak of structure, conduct and performance in discussions of markets. The results presented in this chapter stress the importance of time-varying conduct driven by business cycle conditions and the durability of goods as a key element of market structure in explaining the dynamic behaviour of oligopoly pricing. Little has been said about performance in the traditional sense of the magnitude of price–cost margins, beyond the observation that estimates of mark-ups based on the Solow residual are high enough to suggest tacitly collusive conduct. It has been noted, however, that care must be exercised with respect to any such interpretation, given that there exist theories that predict positive mark-ups as a consequence of price rigidities. Such rigidities have been identified here as being associated with durable goods manufacturing in industries that do not share characteristics necessarily amenable to the maintenance of tacitly collusive arrangements. Significant differences in cyclical behaviour and price rigidity were also a feature of the trigger-strategy group, however, which was selected to approximate the structural characteristics of the models of Green–Porter, Rotemberg–Saloner and Haltiwanger–Harrington. This finding indicates the need for theoretical work on the durable goods oligopolist's problem in the context of dynamic environments, such as supergames.

The oligopoly supergame models examined here must be interpreted as models of non-durable goods industries, and empirical discrimination between them should be based on the empirical results for the non-durable goods sector of the trigger-strategy group. Mark-ups of price over marginal cost as estimated from the Solow residual are highly procyclical in nature for this sector, while prices are mildly countercyclical. Prices exhibit rigidity, less than for durable goods but much more than for the full sample of data for US manufacturing. These results are robust to the inclusion of rational expectations of future demand movements. Although procyclical margins can be rationalized in the context of all three models studied, the overall combination of results appears to support the Rotemberg–Saloner formulation.[35] On the other hand, the Haltiwanger–Harrington model suggests ambiguities that can only be settled empirically, and the results presented here confirm the importance of their emphasis on the consideration of future demand conditions in the analysis of market structure and conduct. Some of the simulation evidence reported by Haltiwanger and Harrington is consistent with the empirical evidence in this chapter as well. In particular, procyclical profits were maintained in the presence of countercyclical prices that served to sustain the collusive outcome in one of the simulated models.

The behaviour of prices and margins in the durable goods sector has not yet been rigorously explained in the context of dynamic oligopoly theory, but alternative explanations for the strong countercyclical behaviour and rigidity of prices and the acyclical to countercyclical behaviour of price–cost margins were mentioned along the way. The most notable reference is the work of Bils (1987) on monopolistic competition. Some supporting empirical evidence also exists that has escaped mention. Lebow (1988) presents results on the countercyclical behaviour of prices in concentrated durable goods industries, and his results suggest acyclical behaviour for price–cost margins. Morrison (1989) finds strong counter-cyclical behaviour of margins in durable goods manufacturing based on a production-theory approach.

The results of this chapter indicate the need for further investigation of such a production-theoretic approach, but in a dynamic context. A fruit-ful direction seems to be the investigation of multi-stage games, in which a strategic commitment such as investment is made, followed by a price or quantity-setting supergame. Shapiro (1989a, 1989b) contains discussion and references to such models. A particular example is provided by the work of Staiger and Wolak (1990) incorporating a capacity-setting stage before each period of a Rotemberg–Saloner-style stage game. In such a setting, capacity constraints are emphasized as one means to approach the dynamic interaction between business cycle conditions and costs. The resolution of the empirical behaviour of mark-ups on the one hand, and prices on the other, indeed requires the investigation of the relative fluc-tuation of costs, not just prices, over the cycle, in a dynamic game-theoretic framework.

NOTES

1. The latter was emphasized as early as in the classic article by Stigler (1964), which still motivates many of the important developments in oligopoly pricing today.
2. On the empirical front, see the discussion of the 'new empirical industrial organization' in Bresnahan (1989). An example in theory is provided by the companion articles by Fisher (1989) and Shapiro (1989a) dealing with the usefulness of game theory in understanding industrial structure.
3. Local industry demand effects not accounted for by aggregate cyclical fluctuations are investigated in Domowitz, Hubbard and Petersen (1986a). Such differential local effects were not found to be nearly as significant quantitatively as aggregate demand movements in explaining the effects of industry concentration and capital on price–cost margins. For a discussion of the impact of industry structure on macroeconomic thought, see Carlton (1989).
4. The precise meaning of 'market power' is an issue itself. Conventional models relate such power to small numbers of firms and particular demand configurations. See Bresnahan (1989) for a summary characterization of power as an 'unknown parameter to be estimated'.
5. The first systematic empirical investigation of this effect is Domowitz, Hubbard and Petersen (1987b).
6. The work of Bils (1987) on monopolistic competition is closely related and discussed in Section 3. Ausubel and Deneckere (1986) study the durable goods monopolist's problem in a supergame setting. For an early reference, see Coase (1972).
7. Bresnahan (1989) provides an excellent survey of empirical studies of industries pre-

sumed to display market power. His Table 1 contains a list of industry studies that emphasize calculation of performance (in the form of the Lerner index), and reviews of work emphasizing tests of conduct are given elsewhere in the paper. Although Shapiro (1989b) does not review empirical contributions, his survey of theories of oligopoly pricing and behaviour should be required reading, especially with regard to two-stage dynamic games. There is no empirical work relating to the latter of which I am aware.

8. A partial listing of such papers includes Sullivan (1985), Ashenfelter and Sullivan (1987), Roberts (1984), Appelbaum (1979) and Gasmi and Vuong (1988). Empirical methodology papers without applications that are also based on static equilibria include Panzer and Rosse (1987) and Bresnahan and Reiss (1989). I hasten to point out that I have high regard for all these papers cited. I simply believe that further progress must be in the dynamics of equilibrium, and that conclusions based on static models in dynamic environments must be treated with extreme caution. I also note an analogy in another area of economics: the movement to estimate explicitly dynamic equilibrium models in macroeconomics was termed a 'revolution' not so long ago.

9. A major exception is the work of Slade (1991a) on gasoline price wars. In that particular industry environment, 'stable' or stationary periods are uninteresting, being characterized by identical, constant, posted prices. Her data are restricted to unstable periods, and a time-varying parameter methodology is used to model intertemporal reactions.

10. Osborne (1976) must be given credit for first delineating the information structure allowing implementation of a collusive agreement that maximizes profits and deters cheating. His rule implied a game in which history matters, but was not formalized as such. See Geroski, Phlips and Ulph (1985) for an overview in the broader context of oligopoly pricing.

11. See Shapiro (1989b) for a discussion of the problem of finite horizons.

12. I differentiate here between the common usage of the term 'supergame' and multi-stage games of business strategy, in which history matters owing to some irreversible commitment such as capacity investment. See Shapiro (1989a) and references therein for discussion of this area.

13. This claim ignores numerous difficulties and refinements along the way, including refinements of equilibrium concepts, analysis of types of credible punishments, and characterization of multiplicity of equilibria, to name only a few. Over 150 references appear in the Shapiro (1989b) survey, many pertaining to supergame theory.

14. See also Porter (1983) for an empirical test of price wars in a railroad cartel, and Porter (1985) for a game that focuses on market share as the relevant concept.

15. Domowitz, Hubbard and Petersen (1987a) also examine a second major prediction of the model, namely the incidence of periodic steep price declines. Although no evidence is found of this effect, the data used are longitudinal with annual observations only, and such evidence must be considered inconclusive.

16. Bils (1985) provides empirical evidence that marginal cost is indeed procyclical in US manufacturing.

17. This effect in particular was examined in Domowitz, Hubbard and Petersen (1987a). Controlling for aggregate economic activity, industry growth rates were found to influence prices in a procyclical direction for highly concentrated industries, regardless of the level of the price–cost margin.

18. Note that

$$\frac{P-AVC}{P} = \frac{P-MC}{P} + \frac{MC-AVC}{P}.$$

Procyclical movements in Census price-cost margins can be associated with any form of cyclicality in the Lerner index, depending on the relationship between marginal cost and variable cost over the business cycle. Using the methodology described in the text, it is possible to construct $(MC-AVC)/P$ for the industries in the sample. Regressions of this dependent variable on aggregate capacity utilization (as a measure of macroeconomic activity) and industry capital/output ratios reveal that $(MC - AVC)/P$ is countercyclical overall and this effect does not depend on the level of industry concentration. This difference is strongly procyclical, however, for concentrated durable goods industries, implying that, for the durable goods sector, the census margin can be procyclical while the true Lerner index is countercyclical. This combination of findings rationalizes the agreement of the results on procyclicality of mark-ups overall based on census data in Domowitz, Hubbard and Petersen (1986a, 1986b, 1987a) with the findings in Domowitz, Hubbard and Petersen (1988) based on parametric estimates of the mark-up.

19. I return to this point later, because an argument can be made against it. In particular, the theory of 'real business cycles' invalidates the assumption. Alternative identifying instruments can, and are, found to statistically identify and estimate the margin.

20. The use of capacity utilization instead of other possible measures of aggregate activity follows Schmalensee (1987) and is consistent with Domowitz, Hubbard and Petersen (1987b, 1988). Other measures yield similar results; capacity utilization does not exhibit as strong a trend component as other possibilities such as unemployment.

21. The producer–consumer classification is taken from Ornstein (1975). Ornstein's classification is based on the percentage of shipments of output of final demand in four categories: consumption, investment, materials and government. If 50 per cent or more of an industry's output went to consumption, it was classified as a consumer-goods industry; if 50 per cent or more went to investment plus materials, it was classified as a producer-goods industry.

22. The standard measure of market concentration in cross-sectional studies is the census four-firm concentration ratio. There are a number of acknowledged problems with this measure, including inappropriate specification of product and geographic market boundaries. A second important consideration is foreign competition, which has become increasingly more important in US manufacturing, particularly in concentrated industries (Domowitz, Hubbard and Petersen, 1986a). A direct adjustment to the concentration ratio is to reduce it by the share of imports in domestic sales – I/S (Waterson, 1984). The adjusted concentration measure $(C4A)$ that we employ is defined as $C4A_{it} = C4_{it}(1 - (I/S)_{it})$, where $C4$ is the adjusted concentration measure derived by Weiss and Pascoe (1981). These adjusted measures are used for all references to industry concentration in the remainder of the chapter.

23. The importance of this distinction in the list of instrumental variables was explored in Domowitz, Hubbard and Petersen (1988) using a Hausman-style test statistic based on theory contained in Domowitz and White (1982). Although the null hypothesis of identical coefficient estimates (in equations such as (9.6) and using a larger sample) across different instrument specifications for most industry categories could not be rejected, the hypothesis was rejected in the case of durable goods. Since a focus of much of the work below is indeed on the distinction between the durable and non-durable sectors, the empirical analysis uses the more defensible set of instrumental variables. See also Hall (1988) on this point.

24. High margin industries are defined to be those with census price-cost margins greater than the mean for all industries; the low margin group has census margins below the mean. See Domowitz, Hubbard and Petersen (1986a) for details as to the construction of the margins from census data.

25. See also Domowitz, Hubbard and Petersen (1988), Table 3, for comparisons of estimated and census margins by two-digit industry classifications. The average correlation between the alternative measures reported there is 0.77.

26. Expectations were estimated using standard rational expectations methodology, instrumenting out future values of capacity utilization. Instrumental variables used included lagged values of capacity utilization and current and lagged values of the growth in military expenditures.

27. Durable-goods and non-durable-goods industries were defined as follows. Durable goods are assumed to be capital goods – for use either by households or by firms. With

few exceptions, the set of durable goods industries includes the following two-digit categories: 25 (Furniture), 35 (Machinery Except Electrical Machinery), 36 (Electronic Equipment), 37 (Transportation Equipment), and 38 (Instruments and Related Products).

28. See Bulow (1982), Stokey (1981) and Bond and Samuelson (1984) on the monopolist's problem. For example, Carlton and Gertner (1988) study the oligopolist's durable goods problem in a static setting, concluding that the sale of durable goods creates strategic externalities that produce greater competitive behaviour (that is, greater production) than expected. It is difficult to draw conclusions concerning relative cyclical behaviour of mark-ups from their work, however.

29. See Carlton (1989), who provides empirical evidence from transactions prices but notes that simple oligopoly models do not have any prediction relating price rigidity to the degree of market concentration.

30. The approximation, $\log(1 + z) - z$ for small z is used here.

31. Equation (9.11) lacks observable industry-specific components as formulated here. At a minimum, the size and behaviour of the mark-up is expected to change with the degree of market concentration. This is achieved here by dividing the sample according to discrete concentration categories in a fashion consistent with the analysis of the last section. The addition of individual industry growth rates, for example, was examined in Domowitz, Hubbard and Petersen (1987a), but such effects were estimated with very large standard errors.

32. Industry output price indexes are obtained from the four-digit SIC data base constructed by the Penn-SRI-Census project and updated and extended at the National Bureau of Economic Research. Unit cost data for labour and materials were used in the construction of c; see Domowitz, Hubbard and Petersen (1987a). The instrument list includes current and lagged values of the percentage change in military expenditures, and percentage changes in cost and output prices lagged two periods. The first lag of the last two variables was not included, owing to the nature of the error term given the interpretation of (9.12) as a fixed-effects estimating equation of a price equation in log levels with a secular time trend and unit root error. All regressions reported in this section were also estimated with an instrument list that replaced military expenditure with capacity utilization, but the results hardly differed in any particular and are, therefore, not reported here. Differences were observed when lagged GNP was used in the instrumental variables list, but problems with this instrument have already been discussed in the context of the price–cost margin models. Finally the bias in coefficient estimates to be expected in a fixed-effects scheme with a lagged dependent variable is negligible here, owing to the length of the sample in the time dimension; see Nickell (1986).

33. It must be noted, however, that price flexibility is measured in terms of the time discount factor in their model, not in terms of the serial correlation in the change or in the rate of change of prices.

34. This is not a simple artifact of the sample design. Only 15 industries classified as 'durable goods' appear in the group of 57 trigger-strategy industries; 11 durable goods industries appear in the group of 39 'high margin' trigger-strategy industries.

35. Procyclical mark-ups also are consistent with a variation of the Rotemberg–Saloner model in which a capacity-setting stage precedes each stage-game; such a model is due to Staiger and Wolak (1990). Their model predicts procyclical pricing in general. The authors note, however, that, if demand is sufficiently weak and excess capacity is so large that potential defectors do not face capacity constraints, countercyclical pricing is still possible. See Domowitz, Hubbard and Petersen (1988) for discussion of excess capacity in US manufacturing, in which fixed labour costs are differentiated from capital costs.

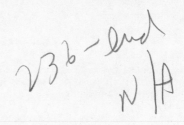

Bibliography

Abreu, D. (1986), 'External equilibria of oligopolistic supergames', *Journal of Economic Theory*, vol. 39, pp. 191–225.

Abreu, D., D. Pearce and E. Stracchetti (1986), 'Optimal cartel equilibria in supergames', *Journal of Economic Theory*, vol. 39, pp. 251–69.

Aghion, P. and P. Bolton (1987), 'Contracts as a barrier to entry', *American Economic Review*, vol. 77, pp. 388–401.

Aoki, M., B. Gustafsson and O.E. Williamson (eds) (1990), *The Firm as a Nexus of Treaties*, London: Sage.

Appelbaum, E. (1979), 'Testing price taking behaviour', *Journal of Econometrics*, vol. 9, pp. 283–94.

Arrow, K. (1962), 'Economic welfare and the allocation of resources for inventions', in R.R. Nelson (ed.), *The Rate and Direction of Inventive Activity*, Princeton: Princeton University Press.

Arvan, L. (1985), 'Some examples of dynamic Cournot duopoly with inventory', *Rand Journal of Economics*, vol. 16, pp. 569–78.

Ashenfelter, O. and D. Sullivan (1987), 'Nonparametric tests of market structure: An application to the Cigarette Industry', *Journal of Industrial Economics*, vol. 35, pp. 483–98.

Aumann, R. J. (1974), 'Subjectivity and correlation in randomized strategies', *Journal of Mathematical Economics*, vol. 1, pp. 67–96.

Aumann, R. J. (1985), 'Repeated games', in G. R. Feiwell (ed.), *Issues of Contemporary Microeconomics and Welfare*, London: Macmillan.

Aumann, R. J. (1987), 'Correlated equilibrium as an expression of Bayesian rationality', *Econometrica*, vol. 55, pp. 1–18.

Aumann, R. J. and S. Sorin (1989), 'Cooperation and bounded rationality', *Games and Economic Behavior*, vol. 1, pp. 5–39.

Ausubel, L. and R. Deneckere (1986), 'Reputation in Bargaining and Durable Goods Monopoly', discussion paper No. 695, Center for Mathematical Studies in Economics and Management Science, Northwestern University.

Axelrod, R. (1984), *The Evolution of Cooperation*, New York: Basic Books.

Azariadis, C. (1975), 'Implicit contracts and underemployment equilibria', *Journal of Political Economy*, vol. 83, pp. 1183–1201.

Babbage, C. (1832), *On the Economy of Machinery and Manufactures*, London: C. Knight.

Bain, J. (1956), *Barriers to New Competition*, Cambridge, Mass.: Harvard University Press.

Bain, J. (1968), *Industrial Organization*, New York: Wiley.

Baldwin, W. and J. Scott (1987), *Market Structure and Technological Change*, Chur: Harwood Academic Publishers.

Barham, B. and R. Ware (1990), 'Excess Capacity, Entry Deterrence and Market Structure: A Note', Discussion Paper, Queens University.

Beath, J., Y. Katsoulacos and D. Ulph (1989), 'The game-theoretic analysis of innovation: A survey', *Bulletin of Economic Research*, vol. 41(3), pp. 163–84.

Beckmann, M. (1976), 'Spatial price policies revisited', *Bell Journal of Economics*, vol. 7, pp. 619–30.

Benoit, J. P. and V. Krishna (1985), 'Finitely repeated games', *Econometrica*, vol. 53, pp. 905–22.

Benson, B. L., M. L. Greenhut and G. Norman (1990), 'On the basing point system', *American Economic Review*, vol. 80, pp. 584–8.

Bental, B. and M. Spiegel (1984), 'Horizontal product differentiation, prices and quantity selection of a multi-product monopolist', *International Journal of Industrial Organisation*, vol. 2, pp. 99–104.

Bernheim, B. D. (1986), 'Axiomatic characterization of rational choice in strategic environments', *Scandinavian Journal of Economics*, vol. 8, pp. 473–88.

Bertrand, J. (1883), 'Review of "Théorie mathématique de la richesse sociale" and "Recherches sur les principes mathématiques de la théorie des richesses" ', *Journal des Savants*, pp. 499–508.

Bester, H. (1989), 'Noncooperative bargaining and spatial competition', *Econometrica*, vol. 57, pp. 97–103.

Bils, M. (1985), 'The Cyclical Behavior of Marginal Cost and Price', working paper No. 30, Rochester Center for Economic Research.

Bils, M. (1987), 'Cyclical Pricing of Durable Goods', unpublished manuscript, University of Rochester.

Bond, E. W. and L. Samuelson (1984), 'Durable good monopolies with rational expectations and replacement sales', *Rand Journal of Economics*, vol. 15, pp. 336–45.

Bork, R. H. (1978), *The Antitrust Paradox*, New York: Basic Books.

Boyer, M. and M. Moreaux (1989), 'Les équilibres de marché avec meneur en information complète', Université des Sciences Sociales de Toulouse, Gremaq, Cahier 8919.

Brander, J. A. and J. Eaton (1984), 'Product line rivalry', *American Economic Review*, vol. 74, pp. 323–34.

Brander, J. A. and T. R. Lewis (1986), 'Oligopoly and financial structure: The limited-liability effect', *American Economic Review*, vol. 76, pp. 956–70.

Brander, J. A. and B. Spencer (1983), 'Strategic commitment with R&D: The symmetric case', *Bell Journal of Economics*, vol. 14, pp. 225–35.

Bresnahan, T. (1987), 'Competition and Collusion in the American Automobile Industry: The 1955 Price War', *Journal of Industrial Economics*, vol. 35, pp. 457–82.

Bresnahan, T. (1989), 'Empirical Studies of Industries with Market Power', Chapter 17 in R. Schmalensee and R. Willig (eds), *Handbook of Industrial Organization*, Amsterdam: North Holland.

Bresnahan, T. F. and P. C. Reiss (1989), 'Empirical Models of Discrete Games', unpublished manuscript, Stanford University.

Bulow, J. I. (1982), 'Durable-goods monopolists', *Journal of Political Economy*, vol. 90, pp. 314–32.

Cannan, E. (1893), *A History of the Theories of Production and Distribution in English Political Economy from 1776 to 1848*, London: Percival.

Cantillon, R. (1755), *Essai sur la Nature du Commerce en Général* (ed. H. Higgs), London: Macmillan (1931).

Carlton, D. W. (1989), 'The Theory and the Facts of How Markets Clear: Is Industrial Organization Valuable for Understanding Macroeconomics?' in R. Schmalensee and R. Willig (eds), *Handbook of Industrial Organization*, Amsterdam: North-Holland.

Carlton, D. W. and R. Gertner (1988), 'Market Power and Mergers in Durable Good Industries', unpublished manuscript, University of Chicago.

Casson, M. C. (1982), *The Entrepreneur: An Economic Theory*, Oxford: Martin Robertson.

Casson, M. C. (1990), *Enterprise and Competitiveness: A Systems View of International Business*, Oxford: Clarendon Press.

Casson, M. C. (1991), *Economics of Business Culture: Game Theory, Transaction Costs and Economic Welfare*, Oxford: Clarendon Press.

Chamberlin, E. H. (1929), 'Duopoly: Value where sellers are few', *Quarterly Journal of Economics*, vol. 43, pp. 63–100.

Chamberlin, E. H. (1962), *The Theory of Monopolistic Competition*, 8th edn, Cambridge, Mass: Harvard University Press.

Coase, R. H. (1937), 'The nature of the firm', *Economica* (N.S.), vol. 4, pp. 386–405.

Coase, R. H. (1972) 'Durability and monopoly', *Journal of Law and Economics*, vol. 15, pp. 143–9.

Commission of the European Communities (1988), 'Proposal for a

Council Directive on the Legal Protection of Biotechnological Inventions', Brussels, 17 October 1988.

Cordero, H. G. and L. H. Tarring (1960), *Babylon to Birmingham*, London: Quinn Press Ltd.

Cournot, A. (1838), *Recherches sur les Principes Mathématiques de la Théorie des Richesses*, Paris: Hachette.

Dasgupta, P. (1986), 'The Theory of Technological Competition', in J. Stiglitz and F. Mathewson (eds), *New Developments in the Analysis of Market Structure*, London: Macmillan.

Dasgupta, P. and E. Maskin (1986), 'The Existence of Equilibrium in Discontinuous Economic Games', *Review of Economic Studies*, vol. 52, pp. 1–26 (Part I: Theory) and pp. 27–41 (Part II: Applications).

Dasgupta, P. and J. Stiglitz (1980), 'Uncertainty, industrial structure and the speed of R&D', *Bell Journal of Economics*, vol. 11(1), pp. 1–28.

d'Aspremont, C. and A. Jacquemin (1988), 'Cooperative and noncooperative R&D in duopoly with spillovers', *American Economic Review*, vol. 78, pp. 1133–1137.

d'Aspremont, C., J. J. Gabszewicz and J. F. Thisse (1979), 'On Hotelling's stability in competition', *Econometrica*, vol. 47, pp. 266–93.

d'Aspremont, C., A. Jacquemin, J. J. Gabszewicz and J. Weymark (1983), 'On the stability of collusive-price leadership', *Canadian Journal of Economics*, vol. 16, pp. 17–25.

Daughety, A. (ed.) (1988), *Cournot Oligopoly-Characterization and Applications*, Cambridge: Cambridge University Press.

Demsetz, H. (1982), 'Barriers to entry', *American Economic Review*, vol. 72, pp. 47–57.

Deneckere, R. and C. Davidson (1985), 'Incentives to form coalitions with Bertrand competition', *Rand Journal of Economics*, vol. 16, pp. 473–86.

de Palma, A., V. Ginsburgh, Y. Papageorgiou and J. F. Thisse (1985), 'The principle of minimum differentiation holds under sufficient heterogeneity', *Econometrica*, vol. 53, pp. 767–82.

Dick, A. R. and J. Lott (1990), 'The role of potential competition in industrial organization: comment', *Journal of Economic Perspectives*, vol. 4, pp. 213–15.

Dixit, A. K. (1980), 'The role of investment in entry deterrence', *Economic Journal*, vol. 90, pp. 95–106.

Domowitz, I., R. G. Hubbard and B. C. Petersen (1986a), 'Business cycles and the relationship between concentration and price–cost margins', *Rand Journal of Economics*, vol. 17, pp. 1–17.

Domowitz, I., R. G. Hubbard and B. C. Petersen (1986b), 'The intertemporal stability of the concentration–margins relationship', *Journal of Industrial Economics*, vol. 35, pp. 13–34.

Domowitz, I., R. G. Hubbard and B. C. Petersen (1987a), 'Oligopoly supergames: Some empirical evidence on prices and margins', *Journal of Industrial Economics*, vol. 36, pp. 379–98.

Domowitz, I., R. G. Hubbard and B. C. Petersen (1987b), 'Market Structure, Durable Goods and Cyclical Fluctuations in Markups', unpublished manuscript, Northwestern University.

Domowitz, I., R. G. Hubbard and B. C. Petersen (1988), 'Market structure and cyclical fluctuations in U.S. manufacturing', *Review of Economics and Statistics*, vol. 70, pp. 55–66.

Domowitz, I. and H. White (1982), 'Misspecified models with dependent observations', *Journal of Econometrics*, vol. 20, pp. 35–58.

Eaton, B. C. (1976), 'Free entry in one-dimensional models: pure profits and multiple equilibria', *Journal of Regional Science*, vol. 16, pp. 21–33.

Eaton, B. C. and R. G. Lipsey (1978), 'Freedom of entry and the existence of pure profit', *Economic Journal*, vol. 88, pp. 455–69.

Eaton, B. C. and R. G. Lipsey (1979), 'The theory of market preemption: The persistence of excess capacity and monopoly in growing spatial markets', *Economica*, vol. 46, pp. 149–58.

Eaton, B. C. and R. G. Lipsey (1980), 'Exit barriers are entry barriers: The durability of capital as a barrier to entry', *Bell Journal of Economics*, vol. 11, pp. 721–9.

Eaton, B. C. and R. G. Lipsey (1981), 'Capital, commitment and entry equilibrium', *Bell Journal of Economics*, vol. 12, pp. 593–604.

Eaton, B. C. and R. Ware (1987), 'A theory of market structure with sequential entry', *Rand Journal of Economics*, vol. 18, pp. 1–16.

Eatwell, J., M. Milgate and P. Newman (1989), *The New Palgrave. Game Theory*, New York: Norton.

Edgeworth, F. (1897), 'La teoria pura del monopolio', *Giornale degli Economisti*, vol. 40, pp. 13–31.

Edgeworth, F. Y. (1925), *The Pure Theory of Monopoly*, London: Macmillan.

Erkkila, J. (1986), 'Copyright law, photocopying and price discrimination: comment' in J. Palmer (ed.), *Research in Law and Economics*, Greenwich: JAI Press.

Farrell, J. and G. Saloner (1985), 'Standardization, compatibility and innovation', *Rand Journal of Economics*, vol. 16, pp. 70–83.

Farrell, J. and G. Saloner (1986a), 'Standardization and variety', *Economic Letters*, vol. 20, pp. 71–4.

Farrell, J. and G. Saloner (1986b), 'Installed base and compatibility: Innovation, product preannouncements and predation', *American Economic Review*, vol. 76, pp. 940–55.

Farrell, J. and C. Shapiro (1990), 'Horizontal Mergers: An Equilibrium Analysis', *American Economic Review*, vol. 80, pp. 107–26.

Fisher, F. M. (1989), 'Games economists play: A noncooperative view', *Rand Journal of Economics*, vol. 20, pp. 113–24.

Forges, F. (1988), 'Repeated games of incomplete information: non-zero sum', CORE Discussion Paper 8805. To appear as Chapter 6 in *Handbook of Game Theory with Economic Applications*.

Fraas, A. G. and D. F. Greer (1977), 'Market structure and price collusion: An empirical analysis', *Journal of Industrial Economics*, vol. 26, pp. 21–44.

Fraysse, J. and M. Moreaux (1985), 'Collusive equilibria in oligopolies with finite lives', *European Economic Review*, vol. 27, pp. 45–55.

Friedman, J. W. (1968), 'Reaction functions and the theory of oligopoly', *Review of Economic Studies*, vol. 35, pp. 257–72.

Friedman, J. W. (1971), 'A non-cooperative equilibrium for supergames', *Review of Economic Studies*, vol. 38, pp. 1–12.

Friedman, J. W. (1977), *Oligopoly and the Theory of Games*, Amsterdam: North Holland.

Friedman, J. W. (1985), 'Cooperative equilibria in finite horizon, noncooperative supergames', *Journal of Economic Theory*, vol. 35, pp. 390–8.

Friedman, J. W. (1990), *Game Theory with Applications to Economics*, 2nd ed, Oxford: Oxford University Press.

Fudenberg, D. and J. Tirole (1984), 'The Fat-Cat Effect, the Puppy-Dog Ploy, and the Lean-and-Hungry Look', *American Economic Review*, vol. 74, pp. 361–6.

Fudenberg, D. and J. Tirole (1989), 'Noncooperative game theory for industrial organization. An introduction and overview', in R. E. Schmalensee and R. Willig (eds), *Handbook of Industrial Organization*, Amsterdam: North-Holland, pp. 259–327.

Gabszewicz, J. J. and J. F. Thisse (1979), 'Price competition, quality and income disparities', *Journal of Economic Theory*, vol. 20, pp. 340–59.

Gabszewicz, J. J. and J. F. Thisse (1980), 'Entry (and exit) in a differentiated industry', *Journal of Economic Theory*, vol. 22, pp. 327–38.

Gabszewicz, J. J. and J. F. Thisse (1986), *Location Theory*, London: Harwood Academic Publishers.

Gabszewicz, J. J. and J. F. Thisse (1989), 'Location', CORE Discussion Paper 8928. To appear as Chapter 9 in *Handbook of Game Theory and Economic Applications*.

Gal-Or, E. (1985), 'First mover and second mover advantages', *International Economic Review*, vol. 26, pp. 649–53.

Gal-Or, E. (1988), 'Oligopolistic non-linear tariffs', *International Journal of Industrial Organisation*, vol. 6, pp. 199–221.

Gaskins, D. (1971), 'Dynamic limit pricing: Optimal pricing under threat of entry', *Journal of Economic Theory*, vol. 2, pp. 306–22.

Gasmi, F. and Q. H. Vuong (1988), 'An Economic Analysis of Some Duopolistic Games in Prices and Advertising', unpublished manuscript, University of Southern California.

Gaudet, G. and S. W. Salant (1989), 'The Profitability of Exogenous Output Contractions: A Comparative-Static Analysis with Applications to Strikes, Mergers and Export Subsidies', CREST Working Paper No. 89–09, Ann Arbor, University of Michigan, Department of Economics.

Gaudet, G. and S. W. Salant (1991a), 'Increasing the Profits of Firms in Oligopoly Models with Strategic Substitutes', *American Economic Review*, vol. 81, pp. 658–65.

Gaudet, G. and S. W. Salant (1991b), 'Uniqueness of Cournot Equilibrium: New Results from Old Methods', *Review of Economic Studies*, vol. 58, pp. 399–404.

Gaudet, G. and S. W. Salant (1991c), 'The Limits of Monopolization through Acquisitions: Further Results', mimeo, Ann Arbor, University of Michigan, Department of Economics.

Gee, J. M. A. (1976), 'A model of locational efficiency with free entry', *Quarterly Journal of Economics*, vol. 90, pp. 557–74.

Geroski, P. (1988), 'In pursuit of monopoly: Recent quantitative work in industrial organization', *Applied Econometrics*, vol. 3, pp. 107–25.

Geroski, P., R. Gilbert and A. Jacquemin (1990), 'Barriers to entry and strategic competition', in J. Lesourne and H. Sonnenschein (eds), *Fundamentals of pure and applied economics*, New York: Harwood.

Geroski, P. A., L. Phlips and A. Ulph (1985), 'Oligopoly, competition and welfare: Some recent developments', *Journal of Industrial Economics*, vol. 33, pp. 369–86.

Geroski, P., A. Ulph and D. Ulph (1986), 'A model of the crude-oil market in which conduct varies over time', *Economic Journal*, vol. 97, pp. 77–86.

Gilbert, R. (1989a), 'Mobility barriers and the value of incumbency', in H. Sonnenschien and R. Willig (eds), *Handbook of Industrial Organization*, New York: North-Holland.

Gilbert, R. (1989b), 'The role of potential competition in industrial organisation', *Journal of Economic Perspectives*, vol. 3(3), pp. 107–27.

Gilbert, R. and D. Newbery (1982), 'Preempting patenting and the persistence of monopoly', *American Economic Review*, vol. 72, pp. 514–26.

Gilbert, R. and C. Shapiro (1990), 'Optimal Patent Breadth and Length', *Rand Journal of Economics*, vol. 21, pp. 106–12.

Gilbert, R. and X. Vives (1986), 'Entry deterrence and the free rider problem', *Review of Economic Studies*, vol. 53, pp. 71–83.

Goldman, M., H. Leland and D. Sibley (1984), 'Optimal non-uniform pricing', *Review of Economic Studies*, vol. 51, pp. 305–20.

Gravelle, H. and R. Rees (1980), *Microeconomics*, London: Longman.

Green, E. and R. Porter (1984), 'Noncooperative collusion under imperfect price information', *Econometrica*, vol. 52, pp. 87–100.

Greenhut, J. and M. L. Greenhut (1975), 'Spatial price discrimination, competition and locational effects', *Economica*, vol. 42, pp. 401–19.

Greenhut, M. L., G. Norman and C. S. Hung (1987), *The Economics of Imperfect Competition: a spatial approach*, Cambridge: Cambridge University Press.

Grossman, G. M. and C. Shapiro (1984), 'Informative advertising with differentiated products', *Review of Economic Studies*, vol. 51, pp. 63–81.

Grossman, G. and C. Shapiro (1987), 'Dynamic R&D competition', *Economic Journal*, vol. 97, no. 386, pp. 372–87.

Hall, R. E. (1987), 'A Non-Competitive, Equilibrium Model of Fluctuations', mimeo, Stanford University.

Hall, R. E. (1988), 'The Relation between Price and Marginal Cost in W. S. Industry', *Journal of Political Economy*, vol. 96, pp. 921–47.

Haltiwanger, J. and J. E. Harrington Jr. (1988), 'The Impact of Cyclical Demand Movements on Collusive Behavior', *Rand Journal of Economics*, vol. 22, pp. 89–106.

Hamilton, J. H. and S. M. Slutsky (1990), 'Endogenous timing in duopoly games: Stackelberg or Cournot equilibria', *Games and Economic Behavior*, vol. 2, pp. 29–46.

Harper, D. (1990), 'The Process of Interpersonal Criticism with the External Capital Market', mimeo, New Zealand Institute of Economic Research, Wellington.

Harsanyi, J. C. (1967–8), 'Games with incomplete information played by Bayesian players', *Management Science*, vol. 14, pp. 159–82, 320–34, 486–502.

Hay, G. A. and D. Kelly (1974), 'An empirical survey of price-fixing conspiracies', *Journal of Law and Economics*, vol. 17, pp. 13–38.

Hayek, F. A. (1937), 'Economics and Knowledge', *Economica* (N.S.), vol. 4, pp. 33–54, reprinted in F. A. Hayek, *Individualism and Economic Order*, London: Routledge & Kegan Paul (1959), pp. 77–91.

Hoover, E. M. (1937), 'Spatial price discrimination', *Review of Economic Studies*, vol. 4, pp. 182–91.

Hoover, E. M. (1945), *The Location of Economic Activity*, New York: McGraw Hill.

Hotelling, H. (1929), 'Stability in competition', *Economic Journal*, vol. 39, pp. 41–57.

Ireland, N. J. (1987), *Product Differentiation and Non-Price Competition*, Oxford: Basil Blackwell.

Jacquemin, A. (1987), *The New Industrial Organization*, Cambridge, Mass.: MIT Press.

Jacquemin, A. (1988), 'Collusive behavior, R&D, and European economic policy', *European Economic Review*, vol. 32, pp. 551–60.

Jacquemin, A., T. Nambu and I. Dewez (1981), 'A dynamic analysis of export cartels', *Economic Journal*, vol. 91, pp. 685–96.

Jacquemin, A. and M. Slade (1989), 'Cartels, Collusion and Horizontal Merger', Chapter 7 in R. Schmalensee and R. Willig (eds), *Handbook of Industrial Organization*, Amsterdam: North-Holland, pp. 415–73.

Judd, K. L. (1985), 'Credible spatial preemption', *Rand Journal of Economics*, vol. 16, pp. 153–66.

Kalai, E. and W. Stanford (1985), 'Conjectural-variations strategies in accelerated Cournot games', *International Journal of Industrial Organization*, vol. 3, pp. 133–54.

Kaldor, N. (1934), 'The equilibrium of the firm', *Economic Journal*, vol. 44, pp. 60–76.

Kamien, M. and N. Schwartz (1982), *Market Structure and Innovation*, Cambridge: Cambridge University Press.

Kamien, M. I. and I. Zang (1990), 'The Limits of Monopolization Through Acquisition', *Quarterly Journal of Economics*, vol. 105, pp. 465–500.

Katz, M. (1983), 'Non-uniform pricing, output and welfare under monopoly', *Review of Economic Studies*, vol. 50, pp. 37–56.

Katz, M. (1986), 'An analysis of cooperative research and development', *Rand Journal of Economics*, vol. 17, pp. 527–43.

Katz, M. and C. Shapiro (1985), 'Network externalities, competition and compatibility', *American Economic Review*, vol. 75, pp. 424–40.

Katz, M. and C. Shapiro (1986), 'Technology adoption in the presence of network externalities', *Journal of Political Economy*, vol. 94, pp. 822–41.

Kihlstrom, R. E. and J. J. Laffont (1979), 'A general equilibrium entrepreneurial theory of firm foundation based on risk aversion', *Journal of Political Economy*, vol. 87, pp. 719–48.

Kirzner, I. M. (1973), *Competition and Entrepreneurship*, Chicago: University of Chicago Press.

Kirzner, I. M. (1979), *Perception, Opportunity and Profit*, Chicago: University of Chicago Press.

Klemperer, P. (1990), 'How broad should the scope of patent protection be?', *Rand Journal of Economics*, vol. 21(1), pp. 113–30.

Knight, F. H. (1921), *Risk, Uncertainty and Profit*, Boston: Houghton Mifflin Co.

Kreps, D. (1990), *A Course in Microeconomic Theory*, Princeton: Princeton University Press.

Kreps, D., P. Milgrom, J. Roberts and R. Wilson (1982), 'Rational cooperation in the finitely repeated prisoner's dilemma', *Journal of Economic Theory*, vol. 27, pp. 245–52.

Kreps, D. and J. Scheinkman (1983), 'Quantity precommitment and Bertrand competition yield Cournot outcomes', *Bell Journal of Economics*, vol. 14, pp. 326–37.

Kuhn, H. (1953), 'Extensive games and the problem of information', in H. Kuhn and A. Tucker (eds), *Contributions to the Theory of Games*, vol. II, Princeton: Princeton University Press.

La Manna, M., R. MacLeod and D. de Meza (1989), 'The case for permissive patents', *European Economic Review*, vol. 33(7), pp. 1427–43.

La Manna, M. (1991), 'Patents as early warning signals. The effects of alternative patent regimes on industry structure and social welfare', in G. Norman and A. Gee (eds), *Market Strategy and Structure*, Wheatsheaf, forthcoming.

La Manna, M. (1992), 'Optimal Patent Life vs Optimal Patentability Standards', *International Journal of Industrial Organization*, forthcoming.

Lancaster, K. (1966), 'A new approach to consumer theory', *Journal of Political Economy*, vol. 74, pp. 132–57.

Lancaster, K. (1979), *Variety, Equity and Efficiency*, New York: Columbia University Press.

Lebow, D. (1988), 'Imperfect Competition and Business Cycles: An Empirical Investigation', unpublished manuscript, Princeton University.

Lederer, P. J. and A. P. Hurter (1986), 'Competition of firms, discriminatory pricing and locations', *Econometrica*, vol. 54, pp. 623–40.

Lieberman, M. (1984), 'The learning curve and pricing in the chemical processing industries', *Rand Journal of Economics*, vol. 15, pp. 213–28.

Liebovitz, S. (1986), 'Copyright law, photocopying and price discrimination', in J. Palmer (ed.), *Research in Law and Economics*, Greenwich: JAI Press.

Littlechild, S. (1975), 'Two-part tariffs and consumption externalities', *Bell Journal of Economics*, vol. 6, pp. 661–70.

Luce, R. D. and H. Raiffa (1957), *Games and Decisions*, New York: J. Wiley and Sons.

Lyons, B. R. (1984), 'The pattern of international trade in differentiated products: an incentive for the existence of multi-national firms', in H. Kierzkowski (ed.), *Monopolistic Competition and International Trade*, Oxford: Clarendon Press.

Machlup, F. (1949), *The Basing Point System*, Philadelphia: Blakiston.

McKinnon, J. and N. Olewiler (1980), 'Disequilibrium estimation of the demand for copper', *Bell Journal of Economics*, vol. 11, pp. 197–211.

McLean, R. P. and M. H. Riordan (1989), 'Industry structure with sequential technology choice', *Journal of Economic Theory*, vol. 47, pp. 1–21.

MacLeod, W. B., G. Norman and J. F. Thisse (1988), 'Price discrimination and equilibrium in monopolistic competition', *International Journal of Industrial Organization*, vol. 6, pp. 429–46.

McNicol, D. L. (1975), 'The two price systems in the copper industry', *Bell Journal of Economics*, vol. 6, pp. 50–73.

Mathewson, G. F. and R. A. Winter (1984), 'An economic theory of vertical restraints', *Rand Journal of Economics*, vol. 15, pp. 27–38.

Mertens, Y. (1990), 'Modelling price behaviour in the European car market: 1970–1985', The Economics of Industry Group, paper E1/1, London School of Economics.

Milgrom, P. and J. Roberts (1982), 'Limit pricing and entry under incomplete information: an equilibrium analysis', *Econometrica*, vol. 50, pp. 443–59.

Milgrom, P. and J. Roberts (1987), 'Informational asymmetries, strategic behavior, and industrial organization', *American Economic Review*, vol. 77, pp. 184–93.

Modigliani, F. (1958), 'New developments on the oligopoly front', *Journal of Political Economy*, vol. 66, pp. 215–32.

Morrison, C. J. (1989), 'Markup Behavior in Durable and Nondurable Manufacturing: A Production Theory Approach', working paper no. 2941, National Bureau of Economic Research.

Moulin, H. (1982), *Game Theory for the Social Sciences*, New York: New York University Press; 2nd edition, 1986.

Murphy, K., A. Shleifer and R. Vishny (1989), 'Increasing Returns, Durables and Economic Fluctuations', paper prepared for the National Bureau of Economic Research 10th Anniversary Research Meeting of the Program on Economic Fluctuations, NBER.

Mussa, R. and S. Rosen (1978), 'Monopoly and product quality', *Journal of Economic Theory*, vol. 18, pp. 301–17.

Nash, J. F. (1950), 'The bargaining problem', *Econometrica*, vol. 18, pp. 155–62.

Nash, J. F. (1951), 'Non-cooperative games', *Annals of Mathematics*, vol. 54, pp. 286–95.

Neven, D. and L. Phlips (1985), 'Discriminating oligopolists and common markets', *Journal of Industrial Economics*, vol. 74, pp. 133–49.

Nickell, S. (1986), 'Biases in dynamic models with fixed effects', *Econometrica*, vol. 45, pp. 1417–26.

Nordhaus, W. (1969), *Invention, Growth and Welfare*, Cambridge, Mass: MIT Press.

Norman, G. (1983), 'Spatial pricing with differentiated products', *Quarterly Journal of Economics*, vol. 98, pp. 291–310.

Oi, W. Y. (1971), 'A Disneyland dilemma: two-part tariffs for a Mickey Mouse monopoly', *Quarterly Journal of Economics*, vol. 85, pp. 77–90.

Ordover, J. and G. Saloner (1989), 'Predation, Monopolization and Antitrust', in R. Schmalensee and R. Willig (eds), *Handbook of Industrial Organization*, Amsterdam: North Holland, Chapter 9.

Ordover, J. and R. Willig (1985), 'Antitrust for high-technology industries: Assessing research joint ventures and mergers', *Journal of Law and Economics*, vol. 28, pp. 311–34.

Oren, S., S. Smith and R. B. Wilson (1983), 'Competitive non-linear tariffs', *Journal of Economic Theory*, vol. 29, pp. 49–71.

Osborne, D. K. (1976), 'Cartel problems', *American Economic Review*, vol. 66, pp. 835–44.

Osborne, M. J. and M. Pitchik (1987), 'Equilibrium in Hotelling's model of spatial competition', *Econometrica*, vol. 55, pp. 911–22.

Panzar, J. and J. N. Rosse (1987), 'Testing for "Monopoly" equilibrium', *Journal of Industrial Economics*, vol. 35, pp. 443–56.

Phlips, L. (1983), *The Economics of Price Discrimination*, Cambridge: Cambridge University Press.

Phlips, L. (1988a), 'Price discrimination: a survey of the theory', *Journal of Economic Surveys*, vol. 2, pp. 135–67.

Phlips, L. (1988b), *The Economics of Imperfect Information*, Cambridge: Cambridge University Press.

Pigou, A. C. (1932), *The Economics of Welfare*, (4th edn), London: Macmillan.

Porter, R. H. (1983), 'A study of cartel stability: The Joint Executive Committee, 1880–1886', *Bell Journal of Economics*, vol. 14, pp. 301–14.

Porter, R. H. (1985), 'On the incidence and duration of price wars', *Journal of Industrial Economics*, vol. 33, pp. 415–26.

Prescott, E. C. and M. Visscher (1977), 'Sequential location among firms with foresight', *Bell Journal of Economics*, vol. 8, pp. 378–93.

Radner, R. (1980), 'Collusive behavior in non-cooperative epsilon-equilibria in oligopolies with long but finite lives, *Journal of Economic Theory*, vol. 22, pp. 136–54.

Rasmusen, E. (1989), *Games and Information*, Oxford: Basil Blackwell.

Reinganum, J. (1985), 'A two-stage model of research and development with endogenous second-mover advantages', *International Journal of Industrial Organization*, vol. 3, pp. 275–92.

Rives, N. W. (1975), 'On the history of the mathematical theory of games', *History of Political Economy*, vol. 7, pp. 549–65.

Roberts, M. (1984), 'Testing oligopolistic behavior: An application of the variable-profit function', *International Journal of Industrial Organisation*, vol. 2, pp. 367–83.

Robinson, J. (1933), *The Economics of Imperfect Competition*, London: Macmillan.

Rosen, J. B. (1965), 'Existence and uniqueness of equilibrium points for concave N-person games', *Econometrica*, vol. 33, pp. 520–34.

Rotemberg, J. J. (1982), 'Sticky prices in the United States', *Journal of Political Economy*, vol. 90, pp. 1187–1212.

Rotemberg, J. J. and G. Saloner (1986), 'A supergame-theoretic model of business cycles and price wars during booms', *American Economic Review*, vol. 76, pp. 390–407.

Rotemberg, J. J. and L. H. Summers (1987), 'Labor Hoarding, Inflexible Prices and Procyclical Productivity', mimeograph, Massachusetts Institute of Technology.

Rothschild, M. and J. Stiglitz (1976), 'Equilibrium in competitive insurance markets: an essay on the economics of imperfect information', *Quarterly Journal of Economics*, vol. 90, pp. 629–50.

Rubinstein, A. (1982), 'Perfect Equilibrium in a Bargaining Model', *Econometrica*, vol. 50, pp. 97–109.

Salant, S. W., S. Switzer and R. J. Reynolds (1983), 'Losses from horizontal merger: The effects of an exogenous change in industry structure on Cournot–Nash equilibrium', *Quarterly Journal of Economics*, vol. 98, pp. 185–99.

Salop, S. C. (1979), 'Monopolistic competition with outside goods', *Bell Journal of Economics*, vol. 10, pp. 141–56.

Salop, S. C. and D. Scheffman (1983), 'Raising rivals' costs', *American Economic Review*, vol. 73, pp. 267–71.

Salop, S. C. and D. Scheffman (1986), 'Cost-raising strategies', working paper no. 146, Federal Trade Commission, Bureau of Economics.

Samuelson, L. (1987), 'Nontrivial supergame perfect duopoly equilibria can be supported by continuous reaction functions', *Economics Letters*, vol. 24, pp. 207–11.

Schelling, T. (1960), *The Strategy of Conflict*, Cambridge, Mass: Harvard University Press.

Scherer, F. M. (1972), ' "Nordhaus" Theory of Optimal Patent Life: A Geometric Representation', *American Economic Review*, vol. 62, pp. 4222–7.

Scherer, F. M. (1980), *Industrial Market Structure and Economic Performance*, Chicago: Rand McNally.

Scherer, F. M. and D. Ross (1990), *Industrial Market Structure and Economic Performance* (3rd edn), Boston: Houghton Mifflin.

Schmalensee, R. (1978), 'A model of advertising and product quality', *Journal of Political Economy*, vol. 86, pp. 485–504.

Schmalensee, R. (1981), 'Output and welfare effects of monopolistic third-degree price discrimination', *American Economic Review*, vol. 71, pp. 242–7.

Schmalensee, R. (1982), 'Monopolistic two-part pricing arrangements', *Bell Journal of Economics*, vol. 13, pp. 354–68.

Schmalensee, R. (1983), 'Advertising and entry deterrence: An exploratory model', *Journal of Political Economy*, vol. 90, pp. 636–53.

Schmalensee, R. (1987), 'Intra-Industry Profitability Differences in U.S. Manufacturing: 1953–1983', unpublished manuscript, Massachusetts Institute of Technology.

Schumpeter, J. A. (1934), *The Theory of Economic Development*, Cambridge, Mass.: Harvard University Press.

Schumpeter, J. A. (1939), *Business Cycles: A Theoretical, Historical and Statistical Analysis of the Capitalist Process*, New York: McGraw-Hill.

Schwartz, M. and M. Baumann (1988), 'Entry-deterrence externalities and relative firm size', *International Journal of Industrial Organization*, vol. 6, pp. 181–97.

Selten, R. (1965), 'Spieltheoretische Behandlung eines Oligopolmodells mit Nachfragetragheit', *Zeitschrift für die gesamte Staatswissenchaft*, vol. 121, pp. 301–24 and 667–89.

Selten, R. (1975), 'Reexamination of the perfectness concept for equilibrium points in extensive games', *International Journal of Game Theory*, vol 4, pp. 25–55.

Selten, R. (1978), 'The chain store paradox', *Theory and Decision*, vol. 9, pp. 127–59.

Shaked, A. and J. Sutton (1982), 'Relaxing price competition through product differentiation', *Review of Economic Studies*, vol. 49, pp. 3–13.

Shaked, A. and J. Sutton (1983), 'Natural oligopolies', *Econometrica*, vol. 41, pp. 1469–84.

Shaked, A. and J. Sutton (1987), 'Product differentiation and industrial structure', *Journal of Industrial Economics*, vol. 36, pp. 131–46.

Shapiro, C. (1989a), 'The theory of business strategy', *Rand Journal of Economics*, vol. 20, pp. 125–32.

Shapiro, C. (1989b), 'Theories of Oligopoly Behavior', in R. Schmalensee and R. Willig (eds), *Handbook of Industrial Organization*, Amsterdam: North Holland.

Siemaan, M. and J. B. Cruz (1973), 'On the Stackelberg strategy in non-zero sum games', *Journal of Optimisation Theory and Applications*, vol. 11, pp. 533–55.

Singh, N. and X. Vives (1984), 'Price and quantity competition in a differentiated oligopoly', *Rand Journal of Economics*, vol. 15, pp. 546–54.

Slade, M. E. (1986), 'Conjectures, firm characteristics and market structure', *International Journal of Industrial Organization*, vol. 4, pp. 347–70.

Slade, M. E. (1987a), 'Interfirm rivalry in a repeated game: An empirical test of tacit collusion', *Journal of Industrial Economics*, vol. 35, pp. 499–516.

Slade, M. E. (1989a), 'Price wars in price setting supergames', *Economica*, vol. 56, pp. 295–310.

Slade, M. E. (1989b), 'The fictitious payoff function: two applications to dynamic games', *Annales d'Economique Statistique*, vol. 15/16, pp. 193–216.

Slade, M. E. (1991a), 'Vancouver's Gasoline-price wars: an empirical exercise in uncovering supergame strategies', *Review of Economic Studies* (forthcoming).

Slade, M. E. (1991b), 'Strategic pricing with customer rationing: the case of primary metals', *Canadian Journal of Economics*, vol. 24, pp. 70–100.

Solow, R. M. (1957), 'Technical change and the aggregate production function', *Review of Economics and Statistics*, vol. 39, pp. 312–20.

Sonnenschein, H. (1968), 'The dual of duopoly is complementary monopoly: Or, two of Cournot's theories are one', *Journal of Political Economy*, vol. 76, pp. 316–18.

Sorin, S. (1988), 'Repeated games with complete information', CORE Discussion Paper 8822. To appear as Chapter 4 in *Handbook of Game Theory with Economic Applications*.

Spence, A. M. (1977a), 'Non-linear price and welfare', *Journal of Public Economics*, vol. 8, pp. 1–18.

Spence, A. M. (1977b), 'Entry, capacity investment, and oligopolistic pricing', *Bell Journal of Economics*, vol. 8. pp. 534–44.

Spence, A. M. (1980), 'Multi-product quantity-dependent pricing and profitability constraints', *Review of Economic Studies*, vol. 51, pp. 353–8.

Spiller, P. and E. Favaro (1984), 'The effects of entry regulation on oligopolistic interaction: The Uruguayan banking sector', *Rand Journal of Economics*, vol. 15, pp. 244–54.

Staiger, R. W. and F. A. Wolak (1990), 'Collusive Pricing with Capacity Constraints in the Presence of Demand Uncertainty', unpublished manuscript, Stanford University.

Stigler, G. (1964), 'A theory of oligopoly', *Journal of Political Economy*, vol. 47, pp. 432–49.

Stigler, G. (1968), *The Organization of Industry*, Homewood, Ill.: Richard D. Irwin, Inc.

Stiglitz, J. (1977), 'Monopoly, non-linear pricing and imperfect information: the insurance market', *Review of Economic Studies*, vol. 44, pp. 407–30.

Stiglitz, J. (1984), 'Price rigidities and market structure', *American Economic Review*, vol. 74, pp. 350–5.

Stiglitz, J. and F. Mathewson (eds) (1986), *New Developments in the Analysis of Market Structure*, Cambridge, Mass.: MIT Press.

Stokey, N. L. (1981), 'Rational expectations and durable goods pricing', *Bell Journal of Economics*, vol. 12, pp. 112–28.

Sullivan, D. (1985), 'Testing hypotheses about firm behavior in the Cigarette Industry', *Journal of Political Economy*, vol. 93, pp. 586–98.

Suslow, V. Y. (1986), 'Estimating monopoly behavior with competitive recycling: An application to Alcoa', *Rand Journal of Economics*, vol. 17, pp. 389–403.

Suslow, V. Y. (1988), 'Stability in International Cartels: An Empirical Survey', Hoover Institution Working Paper No. E-88-7, Stanford, California.

Sutton, J. (1986), 'Non-cooperative bargaining theory: An Introduction', *Review of Economic Studies*, vol. 53, pp. 709–24.

Sylos-Labini, P. (1962), *Oligopoly and Technical Progress*, Cambridge, Mass.: Harvard University Press.

Tandon, P. (1982), 'Optimal patents with compulsory licensing', *Journal of Political Economy*, vol. 90, pp. 470–86.

Thisse, J. F. and X. Vives (1988), 'On the strategic choice of spatial price policy', *American Economic Review*, vol. 78, pp. 123–37.

Tirole, J. (1988), *The Theory of Industrial Organization*, Cambridge, Mass.: MIT Press.

US Federal Trade Commission (1981), 'Initial Decision in re Ethyl Corp, et al.', Docket No. 9128.

van Damme, E. (1987), *Stability and Perfection of Nash Equilibria*, Berlin: Springer-Verlag.

Varian, H. R. (1989), 'Price discrimination', Chapter 10 in R. Schmalensee and R. Willig (eds), *Handbook of Industrial Organization*, vol. 1, Amsterdam: North-Holland.

Vellturo, C. A. (1988), 'Achieving Costs Efficiencies Through Merger: Evidence for the US Rail Industry', mimeo, Cambridge, Mass.: Massachusetts Institute of Technology.

Vives, X. (1984), 'Duopoly information equilibrium Cournot and Bertrand', *Journal of Economic Theory*, vol. 34, pp. 71–94.

Vives, X. (1986), 'Commitment, flexibility and market outcomes', *International Journal of Industrial Organization*, vol. 4, pp. 217–31.

Vives, X. (1990), 'Nash equilibrium with strategic complementarities', *Journal of Mathematical Economics*, vol. 19, (3), pp. 305–21.

von Mises, L. (1949), *Human Action: A Treatise on Economics*, London: William Hodge.

von Neumann, J. and O. Morgenstern (1944), *Theory of Games and Economic Behavior*, Princeton: Princeton University Press.

von Stackelberg, H. (1934), *Marketform und Gleichgewicht*, Vienna: Julius Springer.

von Weizsäcker, C. (1980), 'A welfare analysis of barriers to entry', *Bell Journal of Economics*, vol. 11, pp. 399–420.

Waldman, M. (1987), 'Non-cooperative entry deterrence, uncertainty and the free rider problem', *Review of Economic Studies*, vol. 51, pp. 301–10.

Ware, R. (1984), 'Sunk costs and strategic commitment: a proposed three-stage equilibrium', *Economic Journal*, vol. 94, pp. 370–8.

Ware, R. (1985), 'Inventory holding as a strategic weapon to deter entry', *Economica*, vol. 52, pp. 93–102.

Waterson, M. (1984), *Economic Theory of the Industry*, Cambridge: Cambridge University Press.

Weiss, L. W. and G. Pascoe (1981), 'Adjusted Concentration Ratios in Manufacturing 1972', mimeo.

Wenders, J. (1971), 'Excess capacity as a barrier to entry', *Journal of Industrial Economics*, vol. 20, pp. 14–19.

West, D. (1982), 'Testing for market preemption using sequential location data', *Bell Journal of Economics*, vol. 12, pp. 129–43.

Williamson, O. (1968), 'Wage rates as barriers to entry: The Pennington case in perspective', *Quarterly Journal of Economics*, vol. 85, pp. 85–116.

Willig, R. (1978), 'Pareto-superior non-linear outlay schedules', *Bell Journal of Economics*, vol. 9, pp. 56–69.

Yarrow, G. (1985), 'Welfare losses in oligopoly and monopolistic competition', *Journal of Industrial Economics*, vol. 33, pp. 515–29.

Zachau, U. (1987), 'Mergers in the Model of an R&D-race', mimeo, Universität Bonn, Institut für Gesellschafts-und Wirtschaftswissenschaften, Germany.

Index